Approaches to Literature

APPROACHES TO LITERATURE

LEE T. LEMON

University of Nebraska

New York
OXFORD UNIVERSITY PRESS
London   1969   Toronto

Preface

I have written *Approaches to Literature* to help students arrive at a group of orderly but flexible ways to think and write about literature. A mature appreciation of literature requires awareness of the questions that may be asked about literary works, and a notion of the complexity of response that sensitive and intelligent answers to those questions are likely to possess. I have attempted to supply here a framework for such appreciation and understanding.

The introductory section discusses some general aspects of literary criticism and critical writing. The text proper is divided into five sections, each of which is built around a single frequently taught work of literature. The works selected—Keats's "Ode on a Grecian Urn," Pope's *The Rape of the Lock,* Sophocles' *Oedipus Rex,* Shakespeare's *Henry IV, Part I,* and Joseph Conrad's *Heart of Darkness*—represent widely different types of literature from widely different backgrounds, and so pose different kinds of literary and critical problems. But all of them are central to the tradition of Western literature, and the problems they raise are relevant to a vast number of other works in the tradition.

Each of the five sections contains four or five pairs of essays. The first essay of each pair describes a practical approach to literature, a specific technique for analyzing literary works; the second applies the technique to an analysis of one of the five works. The result is a balanced combination of literary theory and practical example.

The critical approaches presented vary widely—simple paraphrase, close reading, thematic analysis, archetypal analysis, use of biographical and historical data, considerations of genre, and so on. The book attempts less to indoctrinate students in one method of literary study than to help them attain versatility in critical thought and critical writing. Each of the five sections closes with a group of problems designed to serve as topics for further study, and to suggest useful approaches not presented in detail.

The essays that describe an approach to literature note the uses of the approach, discuss its procedures, survey the sort of questions it is best designed to answer, and consider its limitations. Though the practical critiques are illustrations of the approaches discussed, they are also self-contained essays in criticism. They are written simply, in order to be accessible to the student as readable essays, and I hope they will be used as models. Few of the arguments advanced require either specialized knowledge or an extensive literary background; the essays on the works are not intended to be definitive studies of the literature analyzed. Students of literature should learn two things right away: to limit their critical questions (and thereby their critical essays) to manageable size, and to take account of the fact that about any really excellent work of literature, there is usually a great deal more to be said than can be dealt with in a single, brief essay. I hope *Approaches to Literature* will help the student to think about the literature he reads in an independent way, providing him with techniques which will open his mind to a better understanding and appreciation of the many facets which great works of literature possess.

The five sections are sufficiently self-contained so that an instructor is not bound to the poetry-drama-fiction sequence I have chosen. The book would suitably be used either for a chronological survey of literature or for courses and courses sequences arranged by genre. Although it might be assigned as outside reading, it is intended for use in the classroom. I hope it will provide the opportunity for the kinds of discussion and writing about literature and literary theory that lead to a deeper, fuller and more independent appreciation of the best that has been thought and said.

Lincoln, Nebraska   L.T.L.
January 1969

Contents

V Conrad's *Heart of Darkness,* 192

Approaches to Literature

Introduction

Literature and Criticism

Although no definition of literary criticism is accepted universally, most critics would agree that it is a disciplined attempt to understand and to evaluate works of literature. It begins with a personal response to the work: the response may be as general as a feeling of liking or of disliking, as emotional as slamming the book shut, or as coolly pragmatic as a decision to outline the stages of a poem's development. Whatever the response, it is merely a beginning.

The importance of getting beyond personal responses cannot be overestimated, even though it may be difficult to accept. Most readers feel that they know what they like and that their preferences are their own business. But to be satisfied with the first impression of a literary work is, after all, to assume that we are able to assimilate and to evaluate without much thought the experience of some of humanity's best and most sensitive men. In its own way, a Shakespeare play, a Dostoevsky novel, or a Donne sonnet is as complex as the equations of advanced mathematics, and no less precise as a formulation. The first obligation of any reader, no matter how strong his reaction, is to make certain that he understands the work to the best of his ability. Only thinking about a work critically—that is, only a consideration of all of its parts and how they fit together—justifies any reaction. Consequently, a major part of literary criticism consists in making certain that we, as readers, have not oversimplified or distorted the ~~literature~~. *Hamlet,* to use an example that shall recur frequently, is not merely a three-hour injunction against procrastination, any more than it is merely about youth, ~~or~~ about revenge, ~~or~~ about filial loyalties, or about statecraft, or about Oedipal complexes, or whatever; it is about all of these and more, and to understand the drama we have somehow to know precisely how these various thematic elements are related, the proportion of emphasis each receives, the role of each in Hamlet's suffering, the degree to which Hamlet is or is not responsible for his tragedy, and so on. To do this requires a careful reading of the play and a patient analysis of what each element in the work implies.

Literary criticism assumes that literature is worth understanding. A work of literature is, on the one hand, beautiful in itself, and criticism ought to concern itself with that beauty. There is a certain appeal in the splendid sound of the words in *Hamlet,* a glorious intricacy of design in the play, and a creation of suspense and relief that are appealing apart from any effect that the play may have in educating our sensibilities. Criticism ought to help to make us more aware of that kind of literary value. On the other hand, we can learn from literature, for the best literature is a carefully written record of the kinds of experience that men have found significant, and literature that has endured has done so in part because men in different generations and in a variety of circumstances have felt that significance. But we can receive what literature has to give only by stretching our imaginations and our minds to encompass the work; we receive nothing if we shrink the work to our size.

The education of our sensibilities, then, is not automatic. Reading the best that has been thought and said will not automatically make a reader more intelligent, more sensitive, or more humane, any more than any other kind of experience will make persons more effective and valuable human beings. Like any experience, the reading of literature is an opportunity for understanding, it is not the understanding itself; and like other experience, it becomes valuable as something more than mere momentary satisfaction to the extent that we can experience it objectively—to the extent that we see the experience not merely in relation to ourselves, but in itself and in relation to experiences other than ours. And finally, like other significant experiences, a work of literature cannot be summed up neatly in a little aphorism or in a tidy statement of theme.

Obviously, literature as vicarious experience has certain advantages and certain disadvantages in comparison with real experience. Real experience, by its very nature, can be more personal and more vivid than vicarious experience; most persons would rather eat a steak or fall in love than read about either. Yet the advantages of literary experience are not to be taken lightly. The imaginative reader can live in worlds attainable in no other way; he can discover what it means to be a young man who has been betrayed by his mother's hasty marriage to his father's murderer, or what it means to be obsessed by a white whale that has come to symbolize all of the arbitrary and hostile forces in the universe. The imaginative reader has at his command a range of experience explorable in no other way.

Just as importantly, literature is designed to point up the significance of experience. There never was a whaling crew like the crew that hunts Moby Dick—never in real life that perfect combination of a revengeful and malevolently philosophical captain with the eloquence to impel his crew to certain death, with mates who so conveniently range from the meditative Starbuck to the totally unreflecting Flask, with harpooners to represent all stages of primitive man, with the Captain's own dark whaling crew lurking beneath the deck like Hell's fiends or like something in the primordial unconscious, and with an intelligent and literate narrator who miraculously survives to tell the story. Reading *Moby Dick* may be vicarious experience, but it is experience in which every detail has been calculated to have maximum significance. Unlike day-to-day experience, the experience that grows with the careful but imaginative reading of a literary work has been organized to produce the greatest possible impact.

W. K. Wimsatt once defined a poem as "a feat of style by which a complex meaning is handled all at once," and, with certain qualifications, the definition is true of all worthwhile literature. The problem for the reader is to understand the full complexity of the meaning—which is another way of saying that his problem is to experience as fully as possible the total work—without simplification or distortion. The first step is to make literal sense of the work, a step which is sometimes easy, sometimes even deceptively easy, and sometimes obviously difficult. It requires an act of faith in the poet, an assumption that the words he uses are meaningful and that the over-all work has some kind of meaningful organization. Those two assumptions suggest the basic procedure for ascertaining the literal meaning of a poem: ①understand the individual words②and understand the way they are organized into sentences, paragraphs or stanzas, and finally into larger units.

The first, the understanding of the individual words, may come as easily and as naturally for some readers with some poems as the understanding of a letter from home. Or it may involve anything from simple use of the dictionary to a great deal of background reading in the political and social life of a period, primitive or classical mythology, sixteenth-century theology or late eighteenth-century psychology, the history of a literary genre, or what have you. It is impossible to relive fully the experience embodied in a poem unless the reader is acquainted with the elements that make up the experience. The alternatives are an incomplete reading, one which gives only part of what the poem has to offer, or a garbled translation of the poem into a personal frame of reference.

In "The Canonization," for example, Donne has these lines:

> Call us what you will, wee are made such by love;
>   Call her one, mee another flye,
> We'are Tapers, too, and at our owne cost die.

The poem begins with the narrator responding to someone who has complained about a love affair the narrator has been enjoying; he has, in effect, told the busybody to shut up, to do anything but meddle in his love life; in the second stanza he argues first that—contrary to the conventional exaggerations of Petrarchan love poetry—his love harms no one; then, more aggressively, he argues that his love does less harm than do the activities of doctors, soldiers, or lawyers (the major honorable professions in Donne's time). At the point where these lines occur, he is saying, roughly, "Call us anything you want—flies, a candle, an eagle and a dove; but actually, we're more like the phoenix, the bird that periodically dies and rises again. Our love devours us, and intercourse is a little death, so that we both die for love and are reborn in it. We are, then, martyrs for love; we are saints of love."

The paraphrase does not nearly do justice to the subtlety of the narrator's argument, a subtlety which can be appreciated only after perceiving fully the significance of all of the details. In the quoted lines, for example, it is easy to read quickly over "fly," loosely interpreting it as a generally appropriate term of contempt; the narrator is saying, in effect, call us something trivial and dirty if you must. In this loose sense, any number of words would have done as well— gnat, louse, mouse, or whatever. But for the reader who has done his homework, "fly" is the one word that works fully because flies were commonly regarded as symbols both of lust and of the brevity of life and because of the old belief that each time a couple made love, their lives were shortened. These implications of "fly" are precisely what the narrator attempts to deny in the remainder of the poem: his love is not lust, but rather (like the phoenix) a mysterious union of male and female; it is not destructive, for not only do the lovers arise again after making love, their love will guarantee them a kind of immortality.

Whether one needs to know all this to appreciate the poem is a moot point; the poem certainly can give some pleasure to a reader who knows little of flies and of the phoenix. Yet such knowledge does help the reader perceive the poem's coherence. A somewhat simpler but more striking example of the same kind of thing occurs near the end of the poem. The lovers are canonized, and the narrator is saying that future lovers will pray to the narrator and his mistress. This line occurs:

You, to whom love was peece, that now is rage.

A superficial reader is likely to be momentarily puzzled by "rage," since to a modern it will mean either violent anger or popular fashion (as in "all the rage"). And it is, of course, comparatively easy to fit either meaning into the line and have it make a kind of loose sense. A trip to a good dictionary, however, will show that at one time "rage" meant "excessive desire," including lust. In this sense, "rage" gives the line not a loose meaning, but a very precise meaning.

The general point by this time should be clear: the more fully a reader does his homework, the more knowledge he has; and the more knowledge he has, the more fully he can understand and relive the experience embodied in the poem. Reading without such knowledge may not be entirely valueless, but neither is it as rewarding as reading can be.

There is, of course, no general procedure for acquiring the kind of knowledge that any given reader needs for reading any given work intelligently; there are, however, some standard suggestions. The single most invaluable tool is a good edition, an edition that is not only accurate textually but one that also contains an abundance of relevant information. Ideally, such an edition would make available to the student whatever information is needed to understand the work; the kind of information that is necessary will, naturally, vary from work to work. If necessary, such an edition would explain briefly all but the most obvious allusions in the work (it would tell the reader of Dryden, for example, who MacFlecknoe was). It would define words that are obsolete and also words whose meanings have changed (like "rage" in "The Canonization"). It would briefly note the popular and intellectual traditions relevant to the poem ("fly" from "The Canonization"). It would comment upon the genre of the work and the conventions upon which the author depended (Whitman's "When Lilacs Last in the Dooryard Bloom'd" becomes even more moving when the reader senses how Whitman both used and departed from the conventions of the pastoral elegy). It would explain the broad intellectual and social suppositions upon which the work was based (Thackeray's Becky Sharp in *Vanity Fair* is more understandable if the reader is aware of the unattractiveness of the practical alternatives facing an impoverished but educated Victorian girl).

The second major step in making literal sense of a work involves understanding its organization. Sentences in poetry, drama, and fic-

tion ought to make as much sense as the sentences we read in news-
papers, and the over-all structure of literary works ought to be as
meaningful as the structure of non-literary works. To continue with
"The Canonization," the notion that the lovers are saints, which is
the point made by Donne's argument, is foolish unless very carefully
stated, unless there is a progression of supporting detail that wins
at least a tenuous acceptance of the plausibility of the idea. To see
how Donne supports his argument, we need to look at the complete
text of the poem:

> For Godsake, hold your tongue, and let me love,
>   Or chide my palsie, or my gout,
> My five gray haires, or ruin'd fortune flout,
>   With wealth your state, your minde with Arts improve,
>   Take you a course, get you a place,
>   Observe his honour, or his grace,
> Or the kings reall, or his stampèd face
>   Contemplate, what you will, approve,
>   So you will let me love.
>
> Alas, alas, who's injur'd by my love?
>   What merchants ships have my sighs drown'd?
> Who saies my teares have overflow'd his ground?
>   When did my colds a forward spring remove?
>   When did the heats which my veines fill
>   Adde one more to the plaguie Bill?
> Soldiers finde warres, and Lawyers finde out still
>   Litigious men, which quarrels move,
>   Though she and I do love.
>
> Call us what you will, wee are made such by love;
>   Call her one, mee another flye,
> We'are Tapers, too, and at our owne cost die,
>   And we in us finde the 'Eagle and the Dove.
>   The Phoenix ridle hath more with
>   By us, we two being one, are it.
> So to one neutrall thing both sexes fit,

Wee dye and rise the same, and prove
Mysterious by this love.

Wee can dye by it, if not live by love,
    And if unfit for tombes and hearse
Our legend bee, it will be fit for verse;
    And if no peece of Chronicle wee prove,
        We'll build in sonnets pretty roomes;
        As well a well wrought urne becomes
The greatest ashes, as halfe-acre tombes,
    And by these hymnes, all shall approve
    Us *Canoniz'd* for Love:

And thus invoke us; You whom reverend love
    Made one anothers hermitage;
You, to whom love was peece, that now is rage;
    Who did the whole worlds soule contract, and drove
        Into the glasses of your eyes
        (So made such mirrors, and such spies,
That they did all to you epitomize,)
    Countries, Townes, Courts: Beg from above
    A patterne of your love!

Like a skillful debater, Donne conceals his conclusion, that the lovers are saints, until his readers have granted his supporting arguments. Psychologically, the vexed tone of the first stanza is appropriate; the narrator is entirely on the defensive, and his defense is a somewhat feeble, "Don't you have anything better to do than to meddle in my love life?" In the last half of the second stanza, however, the narrator begins to argue that love is not as harmful as most of the occupations by which men win honor. Merchants and soldiers are responsible for the deaths of others; lawyers promote quarrels. The argument is still not very positive, but it is plausible. The third stanza continues the line of argument begun in the second, but with a variation: if anyone is harmed by the love, it is only the lovers. Then, suddenly but subtly, the narrator begins to counter-attack. He and his mistress are not like flies or candles; more accurately, they resemble the phoenix. When the lovers are joined they are, like the phoenix, both male and female; like the phoenix, they die (a Renaissance metaphor for orgasm) and rise again. But if the lovers die for love, they are indeed martyrs, and also, like more conventional martyrs, will be remembered—in poems if not in chronicles. The record of their love shall prove a model for other lovers, just as the lives of the saints provide models for orthodox Christians.

We have now just barely got into the poem, but what has been revealed is the structure of an argument so carefully and persuasively stated that it enlarges our experience. I wonder, for example, if after following Donne's defense of love, I shall ever be able to feel about *Antony and Cleopatra* or *Romeo and Juliet* as I did before— or, for that matter, whether I shall ever feel quite the same about love as I did before. It is not that anything dramatic has happened or that I expect myself and other readers to find mistresses immediately in order to achieve immortality "in sonnets pretty roomes." More probably, the result of imaginatively re-creating the argument in the poem is to make some adjustment, perhaps major, perhaps minor, in any future perception of the subject matter of the poem.

There is no general procedure for arriving at an understanding of the organization of a literary work, although an attempt to answer the very basic questions—who, what, where, when, and why—will clarify much. In a sense, all of the questions that literary criticism asks are developments of these, for a full appreciation of a work of literature requires that we know who is speaking and his relation to the author. The speaker may be a disembodied voice, as in Wordsworth's "Earth has not anything to show more fair"; or it may be an aspect of the author's personality, as in Keats's "When I have fears that I may cease to be"; or it may be a more or less fictional character who represents the author's values, like Hemingway's old man in *The Old Man and the Sea,* or values opposed to the author's, like the cold-blooded narrator of Swift's "Modest Proposal." We also need to know what is being said, both in terms of the general theme of the work and of the details that lead to that theme. We have to have a sense of the setting of the work, of the where and when; Hardy's Edgon Heath is not Dickens's London, and Dickens's nineteenth-century London is not Shakespeare's sixteenth-century

London; we miss much unless we are aware of the implications of the setting. Most importantly, we have constantly to ask "Why?" Why did the author choose to write the work, why do we meet Horatio before we meet Hamlet, why just these words in just this order? Perhaps all literary criticism, and all literary scholarship, is but an attempt to explore these basic questions and their infinite variations so that we might better experience the full richness that is great literature.

The Discipline of Criticism

Although the questions that literary criticism asks are basic, the answers often require disciplined thought. For many works, the questions will never be answered completely, not because the works themselves are incoherent, but because they are so magnificently and complexly coherent that any analysis changes their meaning, at least slightly. To analyze something is to take it apart, to look at things in isolation that were, in the original, connected. Even if it were possible to analyze all the significant strands of sound and imagery and thought and feeling in a poem, they would be combined in the critical essay in a way in which they are not combined in the poem. Another way of putting this is to observe that the purpose of literature is not the same as the purpose of criticism, any more than the purpose of an automobile is the same as the purpose of its description. Literature at its best, unlike other forms of discourse, is designed to satisfy the whole man—to satisfy man sensing, man feeling, and man thinking. Criticism, on the other hand, is designed to satisfy man thinking and, in particular, man thinking about literature.

To return to "The Canonization" for a moment, Donne gives his reader a series of images, some sharply realized and some only quickly suggested, and a tone of voice to titillate the reader's auditory and visual senses. He builds an elaborate emotional structure, from the opening defensive exclamation, "For Godsake, hold your tongue," through the note of triumph at the end. Donne also, as we have seen, creates a persuasive argument, granted the implications of his metaphors, to explain or motivate the change of emotion within the poem. Very generally, what makes "The Canonization" poetry of the high order it is, is both the fact that Donne does create an appeal to the reader's senses, his feelings, and his intellect, and the fact that these areas of appeal are perfectly integrated. To show their integration adequately would require a complete analysis of the poem, but a quick example will clarify the point. The beginning is, as we have seen, a strongly emotional statement. But it also works on the sensory level; the sound of the line and the strong sentence structure combine to help the reader imagine what kind of a man the speaker is. Moreover, what seems to be merely an angry exclamation, "For Godsake," becomes literally true by the end of the poem; if the lovers are worthy of canonization, then it is literally true that "For God's sake" their love should not be discouraged.

Donne's poem, like literature generally, works by implication, by suggesting an experience to the reader and by providing the reader with the clues necessary to experience the poem's subject. Criticism, a more limited kind of discourse, furthers understanding, which is only one aspect of experience. As Kenneth Burke put it, literature works by complexity and criticism by simplicity, and a simplicity is precisely what a complexity is not.

Several corollaries follow from this inherent limitation of literary criticism. If criticism works essentially by simplifying the work of literature, it is also true that not all simplifications will proceed along the same lines. It might be useful to think of a group of critical essays dealing with the same work as analogous to a group of blueprints showing the same building. Within the building, all of the structural supports, the non-load bearing walls, the ornamentation, the wiring, the plumbing, the space for traffic flow, and so on, will exist neatly within the same unit; but a single blueprint that tried to show the exterior of the building, the interior, the structural supports and non-load bearing walls, and so on, would be far too complex to be useful. What is useful is a set of blueprints showing different aspects of the building. Critical studies, as they simplify, as they try to make clear what was either implicit in the poem or obscured by its context, also tend to concentrate upon a single aspect of the work or upon a group of related aspects. One critical study

of "The Canonization," for example, might work primarily to clarify the imagery of the poem; another might attempt to help make
the reader understand the poem's logic; a third might analyze the
metrical structure in some detail; a fourth might attempt to relate
the poem to the intellectual or poetic tradition in which Donne
wrote. The possibilities are all but endless. But just as the blueprints
of the same building must all be mutually compatible, so ought the
critical studies—if the critic is working properly and if the work is
coherent. If what appears to be a door on the blueprint showing a
traffic flow has pipes passing through the same space on the plumbing diagram, then either the building has been badly designed or else
one of the blueprints is in error. Ordinarily, if the critic is reading
the work properly, the approach he is using should yield conclusions
compatible with conclusions arrived at through other approaches.

No single approach, however, will work equally well for all works.
Even works of the same general type may properly be approached
in widely different ways. Here, for example, are two sonnets:

> Earth has not anything to show more fair:
> Dull would he be of soul who could pass by
> A sight so touching in its majesty;
> This City now doth, like a garment, wear
> The beauty of the morning; silent, bare,
> Ships, towers, domes, theatres, and temples lie
> Open unto the fields, and to the sky;
> All bright and glittering in the smokeless air.
> Never did sun more beautifully steep
> In his first splendour, valley, rock, or hill;
> Ne'er saw I, never felt, a calm so deep!
> The river glideth at his own sweet will:
> Dear God! the very houses seem asleep;
> And all that mighty heart is lying still!
>   (*Wordsworth*)

> I caught this morning morning's minion, king-
>   dom of daylight's dauphin, dapple-dawn-drawn
>   Falcon in his riding

Of the rolling level underneath him steady air,
                         and striding
High there, how he rung upon the rein of a wimpling wing
In his ecstasy! then off, off forth on swing,
         As a skate's heel sweeps smooth on a bow-bend:
                         the hurl and gliding
Rebuffed the big wind. My heart in hiding
Stirred for a bird,—the achieve of, the mastery
                         of the thing!

Brute beauty and valour and act, oh, air, pride,
                         plume, here
Buckle! AND the fire that breaks from thee then,
                         a billion
Times told lovelier, more dangerous, O my chevalier!
         No wonder of it: shéer plód makes plough down sillion
Shine, and blue-bleak embers, ah my dear,
         Fall, gall themselves, and gash gold-vermilion.

                                        (*Hopkins*)

Not only are both of these sonnets, both are religious poems written
by deeply religious men. Yet it also seems clear that the initial difficulties presented by each differ, and that each achieves its effects
by its own means. The metrical form of Wordsworth's sonnet, for
example, is comparatively if not completely regular; that of
Hopkins's sonnet is so irregular that readers often fail to recognize it
as a sonnet. Furthermore, the grammatical complexities of Hopkins's
poem need atention before much can be said about its meaning or
about its effect; Wordsworth's sonnet is comparatively straightforward. Initially at least, Wordsworth's and Hopkins's sonnets suggest
the feasibility of different starting points.

In considering two Shakespearean tragedies, *Hamlet* and *Othello,*
to change the examples, a Freudian analysis of one might illuminate
the former but not the latter. I do not want to open up the old de-
bate of whether or not Hamlet suffers from an Oedipus complex,
but the play does contain a young man who is deeply mystified and
wounded by his mother's remarriage and who treats his girl friend

rather cruelly. It is also significant that the stabbing of Polonius, which results in Claudius's deciding that Hamlet must be murdered, occurs only after Hamlet has had a bitter quarrel with his mother; and Hamlet's delay might also be explained on the Freudian premise that, although the ghost has instructed him to avenge himself on Claudius, the real object of his anger is his mother—some evidence in the play supports this reading. Basically, the ingredients for the Oedipal situation are present in *Hamlet,* and an approach to the play from that perspective might possibly yield interesting results. On the other hand, in *Othello* the ingredients for the Oedipal situation simply are not present. If we try to read that kind of situation into the tragedy, we have to invent from our own resources a father and a mother for Othello—we have to, in other words, go far beyond the situation the author has given us.

One of the initial problems of the critic is, then, to select a pertinent approach or combination of approaches. Even though certain approaches may be more or less irrelevant to a particular work, a large number will remain that will lead to valuable insights and to greater understanding. The Freudian approach, for example, does not explain all of *Hamlet;* at most, it explains certain aspects of Hamlet's motivation for and difficulties in carrying out his duty. As Caroline Spurgeon and others have pointed out, significant strands of imagery run throughout the play (in particular, clusters of images dealing with disease and pollution), and these do much to establish the particular tone that *Hamlet* has and to suggest why Hamlet's is a moral obligation rather than a personal vendetta. Since *Hamlet* is a revenge tragedy, an analysis of the requirements of that sub-genre and the way Shakespeare manages them could contribute to an understanding of the tragedy. It would be possible to go on at some length enumerating the kinds of study of *Hamlet* that would produce meaningful results; the point is, briefly, that there are a variety of approaches that will illuminate the play—and the better the critic, the more able he will be to see any work he is considering from a number of perspectives.

Critical approaches are, in a sense, simply methodologies, techniques designed to give the reader an orderly and relatively thorough entry into one aspect of a work of literature. Critical approaches are

difficult to classify because they are rarely used in complete isolation from each other and because different students of literature
mean somewhat different things by "criticism." I shall use "criticism" to mean any study of literature which focuses upon the work
of literature and which attempts to explain and perhaps to evaluate
the work. A critical approach is a methodology or technique for
concentrating attention upon an aspect of the work. Under this
somewhat arbitrary definition, biography, for example, is not criticism; although it may very likely include some criticism, the chief
focus of biography is upon the man rather than upon the work.
Similarly, a history of Elizabethan stagecraft, a study of printers'
shops in the seventeenth century, a clarification of the kind of theo-
logical debates that engaged Swift and his contemporaries, or a
survey of the nineteenth-century reading preferences would not be
criticism in the sense in which I am using that word, for the emphasis would be on the special subject of the study rather than upon
the literary work. Such background studies are often invaluable for
criticism, but they are the critic's necessary homework rather than
his primary task. On the other hand, a study of the effects of a work
is not criticism, as defined here. It may be useful to know that
Goethe's *Werther* drove young Romantics to suicide or that
Dickens's novels contributed greatly to social reform in Victorian
England. Likewise, it may be very important to assess carefully the
effect of literary works on contemporary readers. Is *Giles Goat-Boy,*
for example, a morally pernicious novel that threatens our values,
or is reading it a liberating experience? To the extent that the
reader answers such questions by thinking in terms of his response
or of the imagined responses of other readers, he is not thinking
critically; to the extent that he attempts to answer such questions in
terms of the work itself, he is.

As defined here, criticism is a kind of close reading. It is concerned with a detailed examination of the work in order to understand it and perhaps, either overtly or by implication, to evaluate it.
Within this conception of criticism, however, are any number of
relatively distinct methodologies, depending upon how thickly or
thinly one prefers to cut his discriminations. For our purposes, we
may borrow the terms "intrinsic" and "extrinsic" criticism from

René Wellek and Austin Warren's *Theory of Literature*. Intrinsic criticism, if it could exist purely, would use no material not present within the literary work; extrinsic criticism would interpret the work in the light of material drawn from outside the work. We might further distinguish between extrinsic criticism that relies on materials that are traditionally considered a part of literary study (the life of the author, intellectual traditions, literary conventions, and so on) and extrinsic criticism that relies on non-literary disciplines (history, psychology, anthropology, sociology, and so on).

In practice, the distinctions are not clear cut; they represent areas along a continuous line rather than distinct compartments. Intrinsic criticism cannot be pure because no reader can forget all that he knows in order to think about a work and because, if he could, he would find the work completely incomprehensible; extrinsic criticism cannot be pure because, in order to be criticism at all, it must be directed at the explanation of the internal workings of literature. Nevertheless, there is sufficient difference among the approaches to make the distinction helpful.

Intrinsic criticism sees the work of literature as a more or less self-contained unity, requiring for its interpretation only the general knowledge that an experienced reader is likely to have. Wordsworth's great sonnet, "Earth has not anything to show more fair," for example, is meaningful without bringing to bear upon it any specific knowledge of Wordsworth's philosophy of nature, his notion of the purpose of poetry, or the sonnet tradition. The poem itself tells us that the narrator is struck with the beauty of London as seen from Westminster Bridge, and that what strikes him especially is the quietness of the city, a quietness that seems in some way to link it with nature.

Intrinsic criticism may take a variety of forms, ranging from the analysis of particular patterns within the work to carefully argued statement of the work's theme. It may, that is, select a particular pattern of images or a group of motifs and attempt to explain the work largely in terms of those; or it may abstract a particular device, such as irony, antithesis, meter, rhyme, and so on, as the key to the meaning and artistry of the work; it may concern itself with point of view, characterization, setting, or the handling of dialogue in order to further the understanding of the work. Or it might, instead of beginning with a particular detail and working toward meaning, reverse the procedure by concentrating primarily on the work's theme, attempting to state as precisely as possible what the theme is, and defending the statement of theme by reference to whatever support the work offers. The hallmark of intrinsic criticism, whatever direction it takes, is concern with the internal coherence of the literary work and the attempt to make obvious in the criticism what was less obvious in the literature.

Extrinsic criticism that relies on traditional literary materials attempts to illuminate the work with materials drawn from the author's life and from the intellectual, social, and literary traditions that helped to shape his work. Although it is possible to understand "Earth has not anything to show more fair" with some degree of accuracy simply by looking at the poem itself, the experience it embodies becomes more meaningful as we learn more of Wordsworth's reverence for nature and his usual aversion to cities, and when we further see that attitude as part of a broad intellectual tradition that Wordsworth shared with many of his contemporaries. With such knowledge we can experience more fully, for example, the implications of the word "heart" in the final line:

And all that mighty heart is lying still!

what was before a rather sentimental but comprehensible metaphor becomes a precisely chosen term that tells us that Wordsworth sees the city as a living being, sharing the almost divine animation of the natural world.

Other works require different kinds of literary knowledge. We shall see later, for example, that part of the effect of Pope's *Rape of the Lock* depends upon our understanding the variations he plays upon the epic and the heroic couplet; a study of Renaissance rhetorical conventions will show one of the backgrounds against which Shakespeare wrote, as would a study of dramatic conventions; much of T. S. Eliot's poetry is so richly and intricately allusive that a major portion of the impact is lost unless the reader has a thorough grasp of the literary traditions Eliot drew upon. Without a knowledge of the allegorical traditions upon which Spenser's *Faerie Queene* is based, it is a rambling and frequently confusing adventure story. Authors are, after all, people deeply interested in literature, and what they do and the way they do it will be shaped in part by their understanding of the literature they have read, the conventions they have absorbed, and the literary theories they consciously or unconsciously accept.

The second type of extrinsic criticism relies upon materials and disciplines not usually considered "literary." Since Aristotle, critics have been aware that literature is closely allied with philosophy and history because literature reflects both what man thinks and what he does. Dante's *Divine Comedy,* for example, was so directly influenced by the philosophy of Thomas Aquinas that it has been called a poetic version of the *Summa Theologica;* it is, of course, much else, but it is certainly a rendering of Thomas's highly abstract metaphysical and ethical principles into concrete poetic form. Wordsworth's "Tintern Abbey," on the other hand, is less a direct transferral of a specific philosophical system into poetry than a loose blending of certain philosophical ideas and sentiments that were part of the intellectual climate at the turn of the nineteenth century. In either case, a knowledge of the relevant philosophical systems adds maturity and support to the ideas expressed in the literature and, equally as important, shows the particular areas where for whatever reason the author disagreed with or added to the philosophical system.

A sense of relevant historical background is equally important. Conrad's *Heart of Darkness* acquires a completely new dimension when we realize that the horrors Marlow describes were not only the mental horrors of a mind discovering a primitive universe, but also the actual results of a totally misguided colonial policy. An intelligent reading of Swift's *Gulliver's Travels* requires that the reader know something of the political history of England in the early 1700's and be aware of the state of early eighteenth-century science. The list could be extended indefinitely, but the principle is that the worlds authors create derive in part from the worlds they know, and the reader cannot know the former fully without knowing something of the latter.

During the twentieth century other disciplines, particularly psychology and anthropology, have given valuable tools for the analysis of literature. The various schools of psychology have given us new sets of concepts to explain man's behavior. With some simplification, for example, Hawthorne's view of man as torn between the impulses of the heart (the urge to goodness, charity, happiness) and the head (the urge to explore and dominate nature, others, and even self) can be translated into and given depth by Freud's analysis of the pleasure principle and death urge. Anthropological studies of ritual, myth, and folklore—with or without Jungian overtones—have contributed much to the understanding of drama and narrative. Shakespeare's Prince Hal and Falstaff are, for example, more understandable as figures in the myth of the prodigal prince than as historical characters, since the actual Prince Hal and Falstaff were quite different from Shakespeare's presentation of them and from the presentations Shakespeare knew.

There is, of course, no way of predicting what disciplines will be most helpful in interpreting a given work. To take two extreme but clear examples, Lewis Carroll's *Through the Looking Glass* means more to a reader who plays chess than to one who does not, and Thomas Mann's *Doctor Faustus* is a richer novel if one knows something of contemporary music theory. The ideal critic would be a man able to bring whatever information is necessary to the work and to show the relevance of that information in assessing the meaning and the value of the work.

Although there are numerous other ways of classifying critical approaches to literature, these describe in a general way the methodologies and materials of most criticism. The choice of any particular approach, or of any combination of approaches, will depend upon the kind of question the critic thinks it most important to answer. But his decision about the most important question should depend not upon his habitual preference, chance interest, or the kind of approach he feels most comfortable with; it should depend upon the nature of the work itself.

The Writing of Literary Criticism

The writing of literary criticism is largely a matter of persuasion, for it is impossible to prove—in the strict sense of that word—that any interpretation of a literary work is the only adequate interpretation, that any reading of the images, for example, is the most legitimate reading, or even that the elements chosen for discussion are those most central to the meaning of the work. As we have pointed out before, an adequate work of literature is always richer, more complex, more completely integrated than the critical discussion of it. The most that the critic can hope to show is that his reading is plausible, and perhaps more plausible than other suggested readings. This does not imply that all readings and all critical essays are equally adequate.

Like other forms of persuasive writing, the critical essay requires a clearly formulated topic, an approach to the topic limited enough to permit a convincing argument in the space available yet central enough to lead to a significant conclusion, a development that both considers the strongest supporting evidence available and counters any valid opposition, and a clear and effective prose style. And like any form of writing intended to be read by someone other than the writer, it requires a willingness to rewrite. Every writer should have a large and frequently used wastebasket.

No method of formulating a topic works consistently for all writers. Ideally, the critic would read a work carefully several times and form certain impressions of it that he would like to verify or certain questions that he feels need to be answered if the work is to be properly understood. He would then jot down the impressions or the questions, organize the supporting evidence, and write his essay. Practically, most writers have to inch their way into the topic. Suppose, for example, that after reading *Hamlet* the critic feels that Hamlet is an unusually noble young man, possibly Shakespeare's portrait of the ideal prince. Initially, Hamlet enlists sufficient sympathy to make the notion plausible. The simple topic sentence of such an essay might be, "Hamlet is Shakespeare's portrait of the ideal prince." Unfortunately, the topic is much too broad; to discuss it adequately would require a knowledge of all of Shakespeare's plays in which royalty appears and a rather thorough grasp of the Renaissance conception of the duties of the prince—few students have either the necessary background or the necessary time to acquire that background. The topic, consequently, needs to be restated; it might be "Hamlet is a good prince." The topic still poses formidable problems, but it has the advantage of not committing the student-critic to an impossible task. A reasonably satisfactory—but not complete—treatment of the topic would entail only a thorough character analysis of Hamlet and of his behavior in the play.

Whether or not the topic should be stated overtly in a topic sentence and, perhaps, again in the conclusion is largely a stylistic matter. Although it is possible through extremely careful structuring of an essay to make the topic clear without openly stating it, the most important responsibility of the writer of an essay is to make certain that his reader knows with perfect clarity what the essay is about. Generally, then, the topic should be stated either at the beginning of the essay or at the conclusion, or both. Even if the topic sentence as such is not used in the essay, however, it is wise for the writer to have it written out and to refer to it frequently. In a well-organized essay every sentence, every detail, is relevant to the topic; one of the most useful practical disciplines in writing is to pause regularly, reread what has just been written, and consider its relation to the general purpose of the essay. If the relation is not immediately clear, the section should either be abandoned or be reworked to make its relevance apparent to the most obtuse reader. Material that is not relevant not only wastes the reader's time, it also distracts him, and, perhaps most importantly, its inclusion usually means the exclusion of material that is significant. Writing is more effective if the writer keeps firmly in mind what his subject is and if he makes certain that the reader cannot mistake his intention.

The proper approach to a topic is one that can be managed reasonably well in the amount of time and space available and that will shed some light on the topic. If the writer has a week to do a short paper on *Hamlet,* he obviously does not have time to make a careful study of Renaissance and Shakespearean ideals of princely virtue and their application to Hamlet; a hastily done survey of a large topic demonstrates very little. The writer might note, however, that there is another young prince in the play, Fortinbras, and that both Hamlet and Fortinbras share the problem of how to avenge a father. A comparison of the two princes begins to emerge as a more likely topic. At this point, any writer who is not blessed with a phenomental memory would go back to the text to study in some detail the similarities and differences between the situations of the two princes, and their way of handling the situations in which they find themselves.

The writer could, of course, isolate other elements in the play to show that Hamlet is a good prince. He could, for example, choose to discuss the impersonal motives that lead Hamlet to take revenge, and attempt to show the necessity of Hamlet's taking the course of action he does, even though it costs the lives of a number of persons, some of them innocent. Or the writer might choose to isolate those elements that Shakespeare seems to have included in order to give his audience a favorable impression of the young prince.

There is, of course, a great deal of evidence to show that Hamlet is a good prince. Horatio, who seems to be the voice of reason throughout the play, admires Hamlet; Hamlet seeks revenge both because the ghost of his father demands it and because he recognizes a moral blight in Denmark that only he can remove; he fulfills his duty at great cost to himself and with a reluctance that drives him near suicide. Yet in planning the development of the topic, the writer has to think in terms of both positive and negative evidence. Negatively, Hamlet's scorn of his mother exceeds the instructions given him by his murdered father; despite his good intention, he drives the lovely, innocent Ophelia to suicide, mistakenly kills her father, and slays her brother in a duel; he callously sends Rosenkrantz, Guildenstern, and the crew of a ship to their deaths. In order to show that Hamlet is a good prince, somehow these difficulties must be overcome. Whether they can or not will depend ultimately upon what one conceives the character of the good prince to be. Perhaps, though, the difficulties ought to suggest a still further refinement of the topic. In considering the negative evidence, the writer is forced to note the relationship between Laertes and Hamlet, and at this point he might possibly be struck by the fact that Hamlet, Laertes, and Fortinbras have each a father to avenge. Furthermore, only Fortinbras is completely successful, for only he succeeds without destroying those around him. Perhaps, then, the topic ought to be changed once more, to a discussion of Fortinbras as the "good prince," the one capable of maintaining the order of the state, and of Hamlet and Laertes as men not able to solve satisfactorily the problems set them.

I do not mean to suggest that the method I have described here is the only way of finding a suitable topic; it does, however, suggest that at every stage in thinking through the essay, in outlining it, or in writing the initial drafts, the writer constantly reconsider and reshape his topic in terms both of what he can practically hope to achieve and of the evidence, negative and positive, drawn from the work he is discussing.

Ideally, a writer should finish what he considers to be the final draft of a paper far in advance of the date due so that before submitting his work he can read it from a fresh point of view and, if necessary, make changes. Most writers, even many professionals, tend to be carried away by their topics; along with the excitement of exploring an idea and making discoveries about it goes an almost inevitable tendency to misjudge the strength of the supporting evidence, to feel that certain connections are obvious that are not, and perhaps simply to let the discoveries that are being made develop a life of their own, so that the conclusion of the essay has little to do with the promises made in the introduction. It is extremely helpful if the writer can put himself in the position of an outsider, with only the dimmest of memories of the interrelations that were so clear when he wrote the paper. Time, even a few days, will often do much to help a writer to an objective view of his own work.

Several techniques are especially helpful in reading the final draft. Very often, it is illuminating to read the introduction, skip to the conclusion, and see if what is concluded is the same as what was introduced. An introduction, among other things, says to the reader, "This is what I intend to do," and the conclusion says, "This is what I have done." If the introduction and the conclusion do not jibe, something has gone wrong in the development of the paper.

At this stage in writing the paper, it is also useful to make an outline, either on paper or mentally. Every section and sub-section should be immediately relevant to the topic, and every sentence, every fact cited, should be relevant to the section in which it occurs. Any irrelevant fact, no matter how interesting in itself, or any digression, no matter how valuable it seems, should be ruthlessly deleted. At this stage, the writer might also note any transitions that seem abrupt, for they are signs that he is moving too rapidly for the reader to follow. A simple transition word or phrase, or an additional sentence, will often justify the inclusion of material that otherwise would seem extraneous.

During one of the proofreadings, the writer should take the stance of the devil's advocate; he should be the hostile reader who disagrees with the topic and who challenges it at every point. No generalization should be permitted to stand unless it is supported by the strongest evidence available. Any argument that would undermine the topic should be considered and dealt with. If the writer can learn to take a hostile attitude toward his own work before his readers see it, he can meet their objections in advance.

Because literary criticism is persuasive writing, it most often reaches conclusions that are matters of considered opinion. Nevertheless, the conclusions must be based upon facts and upon carefully reasoned arguments. A fact, simply, is a bit of data that can be verified beyond reasonable doubt; it has a stolidity and definiteness that opinion can never match. It is a fact, for example, that Hamlet has a quarrel with his mother in Act III of the play; whether or not the quarrel has Freudian overtones is a matter of opinion, of interpretation of the fact of the quarrel, and of the context in which it appears. Also a fact, although of a different order, is the existence of a play resembling Shakespeare's *Hamlet* that probably influenced the writing of *Hamlet*. The critic is expected to be aware of and refer to any facts that are relevant to his discussion of the literature; as a general rule, it is good practice in the early drafts of an essay to be overly generous in the citing of facts to support opinions. A writer will feel much more confident if he is certain that an abundance of evidence supports his interpretations; on the other hand, he ought to feel rather uncomfortable when he discovers an interpretation unsupported by some irrefutable data. In later stages, when the paper is being polished and tightened up, any data that is too well known, or too remote from the topic, or too repetitious, can be deleted.

The proof of persuasive writing is whether or not it is convincing; if the reader feels that he can easily refute the writer's arguments, the essay is worthless. An essay that has a clearly formulated topic, that is well developed, that makes no interpretation unbuttressed by facts, that considers all meaningful negative and positive evidence, will of necessity be convincing.

I

Keats's "Ode on a Grecian Urn"

Paraphrasing Poetry

The first, most necessary, and most maligned step in the understanding of poetry is the paraphrase. A paraphrase is a point-by-
point "translation" of the poem into comparatively simple language.
It is not the whole poem, and in some cases not even an important
aspect of the poem. It is merely a mechanical way of laying out the
large-scale movement of the poem so that the interpretation and
the evaluation may proceed with a minimum of misunderstanding.
In some poems the diction, syntax, and structure are so transparent
that their translation comes automatically and simultaneously with
the reading of the lines; other poems require a conscious and careful translation. Shakespeare's Sonnet 17 shows its meaning and
movement in a fairly straightforward way:

> Who will believe my verse in time to come
> If it were filled with your most high deserts?
> Though yet, Heaven knows, it is but as a tomb
> Which hides your life and shows not half your parts.
> If I could write the beauty of your eyes
> And in fresh numbers number all your graces,
> The age to come would say, "This poet lies,
> Such heavenly touches ne'er touched earthly faces."

> So should my papers, yellowed with their age,
> Be scorned, like old men of less truth than tongue,
> And your true rights be termed a poet's rage
> And stretched meter of an antique song.
> But were some child of yours alive that time,
> You should live twice, in it and in my rhyme.

Few readers looking at this sonnet for even the first time will feel compelled to puzzzle over what it says. Sonnet 94, on the other hand, begins with an unusually difficult sentence:

> They that have power to hurt and will do none,
> That do not do the thing they most do show,
> Who, moving others, are themselves as stone,
> Unmoved, cold, and to temptation slow. . . .

Even after many readings of this particular sonnet, I feel a need each time to translate it into more normal grammatical patterns—a very elementary operation but one basic to an understanding of the poem.

Clearing away grammatical difficulties is, of course, only one of the many reasons for paraphrasing a poem. Rare or obsolete words need looking up, figurative language needs to be translated into literal language and the figures of speech grouped in clearly related patterns, the steps in the progress of the poem clarified, and so on. All of this is necessary because we must recognize what a poem says literally before we can interpret it intelligently.

Perhaps the most important use of the paraphrase, however, is the opportunity it offers for comparison with the original poem. A properly made paraphrase reflects accurately the large-scale happenings of the poem; in somewhat oversimplified terms, it "says" the same thing the poem says. Yet without much coaching most readers sense crucial differences between the prose paraphrase and the finished poem, and the most important aesthetic questions concern the precise definition of those differences. Readers re-read Shakespeare's sonnets; a paraphrase seldom gets more than a single quick once-over. Why? The answer will, naturally, depend upon the poem; in all probability the paraphrase will not use sound as functionally as does the poem; it will not capture the richness of the metaphors; it will reduce complexities of thought and feeling to clichés; it will present coldly and schematically what the poem presents emotionally. Whatever the differences, to locate them specifically is to begin to answer a major critical question.

Because paraphrase is a halfway step between the passive reading of the poem and an interpretation of it, it shares some of the qualities of each. On the one hand, it stays as close as possible to the original in diction, word order, arrangement of large-scale elements, and so on; on the other hand, it clarifies whatever major elements in the original need clarification.

Although not strictly a part of the paraphrase, a system of indicating the exact place in the translation where the paraphrase fails to capture the full meaning of the poem is useful in calling the writer's attention to those parts of the poem that need special consideration. No system is universally used, but a judicious use of three marks of punctuation—the question mark, the slash, and brackets—can simply and clearly mark most of the problem areas the critic will find. All editorial insertions in the paraphrase should be put in brackets [. . .] (not parentheses); in using the paraphrase it is often imperative to know precisely what was stated overtly in the original poem and what was interpreted into it. The slash may be used to indicate alternate readings; it is especially useful when a word or phrase in the poem carries several layers of meaning, all of which are important and not all of which can be clearly stated in normal prose. The question mark, in brackets since it is an editorial insertion, marks passages where there are difficulties that cannot be resolved in the paraphrase.

"Ode on a Grecian Urn"

A PARAPHRASE

THE POEM:

I

Thou still unravish'd bride of quietness,
  Thou foster-child of silence and slow time,
Sylvan historian, who canst thus express
  A flowery tale more sweetly than our rhyme:
What leaf-fring'd legend haunts about thy shape
  Of deities or mortals, or of both
    In Tempe or the dales of Arcady?
What men or gods are these? What maidens loth?
  What mad pursuit? What struggle to escape?
    What pipes and timbrels? What wild ecstasy?

II

Heard melodies are sweet, but those unheard
  Are sweeter; therefore, ye soft pipes, play on;
Not to the sensual ear, but, more endear'd,
  Pipe to the spirit ditties of no tone:
Fair youth, beneath the trees, thou canst not leave
  Thy song, nor ever can those trees be bare;
    Bold Lover, never, never canst thou kiss
Though winning near the goal—yet, do not grieve;
  She cannot fade, though thou hast not thy bliss,
    For ever wilt thou love, and she be fair!

III

Ah, happy, happy boughs! that cannot shed
  Your leaves, nor ever bid the Spring adieu;

And, happy melodist, unwearied,
   For ever piping songs for ever new;
More happy love! more happy, happy love!
   For ever warm and still to be enjoy'd,
     For ever panting, and for ever young;
All breathing human passion far above,
    That leaves a heart high-sorrowful and cloy'd,
     A burning forehead, and a parching tongue.

IV

Who are these coming to the sacrifice?
   To what green altar, O mysterious priest,
Lead'st thou that heifer lowing at the skies,
   And all her silken flanks with garlands dressed?
What little town by river or sea shore,
   Or mountain-built with peaceful citadel,
    Is emptied of this folk, this pious morn?
And, little town, thy streets for evermore
   Will silent be; and not a soul to tell
    Why thou art desolate, can e'er return.

V

O Attic shape! Fair attitude! with brede
   Of marble men and maidens overwrought
With forest branches and the trodden weed;
   Thou, silent form, dost tease us out of thought
As doth eternity: Cold Pastoral!
   When old age shall this generation waste,
    Thou shalt remain, in midst of other woe
Than ours, a friend to man, to whom thou say'st,
   Beauty is truth, truth beauty.—That is all
    Ye know on earth, and all ye need to know.

THE PARAPHRASE:

Thou yet/quiet unviolated bride of quietness, thou foster-child of
silence and slow time, who can [because of the nature of your hus-

band and your parents] express a pleasant/pastoral/ornate tale more sweetly than poetry/my poem, what leaf-fringed pictoral narrative is shown on you? [Are the figures] gods, or mortals, or both? [Is the scene] a valley in Thessaly or in Arcadia? Who are these men or gods? Who are these [fleeing?] maidens? What is this mad pursuit, this struggle to escape? What are these pipes and tambourines? What wild ecstasy is shown here?

Heard melodies are sweet, but those unheard are sweeter; therefore, ye soft pipes, play on, not to the sensual ear, but more endearingly, pipe [soundless?] ditties to the spirit. Fair youth beneath the trees, you cannot leave your song, nor can those trees ever be bare; bold lover, you can never kiss [your beloved], even though you seem always about to overtake her. Yet, do not grieve [because] she [her beauty?] cannot fade; though you do not have what would make you happy, you will always love, and she will always be lovely.

Ah! happy, happy boughs! You cannot shed your leaves nor ever bid spring farewell. And, happy melodist, [you are] unwearied [because you are] forever piping songs forever new. More happy love! more happy, happy love; forever warm and still to be enjoyed; forever panting, and forever young; [you are] far above all of the breathing human passion that leaves a heart greatly [nobly?] sorrowful and cloyed, [that leaves?] a burning forehead and a parching tongue.

Who are these [on the other side of the urn?] coming to the sacrifice? To what green altar, O mysterious priest, do you lead that heifer, lowing at the skies, with all her silken flanks dressed with garlands? What little town by river or sea shore, or what mountain-built town, with peaceful citadel, is emptied of these people on this pious morning? Little town, your streets will forevermore be silent, and not a soul can ever return to tell why you are deserted.

O Attic [Grecian] shape! Fair [just, reasonable, lovely] attitude [arrangement of parts, pose, disposition]! With brede [breed] of overwrought [impassioned/depicted] men and maidens, and with forest branches and trodden weeds—you, silent form, do tease [lure or vex] us out of thought [beyond thought?] as doth eternity. Cold pastoral! When old age shall this generation waste, you shall remain, in midst of other woe than ours, a friend to man, to whom you will say, Beauty is truth, truth beauty—that [the entire preceding sentence or the aphorism] is all you [man/ the urn/ the figures on the urn] know on earth and all you need to know.

After completing the paraphrase, it is often useful to jot down a reminder of the difficulties that were encountered in making literal sense of the poem. The "Ode on a Grecian Urn" presents comparatively few difficulties, but of those few, one is crucial. The entire import of the Ode depends upon the interpretation of the final lines, and those lines contain three pronouns that are, without considerable analysis, ambiguous. Does "that" refer merely to the aphorism, "Beauty is truth, truth beauty," or to some larger preceding element? Do the two "ye's" refer to the urn itself or to the figures on it, so that in effect the ending is an ironic comment by the narrator to the urn or its figures, saying, in effect, "Beauty is truth, truth beauty— that's all *you* know about life and all you need to know"? Or does "ye" refer to those who view the urn, including the narrator, and suggest that the narrator is in agreement with the urn's message?

The Importance of the Text

The major difficulty that our paraphrase found in Keats's "Ode on a Grecian Urn," the ambiguity of the final two lines, has possibly been the most hotly argued crux in all poetry. Although we shall look at the issues later in more detail, one reading of the final lines would suggest a culpable naïveté on the part of Keats; as Irving Babbitt noted cantankerously, men have known since the days of Cleopatra that the beautiful is not always true, and man ought to know that the true is not always beautiful. And to compound the culpability, Keats seems not only to give the empty-headed, patently untrue moral, but also to have the gall to tell his readers that that is all they need to know. On the other hand, the formidable British critic, John Middleton Murry, sees the lines as Keats's heroic affirmation of transcendental values, a recognition that man can attain wholeness only when he renounces the transient and petty concerns of day-to-day living.)

I do not want to attempt to resolve the dispute now, but rather to point out the extremes of opinion the lines have occasioned among thoughtful and usually careful scholar-critics. There are, of course, many ways of attempting to resolve such a quarrel, and [ultimately the critic will have to argue from the evidence presented within the poem; that is, which interpretation is most in keeping with the other things that happen within the Ode?]In later essays, that question will be considered.

Obviously, however, before considering what happens in the text, the critic ought first be certain that he has an accurate text; if changes have been made in the text, he ought to know what they are. Most texts assigned to students are reasonably accurate, although many have modernized details of spelling, punctuation, capitalization, and so on; needless to say, the critic who hinges his interpretation upon a textual inaccuracy or upon the editorially supplied punctuation of a line will have cause for embarrassment. An interesting controversy has been raging recently, for example, over T. H. Johnson's edition of Emily Dickinson's poems. The edition was intended to be the definitive edition—complete, compiled only after exhaustive study of all pertinent materials, and painstakingly recording all variant readings of individual words and lines. The result is a body of oddly punctuated poems, as if Emily Dickinson had developed an intense passion for the dash, which in Johnson's edition of the poems seems a general substitute for most other marks of punctuation. Another scholar, Edith Stamm, however, seems to have discovered that the dashes in Miss Dickinson's manuscripts are quite similar to marks used in contemporary elocution texts to indicate precisely how a line should be read. Any interpretation that argues from the punctuation of the poems, then, will first have to establish the intent of the punctuation.

Few textual problems concerning an author's work are as extensive as the example I have cited. Usually, the student will face no problem more complicated than that of a modernized text in which the editor has normalized the ordinary mechanical details. As a safeguard, especially if the critic is basing his argument upon the

kind of material that was likely to be changed in such moderniza-
tion, he ought to consult a standard scholarly edition to make certain that none of the alterations is vital to his argument.

Quite often, important clues may be inferred from a knowledge
of the changes an author made in his work. Some authors, by
chance or intent, have seen to it that their work reaches the public
only in what they consider its final form; others, by chance or intent, have preserved manuscripts showing the stages through which
the work went, or have even made significant changes in already
published pieces. Often the nature of the revisions will show the
intent of the author in a particular passage or, perhaps, even in the
entire work. Herman Melville's *Billy Budd,* for example, is a much
debated short novel, and whether the reader decides that it is an expression of Melville's acceptance of social order or his rejection of
it will depend in large measure upon his understanding of Captain
Vere, the naval officer who presides at the trial of the innocent
Billy and who personally convinces the court to sentence Billy to
death. Hayford and Sealts's recent fine edition of *Billy Budd* is
based upon an extensive study of the manuscript and some involved speculation concerning the stages it went through; they have
shown that as Melville revised, he was working to make the role of
Vere both larger and more sympathetic. Further evidence suggests
the possibility that the manuscript was not complete at Melville's
death. It might be plausible, then, to assume that had Melville lived
he would have clarified Vere's role in the court-martial, made
Vere's action more acceptable to the reader, and thereby reinforced
the theme of social acceptance.

I must stress that such argument is merely conjecture, and that
even a highly probable assessment of authorial intention does not
prove an interpretation; authors, like the rest of us, do not always
realize their intentions, nor, like the rest of us, do they always know
their intentions well enough to state them accurately. Nevertheless,
the critic ought to be cautious, but not intimidated, if his interpretation runs contrary to the author's stated or probable intention. Once
more, the only final test of an interpretation is the internal context of the work. External data provide clues and support, but no
more.

⌈How much effort the student ought to spend verifying the accuracy of a text and inquiring into the various stages through which a work passed will have to depend upon the work, the nature of his critical problem, and the amount of time he has available.⌋Although the situation varies, as a rule of thumb, the earlier the date of a work, the more the likelihood that there are textual problems. Before the days of modern printing, books were transcribed by hand; copyists frequently made mistakes in transcribing and often wrote their own interpolations into the text. Nor did the transcribers have the moderns' strong sense of the proprietary rights of an author; borrowings went unnoted, and a transcriber might for some reason sandwich one text in with another. Add to this such obvious problems as the difficulty in reading the various hands in which the manuscripts were written, the age and frequently poor condition of the manuscripts, unstandardized punctuation, spelling, syntax, and even in some cases, word usages, and the reader can rest assured that the text he has of any work written before 1475 is the result of a large number of editorial decisions.

As printing became more widespread, the problems that resulted directly from transcription of manuscripts gradually lessened. Nevertheless, problems of authorial propriety, standardization of usage, and so on, remained. In fact, instead of the transcriber, the compositor was now the middleman between the author and his reader, and as anyone knows who has examined a well-annotated edition of Shakespeare, the early compositors were frequently careless and not above "correcting" the author.

The situation gradually improved, but even throughout the nineteenth century pirated and cheap editions were commonplace; many authors, although by now keenly aware of their rights as authors, were too harried or too careless to see their works through a carefully corrected edition. Even so scrupulous an author as Henry James, who perhaps worried as much about the structure of his novels and saw them through the press as carefully as any of his contemporaries, was guilty of letting an edition of *The Ambassadors* be printed with two chapters transposed.

Obviously, a scholarly, accurate edition is less important in some types of studies than in others. Novelists rarely make the kind of large-scale error that James let slip by; usually textual inaccuracies are matters of incorrect wording, punctuation, and so on. They are details, but in certain kinds of study they can be crucial details which make or break an interpretation. Soon we shall see how a textual problem in Keats's "Ode on a Grecian Urn" has greatly complicated the analysis of that poem.

A professional scholar may be expected to go to great lengths to make certain of the accuracy of the text he uses; he is, after all, a professional, and a part of his profession is the accurate establishment of texts and conclusions based upon the best evidence available. A dedicated scholar may make several trips across the Atlantic, spending his summers and his treasured sabbatical attempting to trace down a manuscript or an edition that will give him a more correct version of a work than the ones currently available. He may patiently delay the completion of a favorite project, awaiting the death of an author's long-lived heir and the subsequent release of papers that will make his conclusions more certain. The student cannot be expected to go to such great lengths, but he can be expected to know the textual difficulties that sometimes arise, the limitations of the text he is using, and whether or not those limitations are likely to cause difficulties.

The Textual Problem of the Concluding Lines of "Ode on a Grecian Urn"

Keats's "Ode on a Grecian Urn" ends with an aphorism, "Beauty is truth, truth beauty," and a sweeping generalization on that aphorism, "That is all/Ye know on earth, and all ye need to know." The aphorism, like most aphorisms, can be either defended or attacked. As stated, it may be seen as one of the valid conclusions of several philosophical systems, some of which were prevalent in Keats's day, or it may be seen as an exceptionally obtuse statement contrary to the experience of most persons. And certainly, all readers know that man needs to know much more than that beauty and truth are one.

Those who admire the poem have worked out a number of

strategies for defending it, but most of the strategies take one of three general lines. T. S. Eliot, like some other commentators, chose to write off the final two lines as a "serious blemish on a beautiful poem," a kind of mistake that lessens the value of the Ode without quite destroying it. Other critics, such as A. C. Bradley, have attempted to defend the lines as philosophical comment, either by relating it to various forms of neo-Platonism directly, thereby hoping to give the lines respectable precedent, or by relating them to the total context of Keats's life and thought in an attempt to explain their precise meaning. A third group has argued that within the context of the Ode the lines are properly qualified and make complete sense. Among the more desperate attempts to rescue the final lines—just to show how deeply critics have felt the problem and how much ingenuity they have expended on its solution—are those of G. St. Quintin and Cleanth Brooks. Both accept one of the standard printings of the lines—perhaps the most common version in modern texts—in which the aphorism is surrounded by quotation marks and the comment is not. St. Quintin, accordingly, reads the final lines ironically, contending that the aphorism and the comment are made by two different beings. The urn itself, or the figures on it, say, "Beauty is truth, truth beauty"; the aphorism is in quotation marks because the narrator is quoting his source directly. But, St. Quintin argues, the narrator, or Keats, if you will, is too wise for that kind of nonsense, so he answers the figures on the urn, much as we would answer a simpleton who has made some sweeping generalization, by saying, "that's all you know." And, as St. Quintin points out, the figures on the *Yes!* urn, leading the kind of life they lead, need know no more. I shall comment on this interpretation in a moment. Cleanth Brooks, who also cannot accept the final lines at face value, rescues Keats by arguing that the entire Ode is a dramatic utterance delivered by the chatty urn; although it may be ridiculous for a grown man to say that "Beauty is truth, truth beauty.—That's all you need to know," it is not ridiculous for an urn to say so. This interpretation ignores the fact that the Ode is not a dramatic monologue in the manner of, say, Browning, but rather that it is a verbalization of the poet's inner response to the urn, so that the poet, and not the urn or its figures, is totally responsible for the aphorism and the comment.

If the version of the Ode with quotation marks causes problems in interpretation, why do most editors choose to reprint the troublesome version? As Alvin Whitley pointed out in "The Message of the Grecian Urn," in the *Keats-Shelley Memorial Bulletin* (London, 1953, V, 1–3), most modern editors are merely following one—*and only one*—of the possible texts of the poem as Keats *may* have intended it to read. The printing of the lines that most modern editors have selected is from the 1820 *Lamia* edition of Keats's poems; since no copy of the poem in Keats's handwriting has survived and since the 1820 *Lamia* edition was not seen through the press by Keats himself, the usual punctuation may or may not be the punctuation Keats intended.

The standard punctuation is further suspect because it is atypical of other contemporary versions of the lines. The first printed version of the poem, which appeared in the *Annals of the Fine Arts,* also in 1820, has no quotation marks around the aphorism, a period and a dash after "beauty," and a capital "t" in "That"—

> Beauty is truth, truth beauty.—That is all
> Ye know on earth, and all ye need to know.

Fortunately, contemporaries of Keats made four separate transcripts, quite possibly from Keats's own manuscript of the poem, with the following similarities: no quotation marks around the aphorism, no period after the second "beauty," and dashes after the first "truth" and the second "beauty." The transcripts disagree only in the capitalization of "truth" and "beauty." The transcript made by Richard Woodhouse is typical:

> Beauty is Truth,—Truth Beauty,—that is all
> Ye know on earth, and all ye need to know.

From the textual evidence, then, it would seem most unwise to base an interpretation upon the separation of the aphorism and the comment, since the punctuation made by four of the Ode's contemporary transcribers and in one printed edition omits the quotation marks, and all the transcriptions are punctuated to indicate that the aphorism and the comment are part of one continuous statement. For good or ill, Keats the poet, not the urn or the figures on the urn, must take full responsibility for the final lines.

Actually, a very close look at the poem clears away some of the problems occasioned by the final lines by making certain solutions highly unlikely. Although not strictly textual scholarship in the sense of establishing a text, consideration of the grammar of the text eliminates the possibility that the final comment is addressed to the urn; throughout the Ode, Keats has carefully observed the old singular-plural distinction between "thou" and "ye" respectively; he would hardly begin suddenly to refer to the urn in the plural in the final line of the poem.

The "ye," however, could still refer to the figures on the urn, with the comment to be read ironically despite the lack of quotation marks in four out of five sources for the text of the poem, and it probably can never be proven conclusively that that is not the correct reading. It has the merit of absolving Keats of the stupidity of saying that the only thing man needs to know on earth is that beauty and truth are identical, and it does not attempt to bolster the poem by building a rather unwieldy philosophical scaffolding under it. Despite the possible ironic interpretation, however, Keats has defended himself, for the aphorism is not presented as a simple generalization. It is, rather, the end of a long sentence that begins by stipulating a condition:

> When old age shall this generation waste,
>   Thou shalt remain, in midst of other woe
> Than ours, a friend to man, to whom thou say'st,
>   Beauty is truth, truth beauty.—That is all
>   Ye know on earth, and all ye need to know. *for _ _ _*

In other words, when this generation is gone and a new generation is in the "midst of other woe/Than ours," the urn, like a friend, will give man a specific consolation for his troubles. The consolation is the reminder that under the conditions set forth in the Ode, beauty is truth, and that that is the only consolation man needs for that time. Keats may be saying that beauty is always truth and that truth is always beauty; that would be typical of one aspect of his thought and typical of one aspect of the thought of his period. But he is not saying that that is the only knowledge man needs; it is, rather, the only knowledge he needs when he is in a certain condition. The aphorism is not a panacea, but a specific—in the strict medical sense of those terms. More precisely what that condition is and how it is described in the Ode will be considered in later sections.

The Poem and the Poet

When the interpretation of a work of literature is in doubt, the most natural thing to do seems to be to try to discover what the author felt he wanted to accomplish and, perhaps, had actually accomplished. Many scholars and some aestheticians would, in fact, argue that any work of art is successful only to the extent that it fulfills the artist's intention, and that the proper procedure for analyzing and judging a work of art is, in effect, to consult the artist. If we know through Pope's letters, for example, what he intended to do in *The Rape of the Lock,* then we must, according to this argument, interpret the poem and judge it exclusively in the light of the author's stated purpose.

Despite the naturalness of the approach, it does rest on assumptions that are not always warranted. It assumes, for example, that the writer is in constant control of his material, sharply aware at every moment of all the possible implications of every word he writes; it also assumes that language is a completely pliable medium, one that can be bent precisely to the purposes of the writer. It further assumes that the purpose of criticism is not to understand the work of art, but to understand the work of art as the artist understood it.

How much control a writer has of his materials is always a moot point; it depends upon what one means by "control" and upon the writer. Ben Jonson, one of the most controlled writers of the

English Renaissance, wished that his greater contemporary Shakespeare had blotted a thousand lines—that is, that he had had more control. Perhaps, though, the answer begins with the observation that the author and the critic exercise two distinct types of judgment. The judgment of the critic, because he is trying to explain the author's achievement, must be analytic, precise, and reasonably full. His job is to explain in a careful and logical way the interpretation of a passage or of a work. He must discursively and logically defend his judgment. The artist, on the other hand, may judge intuitively; the great Russian short story writer, Isaac Babel, is said to have rewritten his stories as often as thirty-three times, each time making frequent changes. Must we assume that with each change he went through exactly the same thought processes a critic would? Or may we not assume that, at least much of the time, he simply rewrote until a passage felt right, until something within him said, in effect, "that's it, that's the best I can do here." Although an author may or may not be fully conscious of the implications of his choices, he is under no obligation to explain logically what effect he wanted or how he wanted to attain it; it is enough if, a few times in his life, his judgment that "that's it, that feels right" is supported by the judgment of his readers. The author's control does not necessarily consist in knowing precisely why he does what he does; it may often consist in sensing when he has or has not written as well as he can.

Moreover, language is not a completely pliable medium; it offers an author its own resistances and surprises. As Robert Frost once remarked, the only time that a poet is free is the moment *before* he sets the first word down on paper, for that first word will contain implications of sound and syntax and meaning that the poet will have to choose to ignore or to realize; by the time he gets through the first line, he has set up a meter, a tone, perhaps the start of a pattern of imagery, expectations of a certain kind of grammar and diction, and so on. A line or two more, and he is committed to writing with or without rhyme, and then very quickly to a stanza form. Even if we assume that the poet begins with a clearly conceived non-verbal awareness of what he wants to do (if it is verbal and complete, it is already the poem), the moment he begins to formulate the poem, the potentialities within the words begin to pull him away from his intention. It is not always possible, for example, if one is writing rhymed verse, to find a word that will meet these three sets of requirements: express precisely the correct idea or image in precisely the right way, fit grammatically and metrically at the end of the line, and make the necessary rhyme. In such a situation—rhyme is only the most obvious example of a problem authors constantly face—the author must alter either his intended meaning or his intended pattern. As John Crowe Ransom put it, the poet begins with either a determinate (intended) meaning or a determinate form, or perhaps with both. As he writes, the limitations of his language force him repeatedly to compromise with one or the other set of intentions, or with both, until finally the finished work surprises even its author. Dickens, for example, used to complain that his characters tended to take on lives of their own, doing things that surprised and sometimes even astonished him.

Quite often, too, writers are simply unaware fully of the implications of what they write. Playwrights and novelists, for example, are usually close observers of people; they note what people do, what they say, their coloration, the look in their eyes, whether they suffer from chills or not, and so on. There are, consequently, cases of novelists having given classic descriptions of specific physical ailments long before they were recognized as such by the medical profession. The example is perhaps trivial, but the implication is that authors draw their raw materials from the same source as biologists, sociologists, psychologists, and what have you—their raw material is the world they observe. The author's job, though, is not to explain scientifically what he observes, but to use it as the material for what he is constructing. Shakespeare probably noted that certain ruthless women tended to have other rather masculine characteristics and incorporated those into his portrait of Lady Macbeth; modern psychology has given a number of explanations for the masculine syndrome in some women. It would be foolish to argue that Shakespeare was aware of the syndrome in the same way that a modern psychologist would be, but it would be equally foolish to deny that Lady Macbeth's character shows that syndrome. Undoubtedly Shakespeare and Dr. Ernest Jones—the earliest and best Freudian interpreter of *Hamlet*—saw Hamlet from different perspectives, but both were looking at the same kind of young man.

Nevertheless, I do not want so much to argue against using the author's intention in the interpretation of literature as to suggest its limitations. The chief purpose of attempting to ascertain the author's intention is either to provide corroborative evidence for an interpretation already made—to show, in effect, that someone else agrees—or to gain a clue to the unravelling of an otherwise obscure or ambiguous work. The assumption in this case is not that the author is in complete control of his work or that his say about the meaning of the work has final and irrevocable authority; the assumption is, rather, that the author, like the critic, is an intelligent and interested person who has thought much and deeply about the work he is doing. Without being definitive, his opinion and his beliefs about the work and the ideas relevant to it are worth hearing.

Keats's Letters and the "Ode on a Grecian Urn"

If it is plausible to contend that in the final sentence of the "Ode on a Grecian Urn" Keats is saying that beauty is truth and truth beauty, and that in the midst of some future woe, that knowledge alone will console man, it is reasonable to hope that a study of Keats's other writings will show a similar cluster of motifs—that is, despair or some kind of sorrow, combined with a solace in beauty or truth, or both. The evidence will not prove that in this particular poem Keats is offering the ideal union of beauty and truth as a specific consolation to man "in midst of other woe"; it will, rather, show the possibility of such a reading and, if that interpretation stands up after a close reading of the poem, make that the most probable interpretation.

Keats's letters show that he did have a habitual antidote against "woe." At times he called it "beauty," at other times "imagination," but throughout the letters there is a constant turning toward one of the two as an alternative to the harshness, the ugliness, he sometimes found in the world. As early as November 3, 1817, in a letter to his friend Benjamin Bailey, he asked for a "recourse somewhat independant [*sic*] of the Great Consolations of Religion and undepraved Sensations—of the Beautiful—the poetical in all things—O for a Remedy against such wrongs within the pale of the world!"

In a more famous letter to Bailey (November 22, 1817), one we shall look at in another context in a moment, he links Bailey's time of troubles with the imagination in the kind of *non sequitur* that can be explained only by a long-standing and unshakeable faith. He writes, "O I wish I was as certain of the end of all your troubles as that of your momentary start about the authenticity of the Imagination"—and then he launches not into a discussion of his friend's troubles, but into a discussion of the nature of the imagination.

A month later, in a letter to his brothers, he generalizes upon the "excellence of every art," an excellence he sees as the ability of art to make "all disagreeables evaporate, from their being in close relationship with Beauty and Truth." Further evidence from the letters and other poems could be cited, but it should be sufficiently apparent that Keats was habitually inclined to see art, the bearer of beauty and truth, and imagination, the instrument for seeing them, as effective antidotes for sorrow.

The reason for their effectiveness and the particular application to the Ode will be apparent if we understand more fully what Keats meant by "imagination." His theory of the imagination is complex, partly because his conception of the nature of such related concepts as beauty and truth changed as he matured. Basically, for Keats, imagination is the ability to experience the reality of things. In one aspect, it is what he elsewhere called "negative capability," the ability, chameleon-like, to lose himself in whatever object he contemplated. To the degree that a poet, or anyone perceiving beauty, does not have "negative capability," he projects upon the object his own ideas, his own emotions, his own values. The artist who possesses "negative capability" is so able to empathize with his subject matter, so able to subordinate his personality to whatever he contemplates, that he perceives it as it is. Although Keats does not apply the notion to the spectator of a work of visual art or to the reader of a poem—or, quite pertinently here, to Keats contemplating the urn—"negative capability" would be an ability to transcend completely whatever personal feelings he experienced before losing himself in a thing of beauty. The urn that "dost tease us out of thought" perhaps teases us into "negative capability." As an aesthetic object, then, as an object perfectly designed to elevate man from his personal concerns, it is truly a friend to man "in midst of other woe/Than ours." Fully absorbed in the contemplation of the urn, "all the disagreeables of everyday experience evaporate from their being in close relationship with Beauty and Truth."

This still does not explain the identity of beauty and truth as asserted in the final lines of the Ode, however. Various plausible explanations are possible, but the one that emerges most strongly from Keats's letters is based upon the peculiar power Keats ascribed to the imagination. For Keats, the imagination is not, as it is for Coleridge, exclusively a creative power; it is also a power for perception. In the letter to Bailey in which Keats linked Bailey's time of troubles and the imagination, he writes:

> I am certain of nothing but of the holiness of the Heart's affections and the truth of Imagination—what the Imagination seizes as Beauty must be Truth—whether it existed before or not—for I have the same Idea of all our passions as of love. . . . The imagination may be compared to Adam's dream—he awoke and found it truth.

Almost immediately, Keats exclaims, "O for a Life of Sensations rather than of Thoughts!" and near the end of the letter, attempting to explain how he finds happiness, he gives this example, "If a Sparrow come before my Window I take part in its existence and pick about among the Gravel." If I read this letter aright—and it is typical of one phase of Keats's thought, although atypical in its relatively full development of the ideas—Keats says that anything the imagination perceives must be true. If the imagination perceives what has not existed before, it creates it in the act of perceiving it, and attains its truth that way. When it perceives what has existed—

the sparrow picking among the gravel, for instance—it perceives it with such absorption ("abstraction" is the word Keats uses later in the same letter) in the object that it cannot but perceive it truly.

The Grecian urn, then, is a double monument to the imagination. As a creation of the Grecian artist's imagination, it testifies to the power of the imagination to create beauty. On the other hand, as an object—a fact or a truth, if you want—it is a lure to the spectator, attracting his imagination, teasing him out of thought, out of his transient troubles, and into itself. It is only when the spectator has been teased out of his personal world, preferably by a beautiful object, that he can perceive the object truly; and it is then, when the spectator exercises his imagination fully, that truth and beauty are one.

Metaphor, Poetry, and Meaning

In *The Poetics,* which is both a theory of tragedy and a recipe for the writing of tragedy, Aristotle lists the ingredients necessary for tragedy and their proper proportions; everything that the tragedian needs, Aristotle says, can be taught—everything except how to make a metaphor. The playwright, Aristotle believed, can learn to write in the proper meter, can learn the proper mixture of greatness and ordinariness in his hero, can learn how to find his stories and to limit them properly, but he cannot learn how to use language metaphorically. That is a gift that the playwright, and presumably the poet, either has or has not. And, for many critics since Aristotle, the ability to make metaphors is the one indispensable characteristic of the poet.

The narrow definition of metaphor calls it a comparison without the use of "like" or "as." The ghost in *Hamlet,* for example, says, "The serpent that did thy father sting/Now wears his crown." No great perception is needed to understand that the serpent is Claudius, the murderer of Hamlet's father; "serpent," in this sense, is used metaphorically. More broadly, however, a metaphor is any figurative or non-literal use of language. In this sense, much of our normal language is metaphorical. "It was a tough day" uses "tough" metaphorically; "supercilious" means "with raised eye-brow," but to call someone supercilious is not to say that his eyebrows were necessarily raised. Figurative language in literature goes beyond our everyday language by deliberately attempting to use both the literal level and the figurative level of the word. Normal conversation would be difficult, for example, if we regularly stopped to ask how a day could be "tough"; generally, our everyday language needs to work on only one level, so we can loosely interpret "tough" as hard or difficult, and let it go at that. Poetic language, however, works on several levels at one time; at its best, instead of forcing the listener to be unaware of part of the properties of the words that make it up, it forces him to heighten his awareness of those properties. When Wordsworth in a sonnet on evening writes "The holy time is quiet as a Nun/Breathless with adoration," we are supposed to think both of the nun as Wordsworth describes her *and* of the particularly pleasant hush that certain calm evenings have.

The purpose of metaphor at its best is to call attention to and to specify precisely what the poet wants his reader to experience; metaphor, poetically, is both an attention-getting device and a device for precise expression. By comparing the evening to a nun, for example, Wordsworth both surprises and informs us. Literally, the two things are so unlike that the very novelty excites the imagination to consider precisely what Wordsworth had in mind. Consider, for example, the same line with a trite metaphor—the holy time is quiet as a mouse. Because the metaphor is trite, it demands no attention; it simply does not work.

After the poet has our attention, he must convince us that what we are looking at is worth attending to, that the metaphor works both literally and figuratively. Unless the metaphor does both, one half of it is wasted, and poetry, as an art, cannot tolerate waste. If we consider Wordsworth's metaphor of the nun, we find that the more we think about the nun—in the aspect in which Wordsworth presents her as "Breathless with adoration"—the more accurately a certain kind of evening has been described. Nuns are persons whose lives are dedicated to God; they usually lead quiet lives apart from the world. The rhythm of the lines and the factors that Wordsworth calls attention to suggest that he wants the reader to imagine the nun as stately, unhurried, and dignified. Moreover, "holy," which modifies "time" and precedes the metaphor, helps prepare for the nun and to link without further comment the mood implied by the nun and the mood of the evening. Perhaps without metaphor Wordsworth could have described the kind of evening he had in mind—an evening during which everything is quiet, during which nature seems to be moving slowly as if something gently awesome is about to happen, something that will be worthy of human devotion. It might just be possible to suggest accurately such a mood on such an evening without poetic metaphor, but certainly it could not be done with the conciseness, the surprise, and the tone that Wordsworth achieves. Figurative language, if used properly, is not a way of making a loose analogy, a kind of "you get the idea" discourse; it is, rather, a way of comparing two things so that the appropriate values, ideas, or emotions attach to the subject.

Metaphor in general has still another function, however, and one vital to the nature of poetry. Earlier we said that poetry tends to appeal to the whole man—to his emotions, his senses, his intellect. Metaphor, because it works by bringing together things of different orders, builds a multi-dimensional appeal into poetry. Wordsworth, for example, has taken one order of things—the evening—and compared it to another—a person. The result is that the values usually associated with a life of contemplation dedicated to God are suddenly associated with the evening; areas that were separate in our experience are suddenly united into a totally new experience. Donne's "Canonization," which we looked at earlier, gets part of its effect in the same way. Given the situation of the poem, the reader might naturally expect a mere emotional outburst from the narrator; instead, he gets a flood of figurative language that eventually works the narrator out of his anger and into a metaphorically justifiable spiritual pride. The opening words of the poem, "For Godsake," seem to be used merely as a dead metaphor; in ordinary language when someone says, "For God's sake, let me alone," the first three words are merely an intensifier. In "The Canonization," as we have seen, by the end of the poem we find that they are not a dead metaphor but a literal truth, given Donne's argument.

Even images that are not strictly comparisons may fulfill all the functions of metaphor, in that the image, the statement, or the description of a physical object may in a context suggest a certain idea or group of ideas. In the second stanza of "The Canonization," Donne presents several brief images, several brief pictures of various occupations; and each image, as it is presented, is literally accurate. It is true that because some men are merchants, others drown; it is equally true that soldiers kill and lawyers promote quarrels—that may not be the whole truth about the professions Donne cites, but it is a partial truth and it is the relevant truth for the argument Donne is making. With his presentation of the common feature of several alternate ways of life, Donne implies that what usually passes for respectable occupations often harm others, whereas his life as a lover harms no one. The image as Donne uses it in "The Canonization" and as it is characteristically used in effective poetry satisfies the senses of the reader by presenting a picture or a statement of an object or an experience; but in doing so, it simultaneously involves his emotions and his intellect because the image will be chosen and constructed so as to suggest a certain set of values and a certain set of ideas.

Any number of glossaries of literary terms list the kinds of figurative language. The important thing for the student of literature is not primarily an ability to differentiate among the devices, but a realization that any poetic device is more than mere ornament. Only in inferior poetry, in poetry that is not of the best, is there a distinction between the beauty with which the poet tries to attract his reader and the experience which the poem expresses. If the poet is working well, every element of the language will contribute to the entire experience. To expect less than this is to read the best poetry badly.

The Figurative Language of
"Ode on a Grecian Urn"

We have seen that certain textual and biographical evidence suggests that Keats's "Ode on a Grecian Urn" may be read as an attempt to find consolation for what at the time we can call only "woe." The nature of that woe can best be seen by an analysis of the kind of figurative language Keats uses in the body of the poem. If the Ode is indeed integrated in the sense that poetry ought to be integrated, the various figures will all cluster around either a central idea or a set of related ideas, for if metaphor is to be more than mere poetic decoration, each metaphor must be involved in the central concerns of the poem.

The first striking piece of figurative language in the Ode occurs in the opening address to the urn, the oxymoron "unravished bride." Brides, in a sense, are meant to be ravished, since a bride is not officially a bride until she has been taken by her husband. The figure of speech here begins the establishment of a set of relationships that shall run throughout the Ode. The "unravished bride" can only be so, in reality, for a moment; and, according to one of the standards of value expressed in the poem, that moment is the kind of moment that brings the highest happiness. It is the moment at which the bride and her new husband have all of their expectations before them, their desires are at their height, and there has as yet been no fulfillment and therefore no disappointment, no satiety.

It would, of course, be improper to make so much of this figure of speech if it were not carried throughout the Ode in one form or another. It is, actually, just one of a number of paradoxes that Keats builds on. The urn, though a "foster child of silence," can "express/A flowery tale more sweetly than our rhyme"—in other words, like the bride, it is both the thing it is and the thing it is not. The resolution of the paradox begins in the second stanza, with "soft pipes" playing "unheard melodies," again an apparent contradiction in terms. The "unheard melodies" are "more endear'd," more charming, than real melodies, just as the silent urn is a better historian than the poet and just as the bride is unravished. In the second stanza, however, we discover that it is not just a moment that Keats elevates to contain what *apparently* is the highest happiness, but rather a condition of incompletion. The "unheard melodies" are sweeter because they are heard by the "spirit." The piper will forever play his sweet melodies, just as the tree will forever be green. More importantly, however, the lover depicted on the urn as chasing his beloved will never reach her, and for Keats at this point in the poem, the lover's failure is a cause for joy rather than for sorrow. Like the tree that will be forever green, she will be forever fair and he forever in love.

Ordinarily, when a poet uses paradox, he is attempting to startle our attention into seeing that there is a sense in which the terms involved are not really contradictory, that on a realistic level there is a sense in which they are, in fact, compatible—as in the cliché "the sound of silence," meaning a silence so striking that the ear senses it. Keats, however, is using the paradoxes to move beyond a realistic level to suggest that imaginatively if not actually, man can momentarily attain a world in which beauty does not fade or love wilt.

Keats paints reality as he sees it for the purposes of the Ode quickly and dismally in the third stanza. Suppose, he says in effect, the lover were to overtake the girl and to enjoy her; he would be left with "a heart high-sorrowful and cloy'd,/A burning forehead, and a parching tongue." Reality, by allowing happiness to come to completion, thereby permits it to decay.

If paradox, then, is a verbal technique that permits Keats to depict an ideal world, a world in which the contradictions of this world do not prevail, it is an especially appropriate technique for leading into the final lines of the poem. Although grammatically there is a difference of form between "unravished bride," or "unheard" melodies on the one hand, and "Beauty is truth" on the other, logically they all join terms that in reality are not joined. Partly through this device, and partly through others that we shall consider shortly, Keats leads his reader to posit, at least momentarily, a world in which the usual laws of contradiction do not apply and to create around that world an aura of value, an aura of happiness, that our real world of completion and satiety lacks.

We do not have to believe that such a world actually exists. The first four stanzas of the Ode are, in effect, an example of the failure to exercise "negative capability,"—the ability to become so fully absorbed in an object that one loses all personal emotions, habits of perception, habits of thought, and so on. In part, the first four stanzas are one long image, one long description of the urn and the scenes on it, and the very specification seems to give the scenes a kind of reality. The reality, however, is specious, for the content and the emotional coloration of the scenes as Keats describes them are determined not only by what is on the urn but also by the narrator's mood. The Keats of the letters had asked for a life of sensations rather than of thought, a life of the accurate perception of reality rather than the imposition of intellectual (and probably also emotional) patterns upon it. The narrator's conclusion that the lover who does not catch the girl is happier than if he had caught her imposes the narrator's own values upon the pictures shown on the urn.

In the next section, we shall examine this problem in considerably more detail. At this point, however, we can only comment upon the way Keats uses the extended image. The human interest of the scenes, the very factor that makes it possible for Keats to read his own emotions into the scenes, lures Keats into a contemplation of the urn. Throughout the first four stanzas, it is an impure contemplation, a contemplation marred by an overinterpretation of what he sees on the urn. The images have to be presented fully because Keats must convince the reader both of their appeal and of the delusion upon which they are based. He must also construct them so that they suggest the central concerns of the poem—in general terms, the relationship between beauty and truth, and the consolation that the union of those two transcendentals gives man. It is significant, therefore, that Keats's false perception of the urn gives no consolation. At the beginning of the Ode he expected the urn to answer his questions; throughout the middle two stanzas he compared the urn with the real world, to the detriment of the latter; but in the fourth stanza, the last of the imagistic presentations, Keats concludes with a note of dejection. The urn that he expected to "express a flowery tale" cannot even tell why the little village is desolate.

If I am reading the poem aright, the use of the imagery is highly sophisticated and greatly daring. Keats lures us into the same trap into which the urn had lured him—that of meditating on the scenes of the urn and evaluating them in personal terms. But like the urn, Keats leads us out of the trap. In the final stanza Keats perceives that the urn is more than his interpretation of the scenes upon it; it is, actually, an urn, a "fair shape," and not a bride, not a historian. When Keats can see the urn as it is, when he has, in effect, a true image of the urn, then it is a consolation, and only then is its beauty truth, and its truth beauty.

Analysis of Structure

As a brief study of only one aspect of the figurative language of Keats's "Ode on a Grecian Urn," the preceding essay was confined to emphasizing the implications of that language and showing in a general way its relation to the over-all theme of the Ode. The same kind of theme will emerge from a study that shows how the larger elements of the poem are put together.

Ezra Pound once wrote that poetry ought to be at least as well written as prose; he meant, I take it, that the language of poetry ought to be as precise as the language of prose, and also that the over-all organization of a poem ought to be as functional, as meaningful, as the organization of a prose piece. Except for some kinds of overtly didactic poetry, poetry does not usually attempt to argue logically; as we have seen, it makes its arguments by insinuation. Donne compares himself and his lover to flies, then to candles, then to the eagle and the dove, before deciding that the comparison with the phoenix "has more wit," more pertinence; and after establishing that comparison, he applies its implications to the argument that, like the phoenix, he and his love die and rise again. Keats creates a world in which the inherent contradictions in a set of paradoxes do not apply before reaching his conclusion that "Beauty is truth." Even so light and apparently casual a lyric as Herrick's "Upon Julia's Clothes" makes an argument in its own way:

> Whenas in silks my Julia goes,
> Then, then (methinks) how sweetly flows
> That liquefaction of her clothes.
>
> Next, when I cast mine eyes and see
> That brave Vibration each way free,
> Oh how that glittering taketh me!

The purpose of this poem, or the point of its argument, is to convey to the reader some sense of the impression Julia made on the poet. Herrick's plan of argument is amazingly simple, and amazingly complex. Rather than giving a full description of Julia—five feet two, eyes of blue, and so on—he catches her at a moment when she is most lovely, when she is dressed well and moving gracefully. By impeccable control of the tone and rhythm of the lines, he manages to suggest the rhythm, the elegance, of Julia's movements. The control shown in the poem also, however, says something important about the narrator; the perfectly functional rhythm coupled with the only apparently rigid logical form of the six lines (whenas this, then that; next, that) imply that the narrator is not a man easily charmed; he is a man who keeps his feelings in check. Suddenly, in the final line, the control cracks just a bit; the legalistic mind that constructed its compliment to Julia in a logical form with such non-poetic jargon as "whenas," "liquefaction," and "Vibration," suddenly and completely without warning breaks into an exclamation—"Oh how that glittering taketh me!"

As a result of the way "Upon Julia's Clothes" is put together, the reader does not have to accept Herrick's word for the impression that Julia makes, the quick transition from logical pattern to exclamation shows a narrator that we had been taught to think of as a rather level-headed person astonished by Julia's beauty. None of this in the poem is argued logically; it is simply presented as a sequence of events, and the events speak for themselves. A change of one word in the poem, for example, would radically change the structure of the poem and make it substantially less convincing; suppose the final stanza were changed to:

> Next, when I cast mine eyes and see
> That brave vibration each way free
> *Then* that glittering taketh me.

The change alters the form of Herrick's response so that it seems to remain coldly logical all the way through: we do not see the poet being surprised by Julia's loveliness and bursting into an emotional statement; we have to take his word that the "glittering taketh" him.

Another way of putting this is to point out that in most poems something happens, and that whatever happens must seem plausible if the poem is to succeed. Yeats's "Sailing to Byzantium" * is in many respects a difficult poem; and the concluding stanza, in which Yeats in effect states his ambition, poses difficulties for most readers:

> Once out of nature I shall never take
> My bodily form from any natural thing,
> But such a form as Grecian goldsmiths make
> Of hammered gold and gold enameling
> To keep a drowsy Emperor awake;
> Or set upon a golden bough to sing
> To lords and ladies of Byzantium
> Of what is past, or passing, or to come.

In this final stanza of the poem, Yeats asks that he be reincarnated not as a natural object, but as a golden bird that will sing of the past, the present, and the future. The wish does not seem to make much sense unless we consider the poetic argument that leads up to it. The poem begins:

* Reprinted with permission of The Macmillan Company and A. P. Watt and Son from *Collected Poems* by William Butler Yeats. Copyright 1928 by The Macmillan Company. Renewed 1956 by Georgie Yeats.

> That is no country for old men. The young
> In one another's arms, birds in the trees
> —Those dying generations—at their song,
> The salmon falls, the mackerel-crowded seas,
> Fish, flesh, or fowl, commend all summer long
> Whatever is begotten, born, and dies.
> Caught in that sensual music all neglect
> Monuments of unageing intellect.

The beginning of the poetic argument, then, is an expression of the futility of oncoming age and the desire to escape from a country where everyone is young. Yeats is careful to present the argument for the country he wants to leave at its strongest; the season is the best of the year, life teems everywhere, the young couples make love—it seems idyllic, but it is flawed. The life imagery, Yeats reminds his readers, is also death imagery, for "whatever is begotten" also dies; and those who give their lives to living—and dying—neglect the "monuments of unageing intellect."

What can an aging man do? In the second stanza, Yeats argues that "an aged man is but a paltry thing/ . . . unless/Soul clap its hands and sing." When the body is worn out, only the soul can express joy; and, as Yeats says in the final part of the second stanza, the soul can learn to sing only by studying the works of the soul. Hence he travels to Byzantium, a holy city, a beautiful city, and a city of monuments.

In the third stanza, since the body is worn out, he argues that it might as well die, for once the body dies, the soul can be gathered "into the artifice of eternity." After this argument, the conclusion of the poem is both pertinent and plausible. If the soul is eternal, it must exist somewhere after death; Yeats does not want it linked with the body, for bodies die. Throughout the early stanzas, "song" or singing has been a metaphor for joy, and the enemy has been time, the bringer of both birth and death. As an artificial bird— a kind of monument, to stretch that term a bit—singing of "what is past, or passing, or to come," the poet will have mastered time completely.

Perhaps the simplest terminology describing the way poetry

makes its arguments is that used by the late Yvor Winters, who felt that poetry, as distinguished from other kinds of writing, attempted to present an *emotion,* by which he meant a felt rather than a logical evaluation of an experience. But he also believed that in any successful poem the emotion had to be *motivated;* the causes for making just that evaluation of the experience had to be presented clearly and convincingly. In a sense, the test for a poem, according to this standard, is whether the poet's evaluation of the experience he presents is understandable not in terms of what we know about human nature, the poet's biography, or the intellectual currents of his time, but understandable in terms of the over-all structure of the poem. Whether or not the reader would agree with the poet's evaluation is irrelevant; what is relevant is that from the evidence presented in the poem we understand the basis upon which the poet makes his judgment.

The Structure of the "Ode on a Grecian Urn"

Although the "Ode on a Grecian Urn" is divided into five stanzas, it is in terms of its internal organization essentially a two-part poem. The division occurs between the fourth and fifth stanzas, at the point where Keats suddenly begins to see the urn differently from the way he had seen it earlier. Although the terms will have to be clarified later, for now we can say that in the first four stanzas Keats looks at the urn subjectively; in the last stanza, he looks at it objectively. As a result of both ways of looking at the urn, he is finally able to see it as "a friend to man, to whom thou say'st/Beauty is truth, truth beauty."

Perhaps the quickest way of accounting for the change and for its implications is to indicate the setting of the poem. Since the Ode begins with an apostrophe to the urn, we may assume that the poem's narrator is looking at the urn and meditating on it. The final stanza also begins with an apostrophe to the urn, so we may further assume that throughout the Ode, the narrator continues his meditation.

His first reaction to the urn is a thoroughly natural reaction; it has scenes shown on it, and the narrator reacts the way untutored viewers of art have reacted for generations—he wants to know who the persons shown on the urn are, what they are doing, where they are. He is, in other words, looking at the scene on the urn as if it were, say, a newspaper photograph of a picnic. And, at this point in the Ode, the questions are not idle questions; the narrator expects the urn to answer them, for he thinks of the urn as a "Sylvan historian, who canst thus express/A flowery tale more sweetly than our rhyme."

Paradoxically, however, the so-called realistic questions—who, where, when, what—are in this case also personal questions because they will lead to Keats's perceiving the figures on the urn not as they are but as Keats wants to see them. Strangely enough, the questions are not answered; the second stanza takes off in a different direction altogether. As we saw in the preceding section, instead of pursuing the questions he has just asked, Keats continues with the paradoxes that he set up in the first stanza by meditating not on the identity of the figures, on their prose reality, as it were, but upon their meaning to him.

Indirectly, of course, the prose questions are answered at least partly by the identification of the figures as a piper, and a young woman being chased by a young man. But the answer is given casually, and not in the kind of detail and with the kind of precision that the questions called for, and certainly not with the kind of fullness that the description of the urn as "Sylvan historian" promised. It is as if the figures on the urn had lured Keats beyond his original interest in them and into a new and more profound interest.

The new direction of interest continues through the third stanza, with its overt comparison of the ideal permanence of the life depicted on the urn and the impermanence of life—or, more accurately, of human joy—as it actually is. Thus far, the Ode is primarily a rather loose meditation upon the urn organized through the development of the kind of paradoxes we considered in the preceding section. The fourth stanza, however, returns to the kind of interest Keats began with; turning to the side of the urn opposite the scene with the piper and the boy and girl, Keats asks who the people coming to the sacrifice are, what altar the heifer is being led to, and what town the people are from; these are the same kind of who, what, where questions Keats originally asked. It is almost as if his interest in the theme of completion had ended with the comparison of the ideal world and the real world at the end of the third stanza, and now he turns the urn to its other side and idly inquires about the new scene.⌋

Yet, despite the similarity of the questions that Keats asks in stanzas one and four, the attitude behind the questions has changed completely. ⌈At the opening of the Ode he had expected the urn to answer his questions, and a large part of the first stanza gives, in effect, the qualifications of the urn to answer the questions accurately. But in the fourth stanza, Keats explicitly states that he expects no answer. Addressing the little town depicted in the second scene, he says, "thy streets for evermore/Will silent be; and not a soul to tell/Why thou are desolate, can e'er return." He no longer expects the urn to be a historian—at least not a literal historian who can give him the names of persons and of gods, who can tell him what town the persons are from, and so on. The urn has, in fact, failed as a "Sylvan historian." ⌋

Keats learns yet another lesson through the four stanzas. ⌈The second and third stanzas seemed to present the world on the urn as ideal because time could neither ruin the beauty of the maid nor end the delight of the chase. But as Keats contemplates the second scene, the tone changes drastically; Keats now meditates not on "happy, happy boughs," but upon a "desolate" town. Although he does not develop the notion by contrasting the desolate town on the urn with a real town, as he does with the lovers in the third stanza, he does seem to suggest that a world standing apart from the press of time has its obvious disadvantages. Just as the lovers on the urn will always love—a happy condition—the town will always be desolate—an unhappy condition. Stasis is not, Keats discovers in the fourth stanza, an unmixed blessing. ⌋

If my reading of the Ode is correct so far, Keats must either end the poem after the fourth stanza or radically change the way he perceives the urn. He does the latter, and he does it decisively. In the fifth stanza, his description of the urn is literally accurate. It is a Grecian urn, therefore an "Attic shape"; it is a "fair attitude," and therefore a lovely form; it does not depict gods or maidens loth, but rather a "brede/Of marble men and maidens." For the first time, in other words, Keats is seeing the urn objectively—he is seeing it as a lovely object, worthy of his attention not because the scene is relevant to his subjective feelings but [because it is lovely as an urn.] It is, roughly, the difference between looking at Picasso's *Guernica* because of its depiction of a certain moment of history, and looking at it as a painting, as a wonderful combination of form and color.

[When Keats perceives the urn this way, as it was meant to be perceived, it becomes immensely more valuable. To put this in somewhat different terms, Keats's first perception of the urn was deficient in "negative capability" because he approached the urn with expectations that grew from him rather than from the urn. His second way of looking at it sees it precisely as it is; he sees it objectively, as a "Cold pastoral." In this sense, through the beauty of its form, it "dost tease us out of thought." As a beautifully formed vase, it lures Keats into an impersonal experience of beauty.]

Yet, the urn does not merely lure the spectator away from thought; it does not leave the mind either a blank or with an ineffable surge of emotion. Keats specifies that the urn "dost tease us out of thought/As doth eternity," and the comparison with eternity is most significant. In the first section of the Ode, Keats has been concerned with temporality, the opposite of eternity, in at least two ways. [We have seen already that his revery in the second and third stanzas centers on the theme of time and the stopping of time, and, further, that by the fourth stanza Keats realized that he had to reject the stopping of time as an ideal. In the first and fourth stanzas, his interest in time is somewhat different; the questions he asks the urn are, in effect, historical questions which the urn cannot answer. Through his meditation on the urn in the opening stanzas, despite the fact that it was based on assumptions he had to discard, Keats arrives at a true perception of it as an "Attic shape," a "Cold pastoral." This newly won perception of the urn is both its truth and its beauty.

panacea; a proposed remedy for all ills.

If we review briefly what has happened in the Ode, we can see how literally true it is that the urn does "tease" the beholder out of thought. The figures shown on the urn have literally lured Keats into contemplating them, and through them, the urn. The figures function as a kind of enticement, like the bawdy puns and the drunk scenes in Shakespeare's plays, scenes which catch and hold audience attention with elementary dramatic and verbal fireworks. Keats's response to the figures on the urn is like that of an audience to the opening scene of *Hamlet*—with all the bustle on the stage, the soldiers, the ghost, we want to know what is happening and why. It is a normal enough human reaction for an artist to count on. But once the attention is caught, the work of art, *Hamlet* or the urn, can go about its more serious business. The more serious business in this case is the lesson that the questions dealing with time as history are relatively insignificant and that the idealization of time as stasis is not a sure consolation. In midst of other woe the urn will remain, its figures a lure to contemplation; and through contemplation of the urn, man may learn that beauty must be perceived truly. The urn does not offer man a panacea, but a perception of the endurance of beauty and truth, and in that perception, a consolation against the ravages of time.

Further Possibilities

These five short essays have left a number of topics relevant to the "Ode on a Grecian Urn" either unexamined or examined only superficially. A full list of the relevant topics would be out of place here, although some indication of further possibilities is appropriate.

Nothing, for example, has been said about either the metrics or about the relation of the sound to the meaning of the Ode. Most readers would probably agree that the sound of the poem is appropriate to its effect, and a critic ought to be prepared to analyze— at least crudely, until linguists give us a better way of describing sound effects—just why this particular combination of sounds is right for this particular poem. It is, for example, impossible to read the Ode rapidly; what in the sounds of the words and the way they are joined forces the reader to read slowly? Is the alliteration used functionally so that the words it emphasizes are important enough to deserve such emphasis, or is it merely decorative? Does Keats use the rhyme words functionally—that is, are they words he would want to call special attention to—or is the rhyme scheme in the Ode merely a conventional pattern?

To turn to a different kind of topic, the "Ode on a Grecian Urn" is one of a group of odes that Keats wrote during a brief but intensely creative period in his life. Furthermore, there are some similarities of theme and even of situation among the odes. To study them as a group would quite probably throw light on each of the poems individually, and an analysis of the thematic similarities and differences that mark the odes would be likely to reveal something about Keats both as a thinker and as a craftsman.

Although it is dangerous to read the biography of a poet back into his poems, some consideration of the reasons for Keats's concern with the themes presented in the "Ode on a Grecian Urn" could possibly support a reading of the Ode. In particular, Keats's love for Fanny Brawne may have led him into a certain intensity of mood that he never before or never after achieved. A knowledge of his relationship with Fanny might explain why Keats momentarily found the desirability of the young lady on the urn enhanced by her unapproachability, and why later in the poem he became disillusioned with the notion of a perpetual chase.

Even though we touched upon Keats's conception of the imagination, we did not attempt to consider it fully as it would have been understood by Keats and his contemporaries. The notion of the imagination was one of the key concepts of the period, and a more complete realization of the power that was ascribed to it is helpful in understanding the full import of the final lines of the poem. Along with analysis of the concept of the imagination would go a study of neo-Platonism, and in particular the forms of it that were argued and accepted by Keats and his fellow poets.

This summary of topics is not intended to be exhaustive, nor will every approach be equally well suited to the abilities and interests of every student. It is designed merely to indicate some of the topics available and to suggest that there may be others awaiting exploration. The student is likely to understand literature much better and to appreciate it much more if he can come to it from many sides, if his approaches to it result from a conscious decision to use the methods he thinks best rather than from his ignorance of available alternatives.

II

Pope's *Rape of the Lock*

Literary Determinants

Earlier we noted that after an author makes his initial choice—whether it be of form, theme, or even of opening word—he is no longer absolutely free to write whatever he pleases, at least not if he intends to produce a coherent work. A variety of factors begin to limit what he may reasonably do, and with each decision the author makes, the limits become progressively narrower.

If we return to *Hamlet,* for example, we ought to be able to see that much of what happens in the play can be accounted for by a few general causes that, for the sake of convenience, we will call *literary determinants.* It is, I think, fairly safe to assume that before writing *Hamlet* Shakespeare knew that he was going to write a revenge tragedy based on the story of a Danish prince compelled to avenge his murdered father. With this initial choice of a well-known story and an equally well-known form, both of which he had to accept as givens, Shakespeare greatly limited his freedom. The story requires that he create a cast of characters including Hamlet, Gertrude, Claudius, and the ghost of the murdered king. Since the play is a revenge tragedy, a genre with its own requirements, Shakespeare has to have Hamlet killed *after* taking revenge on Claudius.

All of this is obvious, but not so obvious is the fact that

Shakespeare has also committed himself to much else. An audience for a revenge tragedy would have expected entertainment, and for Shakespeare's audience that tended to include humor and violence. Moreover, the audience would have expected the play to last for a certain length of time, so that Hamlet's revenge upon Claudius would have to be delayed. It would also have expected to see its familiar actors in familiar kinds of roles; and at least part of it would have expected that a tragedy, as one of the high literary forms, have a serious moral theme. Although modern readers and theater-goers may be somewhat more flexible in what they require of a Shakespeare tragedy, one of the reasons that the play has succeeded so well is that it does meet all of these requirements and more.

If we try to generalize now upon the kinds of reasons that will account for the details included in *Hamlet,* we can see several sets of literary determinants, several factors that explain why the play is as it is. I shall list the literary determinants, then discuss them in some detail: (1) the objective source of the literary work—a well-known story, an experience of the author, a story told him, etc.; (2) the conventions of the genre and sub-genre; (3) the need for at least minimal verisimilitude; (4) the need for an acceptable rhythm; (5) the relevant thematic factors. Although the list could be drawn up somewhat differently, these five sets of determinants can explain the inclusion of the details that get into any literary work.

Whether the author is Chaucer retelling the oft-told bawdy anecdote that makes up the "Miller's Tale," Keats looking at an urn, or Bernard Shaw basing a drama upon the history of St. Joan, any work of literature begins with some real or vicarious experience of the author. It may be as personal as Milton considering his blindness or as impersonal as Cooper's reading a Scott novel and deciding he could do better, but one of the things that will determine what happens within a literary work is the kind of objective situation it is based upon. Sometimes the objective experience behind the work is minimal and indirect, perhaps not even worth mentioning either because it is trivial or because nothing certain can be said about it. We may be fairly sure, for example, that Keats did at one time look carefully at a Grecian urn; for a number of reasons, however, whether or not Keats described the urn accurately is irrelevant. It is irrelevant partly because the focus of the poem is upon Keats's meditation and, admittedly on a much lower level, partly because the urn Keats saw is not generally known and so we are content to take Keats's word for what he saw on it. In such a case, the objective source functions minimally as a literary determinant.

In Chaucer's "Miller's Tale," though, or *Hamlet,* or Dryden's *Absalom and Achitophel,* the situation is quite different. In *Absalom and Achitophel,* to take a rather complicated instance, Dryden is basing his poem upon two sets of exterior sources, both of which were well known to his readers. On the one hand, he had to create a cast of characters who in their actions and values reflected the characters in the Biblical story; on the other, he had to create the same set of characters in such a way as to reflect the personalities of the group who attempted to block the succession of James II. The need to consider both objective sources severely limited what Dryden could do in his character portrayals; the necessary casting of Charles II as David, for example, meant that the well-known licentiousness of the King had to be excused and, in fact, the casting provided the excuse by reminding readers that even Biblical kings have concubines and illegitimate children. In general, the better known the situation upon which the writer bases his work, the more limited he is in his treatment of it. Authors can occasionally violate their exterior sources—whether they be literary, historical, or biographical—but they do so at a risk, and readers are likely to feel uncomfortable with a literary work unless somehow the author convinces them that the risk was worth taking.

The genre in which the author is working also sets up its literary determinants. Once a writer decides to compose a Shakespearean sonnet—to take an easy example—he is committed to a rhyme scheme, a length, and a meter; if he breaks the commitment, he may still write a very good poem, but it is not a Shakespearean sonnet. Similarly, a detective story requires a detective, a crime, a criminal, and a solution. All this is elementary, but other requirements of form are more subtle. In a detective story, to return to that example, the rules require that the protagonist solve the crime; he must, consequently, be unusually intelligent (like Sherlock Holmes), unusually peristent (like Mike Hammer), or unusually lucky (like Inspector Pinkerton). And since readers of detective stories tend to lose interest unless the solution to the crime is difficult, the author must further provide complications in the form of a brilliant or ruthless adversary, false clues, or some such device. Moreover, readers are likely to be more interested if the stakes are high, hence the solution to the crime is usually a matter of life and death, great wealth, or national security. Shakespeare's *Hamlet,* to use another example, had to last approximately two hours, because that was what the audience expected; consequently, Hamlet could not kill Claudius immediately, for then the revenge part of the revenge tragedy would be over too quickly; the result is a number of ingenious reasons for Hamlet's delay.

Authors, of course, can and do violate the conventions of their genre, but generally the reader must feel that the violation serves some important purpose. When writing a poem predominantly in heroic couplets, Dryden sometimes included three-line units, thus breaking the pattern; modern literature has created a spate of anti-novels, anti-heroes, anti-poems—that is, novels, heroes, and poems in which the expected conventions are ignored. Such departures from genre conventions work, however, only for one or both of two reasons: either because the departure plays against the convention and gains value because it is recognized as unconventional, or because it suggests some theme that the conventional pattern cannot suggest.

The need for verisimilitude is both pervasive and complex. Most readers will not take an author seriously unless they feel that he knows something about his theme and its relevance to the world. At its simplest level, verisimilitude is the result of having created a world enough like ours so that we do not have that nagging feeling that whatever happens in the fictional world is irrelevant to ours. In *Gulliver's Travels* Swift puts his satire aside for a few pages in each of the four books to provide the kind of detail that will make the reader forget momentarily that Gulliver is a fictional character; he provides him with a family, a home, a profession, a reason for going to sea, and storms and pirates to account for shipwreck—none of which has any direct relevance to the issues that Swift wants to raise in *Gulliver's Travels* but which are vital for the reader's peace of mind. On a much different level, verisimilitude can be as complex as Shakespeare's planting of Mercutio outside the balcony in the famous scene in *Romeo and Juliet*. In the scene between Romeo and Juliet, Shakespeare gives his audience a portrait of youthful and idealistic love; Mercutio, waiting, makes bawdy comments. Robert Penn Warren has pointed out that Mercutio is necessary for a number of reasons, but the one that concerns us now is his use in making the scene believable. The scene between Romeo and Juliet is almost too saccharine; without Mercutio it might just possibly draw the kind of laughter frequently heard in theaters when an audience feels it knows more about life than the author does. Mercutio's bawdy jokes are Shakespeare's way of saying "trust me in this scene; like you, I know that love is not all moonlight and roses and that, to quote Yeats anachronistically—'love has pitched his mansion in the place of excrement'—because I know both sides of love, you may accept this scene seriously." On a very sophisticated level, Mercutio makes the scene believable.

If an author must satisfy his readers' need for verisimilitude, he must also satisfy an equally pressing demand for a kind of rhythm. By *rhythm* I mean a pattern of stresses and relief, problems and solutions, intensity and relaxation, anticipation and satisfaction— no one pair of terms will include all the constituent elements of rhythm that can be found in works of literature. The basis of the demand is the obvious fact that the one sin an author must avoid at all costs is that of boring his readers, and that nothing is more conducive to boredom than monotony. A skilled writer of adventure novels, such as Alexander Dumas père, for example, knows better than to make his novels all adventure, just as a skilled nightclub comedian knows better than to make all of his lines funny. Readers and audiences need time to gather their forces in preparation for surges of laughter, excitement, intellectual or emotional intensity, or whatever might be the major effect the work intends to create. Obviously, the longer the work, the more carefully patterned and more varied the rhythmic devices must be, lest they themselves become monotonous.

The rhythmic devices—perhaps it might be helpful to think of them as patterned contrasts—may be as minute as the rhythmic play of the syllables of a poem against its meter or as large scale as the carefully contrived hour-glass pattern of Henry James's *The Ambassadors*. It is impossible to enter into a full discussion of the types and uses of rhythmic devices that get into literature, but a look at one example might help. Kenneth Burke has a brilliant account of the opening scenes of *Hamlet*. Burke asks why the section up to Hamlet's confrontation with the ghost is so effective and decides that Shakespeare has played masterfully with the expectations of the audience; in our terms, he has created the perfect rhythm for the effect he attempts. *Hamlet* opens with the soldiers on the parapet, the ghost appears and then leaves, the soldiers and Horatio decide it wants to speak to Hamlet. Rhythmically, the scene ends with the audience anticipating some important communication from the ghost. A lesser playwright than Shakespeare would probably have met those anticipations immediately by having Hamlet meet the ghost in the next scene. Instead, Shakespeare switches scenes from the exterior of the castle to the interior and provides normal exposition between the King and Hamlet; lest the audience forget, however, that it is supposed to be waiting eagerly for the ghost, Shakespeare has Horatio tell Hamlet (and thereby remind the audience) that the ghost is waiting. Certainly the next scene would seem to be the place to introduce the ghost, but instead Shakespeare has another long expository scene between Polonius, Ophelia, and Laertes. In the fourth scene, Hamlet is on the parapet, awaiting the ghost, and surely here it ought to appear. Again Shakespeare delays, and underscores the delay by having Marcellus tell the audience that it is after midnight, after the time that ghosts traditionally appear. Hamlet then begins an extremely interesting speech, perhaps the most thematically significant and rhetorically effective speech up to this point in the play. Just as the audience gets caught up in the speech, the ghost appears. Rhythmically, Shakespeare has created in his audience a desire to see the ghost, delayed the satisfaction for as long as possible, then provided the satisfaction at the moment it was least expected. The result is a double satisfaction—we get precisely what we expected, and we are nevertheless surprised when it comes. In the "Ode on a Grecian Urn" Keats uses rhythm in a rather different way; the contrast is between the first four stanzas of the Ode and the last stanza, with the two ways of seeing the urn played off against each other.

It would, of course, be a mistake to speak of *the* rhythmic pattern of a work; any relatively complex piece of literature will have a variety of rhythmic patterns, of contrasts that serve to play upon the expectations and the demands of the audience. It is, however, wise to realize that this need of building properly, of timing, does account for many of the elements that make their way into literature.

Finally, much of what a writer includes in a work will be determined by the theme he intends to express—or, since themes are not always the intention of the writer—lets grow in his work. One of Swift's chief intentions in *Gulliver's Travels,* for example, was to castigate all forms of man's pride. This intention accounts, in part, for many of the scenes in Gulliver—for example, for making the most sensible creatures in the book horses, thereby attacking man's pride in his common sense; for creating the long-lived Struldbruggs, thereby attacking man's physical pride and his pride in his ability to learn; for the scene in which Gulliver in disgust watches the Brobdingnagian women dress, thereby attacking pride in physical beauty; for his picture of the Academy of Projectors, thereby attacking man's pride in his science—and so on. In *Huckleberry Finn,* Twain expresses the theme that a life in nature is better than a life in society; as a literary determinant that theme obviously requires that Twain show life both in nature and in society, and that generally good things happen in the former and bad in the latter. Consequently, when Huck and Jim are on the river alone, the tone tends to become idyllic, Huck and Jim are happy, and Huck progressively develops more and more moral maturity; when Huck is on land he is involved with a brutal father, a feud, a swindle, and a crude practical joke. Twain's theme does not require these things specifically, but it does require them or their equivalents.

What we have, then, is a general set of factors that explain the kinds of details that get into literary work. For the practical critic, two conclusions may be drawn: in no work of any length will all the details be accountable for by any single literary determinant. We cannot assume that everything that happens in *Gulliver's Travels,* for example, is thematically important. *Gulliver's Travels* is in part a mock-travel book, and must be considered partly as a travel book, which means that it must contain the adventures and the wonders that readers of travel books expect; it also must convince the reader of its reality, at least for the moment, and so Swift must give Gulliver a family and a home, or their equivalents.

More importantly, however, the more successful the work, the less the seams will show—the less the reader will be aware that this particular element was put in for verisimilitude, that for comic relief, that for thematic reasons, and so on. One of the reasons that most propaganda literature is so unconvincing and so dull is that the intelligent reader recognizes that everything in the work has been determined by the writer's theme. Even one of the greatest of propaganda novels, *Grapes of Wrath,* suffers from this failure; Steinbeck in *Grapes of Wrath* wanted to fix the blame for the suffering of the impoverished farmers in the 1930's on the rich Eastern bankers and the exploiting California land-owners; the result is a number of scenes whose only function is to show rich people being nasty and poor people being good. If we look at the opening scenes of *Hamlet* again, we can see that not only have the scenes been constructed to achieve the kind of rhythmic effect I indicated, but they also serve a number of other purposes. They satisfy the objective demands by introducing the characters Shakespeare got from his source and establishing them in the conventional relationships; they meet the genre requirements by providing the expected exposition in the expected place; they promote verisimilitude by helping to establish the feeling that this is a real Hamlet in a real world peopled with relatives and courtiers and friends. Although for the sake of analysis it is often possible to say that a particular detail is the result of a particular literary determinant, in any reasonably complex work very little will be present for any single reason; every word, every character, every scene, will function in as many ways as possible.

The Literary Determinants of
The Rape of the Lock

Although *The Rape of the Lock* is a charming and exciting poem even for those who know little of the eighteenth century and its literary conventions and perhaps even less about the poem's source, one of the reasons that literary scholars find it completely fascinating and so artistically masterful is Pope's ability to meet the very complex set of requirements the poem demanded. Later sections will examine in detail the way Pope managed some of the literary determinants of *The Rape of the Lock;* here I shall merely set out generally the kinds of restrictions that the poem imposed on Pope.

The objective source of *The Rape of the Lock* was a quarrel between Lord Petre and Miss Arabella Fermor, and the supporters of each, that began when the Lord cut a lock of hair from the lovely Arabella. A mutual friend of the antagonists and of Pope, Lord Caryll, suggested that Pope try to end the quarrel; Pope chose to write a mock epic retelling of the cutting of the lock, thereby emphasizing the pettiness of the quarrel. Pope's problem was complicated, however, by the need to placate the parties involved. He had, on the one hand, to tell Arabella and her friends—since they were the more belligerent group—that they were acting foolishly, and on the other hand, to control the tone of the poem so that none of the major participants in the quarrel would be angrier after reading the poem than before. In effect, basing his poem on the Petre-Fermor quarrel committed Pope to a set of characters, a specific action with a specific development, and a responsibility for pleasing the principals while actually deploring their pettiness.

For reasons that we shall examine in more detail later, Pope chose as his genre the mock epic, a form which required that he use the major epic conventions while, simultaneously, inverting their usual purpose. The mock epic did not have to contain all the features of the epic; it could, for example, be considerably shorter than the epic, and usually the brevity led to the avoidance of the beginning *in medias res* (chiefly because such a beginning is a unifying device, and a brief form requires fewer unifying devices than a longer one). In choosing the mock heroic form, however, the poet committed himself to using a sufficient number of epic conventions so that the reader would not forget his intention, and further of using those conventions to force the reader to see a contrast between the days when there were heroes and the days when there were merely elegant lords and ladies, or dunces, or bad poets, or whatever group was being castigated.

Even though the mock epic tends toward fantasy because it works chiefly by blowing things beyond their normal proportions, it must still possess some verisimilitude. Usually, the mock epic, despite its humor and its exaggeration, is deadly serious in its intent; when it is a form of satire, it tries to enlighten its readers, and readers simply will not accept the views of a writer unless he gives some evidence that he knows what he is talking about. Pope consequently has to work extremely hard in *The Rape of the Lock* to promote verisimilitude by showing that he knows the relevant details of Belinda's world. Although much else happens, as we shall see, when Belinda sits in front of her mirror primping for the party, one of the reasons that the scene works so effectively is that her dressing table is realistically described. We can visualize it, with its puffs and powders and love letters and combs and all the paraphernalia with which lovely ladies enhance their loveliness. Pope even takes pains to describe with minute fidelity the game of Ombre played in the third Canto; the cards that are dealt could reasonably be played with the result Pope describes. It is perhaps a minor detail, but it is significant because it shows how thoroughly Pope knows the society he is criticizing; it is an unobtrusive yet very forceful way of telling the reader that Pope is completely qualified to evaluate Belinda's world.

In addition, Pope chose to write *The Rape of the Lock* in heroic couplets, a form that limited him to a line composed of five iambic beats, rhyming aa, bb, etc., and with a definite break after each two lines. The pattern requires that the poet think in twenty syllable (two-line) units and still achieve a variety of tone and sentence structure that will keep the reader alert after several hundred lines of a steady monotonously unvaried iambic pentameter.

As a narrative, and especially as a mock epic, *The Rape of the Lock* would be expected to follow a rhythm of rest and violence, eventually rising to a climax and settling to a resolution. In the exposition in the first Canto, for example, Pope has to foreshadow the theft of the lock; yet to do so too directly would be to tell the reader that the worst that will happen to Belinda is the loss of a snippet of hair; he consequently leaves the threat to Belinda vague yet full of portent. Also, to make the subsequent battles appear more exciting, the dominant tone in the early sections must be comparatively calm. Later, in the two epic battles, Pope must carefully describe the symbolic battle of the hand of Ombre somewhat less excitingly than the battle between Belinda and the Baron lest the latter come as an anti-climax; yet the former must be exciting enough to sustain the interest of the reader.

The limitation imposed by the restricted heroic couplet pattern also creates a problem of rhythm, since Pope must, without changing verse form, vary the sounds of his lines sufficiently to keep the reader reading. The result is a series of contrasting sections of exposition, description, narrative, and dialogue, each sufficiently different in tone from the rest to give the lines the required variety.

And, perhaps most important in *The Rape of the Lock,* Pope must let his theme determine many of the elements that he includes. Instead of seeing the quarrel between Lord Petre and Arabella as an isolated instance of peevishness, Pope chose to see it as symptomatic of a basic corruption in eighteenth-century society. He was, consequently, faced with the problem of broadening his material to suggest that somehow all of his society was involved in the kind of childishness that led to the feud. The central childishness that Pope saw in the life of the Beau and Belle was a refusal to grow up, to accept mature responsibilities. For Belinda, the childishness is a refusal to realize that as a maturing young lady, she is made for love, not for egotistical flirtation; for the society as a whole, the childishness is a refusal to admit that jurymen are made for dispensing justice, not for getting to dinner on time, and that queens are made for governing, not for taking tea. Yet, at the same time, Pope chose not to condemn the society thoroughly; his is not the bitterness of a Gulliver, for example, who expects his society to be completely altered within six months. Pope recognized the elegance, the charm, the comfort of the society he had to attack. Perhaps one of the reasons that the wit in *The Rape of the Lock* works so completely is that it is a thoroughly elegant and charming wit; the Pope of *The Rape of the Lock* is not the almost violently angry ironist of either the "Epistle to Dr. Arbuthnot" or *The Dunciad*. By the charm and the elegance of his wit, Pope shows that he can play the game that Belinda's society plays, and that he can do it both without condescending and without forgetting that it is but a game. The result is an unusually balanced critique of the society.

The beauty of *The Rape of the Lock,* however, derives not from its ingredients, not from this precise set of literary determinants, but from their subtle and complete integration into an artistic whole. I have mentioned, for example, that the accuracy of the description of the card game increases the poem's verisimilitude. Yet within that section Pope also attends to the other literary determinants. In terms of the genre, it provides the occasion for an epic battle, a requirement of the epic, while reducing the battle to a mere game of cards, a kind of reduction necessary to the mock epic. Rhythmically, (a) it provides an interlude between the preparations of Belinda and the Baron for their battle of the sexes and thereby gives time to let suspense about Belinda's fate grow; (b) it contrasts in tone with the preceding section; (c) the details of the card game, with the queen falling to a knave, increases suspense by suggesting the possibility of Belinda's ruin. Thematically, the game shows the seriousness with which Belinda's group takes what is essentially a way of passing time and, with the frequent parallels between the card game and the mating game, permits Pope to underscore how foolishly and purposelessly dangerous the life of the coquette is. It is in large part Pope's ability to satisfy simultaneously the requirements of more than one of the specific literary determinants of *The Rape of the Lock* that accounts for the magnificence of the poem.

The Poem and the Objective Source

In discussing Keats's "Ode on a Grecian Urn" we saw that a consideration of Keats's letters could help verify an interpretation of that difficult poem. Seeing how Keats habitually thought about certain concepts strengthened the interpretation of the Ode. It would, of course, be possible to make the same kind of study of Pope's other writings to discover how he habitually thought of his society, in particular the vices and the virtues he ascribed to it, and to use the results to bolster an interpretation of *The Rape of the Lock*. In the case of *The Rape of the Lock,* however, we have more immediate evidence of Pope's intention and the source of the poem.

Although it ought not to be forgotten that *The Rape of the Lock* does not absolutely need support from information external to the poem, such support is helpful. Many readers have been thoroughly charmed by it while considering it merely a fanciful tale, and Pope's mastery of the couplet provides sufficient delight in itself for any reader. Moreover, the content of *The Rape of the Lock* is told with clarity enough that reference to external events is not strictly necessary for an understanding of the narrative. Like all good poems, it is well wrought enough to please the general reader who lacks specific knowledge of its origin. But like many fine poems, it gains as the reader brings more knowledge to bear upon it.

One of the delights of art is the sheer joy of achievement, the pleasure of watching a master perform according to plan. Can Pope meet the requirements of the story he has to tell and still effectively use the epic materials? We will see that he can, and that his ability to do so is a triumph of his artistry. The triumph is even more spectacular, however, if we realize that the story is, in outline at least, true. In making up a story and fitting it to a form, the artist can naturally enough bend the line of his story to the

requirements of the form; but if he sets himself the added task of
telling a true story, the story line simply cannot be bent very much
and still be true. If a part of artistry be skill, an understanding of
the actual event upon which a narrative is based will add to our
appreciation of the author's ability.

Moreover, an understanding of the relationships that existed
between the poet and the persons involved in the story provides
valuable supplementary material in understanding the tone of the
poem itself. The tone of *The Rape of the Lock* is clear without
knowledge of the biographical details, but nevertheless they present valuable corroborative evidence that we have caught the
proper feeling behind the poem. There is some danger, for example, of exaggerating the pointedness of Pope's satire, of assuming
that it is much more biting than it is. After all, Belinda and her
friends are made to appear quite foolish, and that foolishness is
made to appear symptomatic of the evils that existed in Britain in
the early part of the eighteenth century. If we recognize that Pope
wrote the poem as a favor to a very close friend to quiet a feud
between two families, there will be much less inclination to exaggerate the bitterness of Pope's irony. One does not stop a quarrel
by insulting the participants.

The proper use of such information is a matter of experience
and common sense. Strictly speaking, biographical or historical
reference cannot prove an interpretation for the simple reason that
it cannot put something into a work of literature that is not already
there. Nevertheless, such information ought to warn the reader to
proceed with care when his interpretation is contrary to what the
facts would lead him to expect; and it will help him to see more
clearly, more rapidly, and with more certainty, what is in fact
present in the work.

The Rape of the Lock, Miss Fermor, Lord Petre, and Their Friends

Although we do not know exactly when it happened (the best guess
is sometime during the summer of 1711, since the original version

of *The Rape of the Lock* was probably written before October of that year), we do know that Robert, Lord Petre, did indeed snip a lock of hair from the head of a Miss Arabella Fermor. Like Pope, the Petres and the Fermors were Roman Catholic families of some distinction, and Caryll, to whom the poem is dedicated, was a close friend of both families and of Pope. Before the theft of the lock, the Fermors, the Petres, and the Carylls visited each other frequently and, as Catholic families in a predominately Protestant society, formed a closely knit group. The quarrel that arose over the actual rape of the lock was certainly not tragic, but it was serious enough to break up what had been a comfortable friendship among the Fermors and the Petres. As a friend of both families, Caryll suggested that Pope, who probably then knew neither Miss Fermor nor Lord Petre personally, try to restore the peace.

The temptation for anyone less gifted than Pope would surely have been to write a thoroughly charming and inconsequential version of the snipping, designed only to ingratiate the poet with the Lord and the Belle, and the Lord and the Belle with each other. Pope's integrity as a man and as an artist would not let him take the easy course; a bitter family feud over a lock of hair was absurd, and Pope could not let such absurdity go entirely unnoticed. In addition, the fact that intelligent and well-meaning members of British society could take so seriously such an utterly insignificant trifle seemed to indicate a rather grave lack of values in that society. Pope's problem specifically was to chastise the pettiness while pleasing the participants in the quarrel.

This need to praise the two principals is partly, perhaps, the reason for the roles played by Thalestris and Sir Plume. Sir Plume is certainly Sir George Browne and Thalestris his wife. In all probability, Sir George and his wife were present when the lock was cut; Pope would hardly have placed them in such an active role if they had not been. Their close family relationship with Arabella (Sir George was her cousin) and Sir George's well-known foppishness would make it probable that he and his wife would side with the injured lady.

In terms of the thematic structure of the poem, however, Sir Plume and Thalestris serve neatly to divert the reader's attention from the folly of Belinda and the Baron. When Umbriel returns from the Cave of Spleen, he finds the distraught Belinda in the arms of Thalestris, who "fans the rising Fire" (IV, 94) by asserting hysterically that with the removal of the lock, Belinda's honor is gone. Thalestris rants:

> Gods! shall the Ravisher display your Hair,
> While the Fops envy, and the Ladies stare!
> *Honour* forbid! at whose unrival'd Shrine
> Ease, Pleasure, Virtue, All, our Sex resign.
> Methinks already I your Tears survey,
> Already hear the horrid things they say,
> Already see you a degraded Toast,
> And all your Honour in a Whisper lost!
> (IV, 103–10)

Thalestris quickly points out that if Belinda becomes the subject of gossip, she will lose her dearest friends—including, naturally enough, Thalestris herself.

Sir Plume takes up the case with somewhat less eloquence than his wife showed:

> (*Sir Plume,* of *Amber Snuff-box* justly vain,
> And the nice Conduct of a *clouded Cane*)
> With earnest Eyes, and round unthinking Face,
> He first the Snuff-box open'd, then the Case,
> And thus broke out—"My Lord, why, what the Devil?
> "Z—ds! damn the Lock! 'fore Gad, you must be civil!
> "Plague on't! 'tis past a Jest—nay prithee, Pox!
> "Give her the Hair"—he spoke, and rapp'd his Box.
> (IV, 123–30)

After such a display of bad advice from a Lady and such stupidity from a Lord, Belinda, in her emotional condition, has no choice but to answer the Baron with an outburst, especially since Umbriel pours out his vial of sorrows again. In the next book, after Clarissa

makes her appeal to reason, Thalestris reopens the quarrel by calling Clarissa a prude.

Within just a few lines Pope has done a remarkably clever thing.
He has shifted the human guilt for the quarrel from Belinda and
the Baron to Thalestris and Sir Plume, and as he does so he makes
the latter couple appear in the worst light possible. Belinda may
have some justification for being upset; Thalestris, whose own lock
was not shorn, has no legitimate excuse for her anger. She cannot
even plead friendship for Belinda, since she indicates that if
Belinda's reputation falls, her friendship will fall equally. And in
her speech she displays a total lack of any realistic sense of values.
It is she who first equates the loss of the lock with the loss of
Belinda's honor. The reader can forgive Belinda because Pope has
spent so much time describing her loveliness, and a lovely lady
may be forgiven much. But there are comparatively few compli-
ments to Thalestris, and they come only after she has made her
speech and only after the reader has formed his impression of her.

If the portrait of Thalestris makes Belinda appear in a better
light, that of Sir Plume does the same for the Baron. It is said that
the portrait of Sir Plume fits Sir George perfectly, and if so it again
shows Pope's ability to manage the objective source of his poem
effectively. Sir Plume's magnificently inept blustering shows both
his own inanity and that of any cause he would champion. Although objectively the Baron may be acting just as foolishly as Sir
Plume, the Baron conducts himself with such elegance that, like
the lovely Belinda, he can be at least partly forgiven. To Sir
Plume's bluster the Baron replies with extremely cutting courtesy:

> It grieves me much (reply'd the Peer again)
> Who speaks so well shou'd ever speak in vain.
> (IV, 131–32)

Although literally the continuation of the Baron's speech is as
ridiculous as was Sir Plume's, the tone redeems it. It is almost
inconceivable that anyone who could speak as well as the Baron
would actually mean what he says about the lock; his mock seriousness is appropriate to the situation, just as his elegant exag-

geration is appropriate to the mock epic form. Sir Plume's inco-
herence is appropriate to nothing.

The inclusion of Thalestris and Sir Plume, then, furthers Pope's
purpose of settling the quarrel between the Fermors and the
Petres (although it did not do much to assuage the temper of the
original Sir Plume; Lord Browne continued to bluster for some
time after). In their presence, the Baron and Belinda appear as an
attractive and not overly ridiculous couple.

(Although the outcome of the quarrel between the Petres and
the Fermors is not important in the poem, it might be mentioned.
Arabella, womanlike, apparently could not make up her mind
about Pope's masterpiece. At first she accepted it in good grace, but
it did occasion some laughter at her expense. In the dedicatory
epistle written some two years after the first version of the poem
appeared in 1712, Pope makes amends to the young lady by apolo-
gizing for the poem's wide circulation and by some perhaps exaggerated praise of Arabella herself:

> If this Poem had as many Graces as there are in Your Per-
> son, or in Your Mind, yet I could never hope it should pass
> thro' the World half so Uncensured as You have done.

A part of Arabella's chagrin may have resulted from the fact that
she was indeed in love with Lord Petre [Pope mentions in the poem
that there was an "Earthly Lover lurking at her Heart" (III, 144)]
and that shortly before the publication of the poem Lord Petre
married an heiress younger and much richer than Arabella. Arabella apparently did well, however, for two years later she married
a Mr. Perkins, who was wealthy and amiably enough disposed to
permit her to entertain many of the leading writers of the period.
About the time of her marriage, Arabella had her portrait painted,
wearing the cross that, as Pope wrote, "Jews might kiss, and
Infedils adore" [II, 8]. She was, then, seemingly content to be
remembered as the subject of Pope's poem.)

Genre as a Literary Determinant

Modern critics and poets have generally avoided discussing a work by first classifying it in its proper genre or kind. Many writers feel that any good work of art is unique, and that its very uniqueness gives it whatever power it has. A discussion of Hopkins's "The Windhover" that merely classifies it as a sonnet is not especially helpful. There are good sonnets and bad sonnets, sonnets about love and sonnets about war, sonnets that use highly metaphorical language and sonnets that use relatively direct language, sonnets that are euphonious and sonnets that are cacophonous.

Nevertheless, when a reader picks up a book of poems labeled "Sonnets," he does have certain expectations, and his feeling about the work will depend in part upon how well those expectations are met. Even many sophisticated readers, for example, if told that *Moby Dick* is a novel, will expect Melville to spend most of his pages developing either the action or, perhaps, the characterization. After a number of chapters on whales, whale fishing, whiteness, and what have you, they conclude that the book is not satisfactory because it does not do what they expect a novel to do. The early charge against Whitman was that he simply did not write poetry; his work did not rhyme, and so did not meet the requirements of the genre. The fact is that when a writer does call something a poem, a novel, a tragedy, an essay, he in effect invites his reader to compare his work with others of the same kind.

Genre classifications are most helpful when they are most narrow. To call something a poem does not commit the author to much; to call it a sonnet commits him to more; to call it a Shakespearean sonnet commits him to a definite stanza structure. Again, *Pride and Prejudice* and *Moby Dick* are both novels, but to approach both with the same expectations is seriously to misunderstand one or the other. But if we call the former an ironic social novel and the later a lyric novel, we have at least in a minimal way indicated some major differences and suggested that *Pride and Prejudice* ought most properly be compared with—say—*Bar-*

chester Towers and *Moby Dick* with Hudson's *Green Mansions.*
Certainly one way of better understanding and appreciating a work
of literature is to compare it with works which seem roughly
similar.

A knowledge of the intent and use of a genre is particularly
relevant for works written before the last half of the eighteenth
century. Ben Jonson, to take one of the clearest examples, wrote
for a literate audience which he knew had read classical drama
and certain Renaissance critics; when he wrote tragedy, he knew
precisely what his audience would expect. To understand what
happens in a Ben Jonson drama, one must be aware of the conventions of the comic or tragic sub-genre in which he was writing.
A writer such as Jonson, or Dryden, or Pope, felt that much was
to be gained by attempting a work in a strictly defined genre.

The very limitations imposed by the genre quite often force the
artist to extend himself, to create something better than a free
imaginative ramble could produce. Although no theorist would
want to argue that rhyme is a necessity in poetry, a strict rhyme
scheme—like any pattern that an artist decides to follow—fore-
stalls a mere gush of thought or emotion. The fact that he must find
the word that fits into the scheme he has set will very likely lead
him to consider possibilities that he might have otherwise remained
unaware of. No one with the verbal gift of an author will have
trouble merely expressing a thought; the difficulty, and the achievement of literature, comes when the thought is expressed in precisely the right way so that we, as readers, feel that just this word
in just this place has made the experience come alive. Many authors find that the discipline of writing within a genre helps them
to make their choices more deliberately and sensitively. (Other
authors feel that any attempt to impose a pattern on their inspiration, even a metrical pattern, must inevitably distort their
intention.)

Writing within a genre also permits a kind of freedom attainable
in no other way. This works so naturally and so easily that often
we are totally unaware of what has happened. In the *Heart of
Darkness,* for example, the narrator tells a story that in most
printed versions runs about seventy-five pages; such a long mono-

logue is totally unrealistic. Yet the conventions of fiction—the kind of conditioning readers have undergone—permits us to accept the length of Marlow's speech without difficulty. The proscenium stage, with its three closed sides and one open side, is again a convention that most audiences accept without thought. The conventions of a genre permit the author a kind of shorthand that those who know may read without difficulty.

Some genres have the added advantage of being directly allusive, especially those that are direct take-offs on other literary types. Unlike a modern author, Pope could predict with reasonable accuracy what his audience would have read. Most literate persons, especially those with the leisure, the taste, and the training to enjoy the poetry of Pope, would have read Homer and Virgil, and many of them would have even translated parts of the three classical epics in the normal course of their schooling. They would recognize not only such general epic devices as the invocation, the epic simile, the descent into Hades, the epic battle, and so on, they would also recognize particular allusions to particular lines and many would even recall the context of the line alluded to. Consequently, Pope could expect his readers to have two quite different things in mind as they read *The Rape of the Lock*. They would follow the poem and interest themselves in what was happening, the tone, and so on, and they would compare the action with the part of the epic referred to. Thus the poem not only tells the reader of the quarrel between Belinda and the Baron, but also reminds him of the vast difference between the age of Homer and that of Anne. We miss a large part of the poem unless we understand its conventions.

A full understanding of the conventions of a genre involves much more than an ability to list them. Because the conventions in a well-made literary work are more than decoration, they tend to have thematic values associated with them. We have alluded briefly to the tendency of the mock epic to force a comparison between a genuinely heroic or epic society and the author's world; the conventions of other genres similarly suggest other kinds of themes or, in some cases, ways of handling themes. The Shakespearean sonnet, for example, is composed of three quatrains and a concluding couplet; whether the author intends so or not, the conciseness of the concluding couplet lends itself to an aphoristic statement. It is, therefore, difficult (though not impossible) to write a Shakespearean sonnet which is purely descriptive or in which the theme is not stated at the end. The form does not irresistibly force the poet to conclude with an aphoristic statement of the theme, but it strongly nudges him in that direction.

Similarly, the formal demand for a resolution of the conflict in narrative generally, and in particular in pre-twentieth-century narrative, is on one level a formal requirement—that is, a requirement of the genre. It does, nevertheless, have thematic implications of some consequence. The fact that traditional tragedy must end with a resolution of the conflict, to take an obvious example, means that order must be restored at the end of the drama; and for order to be restored, the forces of order must triumph at least momentarily over the forces of chaos. As a result, despite the conflict and agony that is the subject of tragedy, the theme tends to be optimistic. For much the same kind of reason, the decision to write a novel with the conventional cause and effect sequence of events— the kind of novel Dickens writes in *Great Expectations,* for example, or Jane Austen in *Pride and Prejudice*—commits the writer despite his intentions to a deterministic theme. If in the orthodox eighteenth- or nineteenth-century novel the author felt an obligation to motivate every action and decision of his characters and to show that motivation in some detail, he is through the very structure he has chosen implying that man's choices are conditioned by the kind of events that the author has selected to explain the actions of his characters.

Authors may, of course, conceal or even deny the thematic implications of the genres they choose to write in. *King Lear* is perhaps the most stark and most exceptional of Shakespeare's tragedies largely because there is no effective agent at the end of the play who has the authority to restore order. In *Hamlet,* Fortinbras is there to put the pieces back together, and Shakespeare has described Fortinbras in such a way that we can assume that he will do an effective job; in *Othello,* the representatives of the Duke are on hand to see that justice is done and that the tragedy ends with the death of Othello and the punishment of Iago. But at the end of *King Lear,* there is no king, and the whole thematic mood of that tragedy is different from that of Shakespeare's other tragedies. I would suspect that audiences who know Shakespeare's other tragedies are more dismayed, more awe-struck, at the end of *Lear* than audiences who do not know the other works; they know what the conventions are, and they sense the immense significance of the departure from the expected pattern.

A genre, or a literary type, then, is made up of a grouping of certain devices, techniques, or conventional elements; and any particular grouping will for one reason or another tend to express its own kind of thematic values, or its own way of handling the theme. Even though the tendency is not irresistible, it is always present, and even when the author resists it, he must nevertheless take it into account.

The Rape of the Lock as an "Heroi-Comical Poem"

The title page of the 1714 edition of *The Rape of the Lock* calls the narrative "an heroi-comical poem," thereby informing readers that they might expect a miniature epic, and an epic not of glory but of pettiness. The heroi-comical poem—or mock epic, as it is more often called—uses epic conventions as fully as possible while exposing the faults of the poet's society. The genre itself obviously involves a paradox: the comic is not heroic and the heroic is not comic. The paradox becomes even more notable when we consider the epic conventions themselves and one of their chief purposes.

Among the epic conventions Pope uses are the invocation to the muse, the formal statement of theme, the extended simile, the arming of the hero, epic epithets, grand battles, the journey to the underworld, and the intervention of the gods. All of these conventions are used in the epic to glorify the subject of the poem. The muse is invoked because only a deity could possibly inspire a poem on such an important topic; the theme is stated formally to emphasize its high moral seriousness; the extended similes and the arming of the hero give the poet the opportunity to describe almost lovingly the grandeur of the hero and all that belongs to him; the epic epithets were (like the similes) once a mnemonic device, but they also work to identify the character with a specific trait; the battles are, of course, a test of the hero's heroism, and to be effective tests they must be made larger than life and given the appearance of a conflict between super-beings; the journey to the underworld also tests heroism by showing the ability of the hero to survive Hell itself; the intervention of the gods underlines the importance of the heroic action by reminding the reader that even gods are interested in what these particular mortals do. The epic conventions are more than mere tricks of the genre; they are a group of techniques that work together to inflate the hero and everything about him to magnificiently grand proportions.

Pope begins his translation of the *Odyssey* in much the same way he begins *The Rape of the Lock:*

> The man for wisdom's various arts renown'd,
> Long exercised in woes, O Muse! resound;
> Who, when his arms had wrought the destined fall
> Of sacred Troy, and razed her heaven-built wall,
> Wandering from clime to clime, observant stray'd,
> Their manners noted, and their states survey'd.
> On stormy seas unnumber'd toils he bore,
> Safe with his friends to gain his natal shore:
> Vain toils! their impious folly dared to prey
> On herds devoted to the god of day;
> The god vindictive doom'd them never more
> (Ah, men unbless'd!) to touch that natal shore.
> Oh, snatch some portion of these acts from fate,
> Celestial Muse! and to our world relate.

The man, of course, is Odysseus, and the specific subject of the *Odyssey* is his incredibly long and dangerous journey home from the wars. Odysseus, like most epic heroes, is also much concerned with manners and mores because a hero is, after all, expected to serve as a model for lesser mortals. The muse is invoked because the hero's greatness is such that the poet can sing of it only when inspired. An uninspired poet, as Milton acknowledged in the invocation to *Paradise Lost,* is all too likely to droop below epic heights.

In the opening of *The Rape of the Lock,* Pope not only uses the expected epic conventions, he also begins the mockery that will carry through the poem. The offense about which Pope writes is "dire" and the contest "mighty," although the cause is "trivial." Since everything in a mock epic is to be reduced, Belinda, a mortal, rather than the muse inspires the poem. It is important to recognize that from the very beginning the comparison of the taking of the lock and the ensuing quarrel with an epic struggle is not entirely derisive. Pope is quite honest when he writes "Slight is the Subject, but not so the Praise" (I, 5). In this and other essays on *The Rape of the Lock* we shall see that even though Belinda is not a goddess, it is no small compliment to be compared to one.

Possibly Pope's complex attitude toward Belinda and his equally complex use of heroic materials can best be shown by looking closely at the scene in which Belinda arms herself for the battle of the sexes:

> And now, unveil'd, the *Toilet* stands display'd,
> Each Silver Vase in mystic Order laid.
> First, rob'd in White, the Nymph intent adores
> With Head uncover'd, the *Cosmetic* Pow'rs.
> A heav'nly Image in the Glass appears,
> To that she bends, to that her Eyes she rears;
> Th'inferior Priestess, at her Altar's side,
> Trembling, begins the sacred Rites of Pride.
> Unnumber'd Treasures ope at once, and here
> The various Off'rings of the World appear;
> From each she nicely culls with curious Toil,
> And decks the Goddess with the glitt'ring Spoil.
> This Casket *India*'s glowing Gems unlocks,
> And all *Arabia* breathes from yonder Box.
> The Tortoise here and Elephant unite,
> Transform'd to *Combs,* the speckled and the white.
> Here Files of Pins extend their shining Rows,
> Puffs, Powders, Patches, Bibles, Billet-doux.
> Now awful Beauty puts on all its Arms;

> The Fair each moment rises in her Charms,
> Repairs her Smiles, awakens ev'ry Grace,
> And calls forth all the Wonders of her Face;
> Sees by Degrees a purer Blush arise,
> And keener Lightnings quicken in her Eyes.
> The busy *Sylphs* surround their darling Care;
> These set the Head, and those divide the Hair,
> Some fold the Sleeve, while others plait the Gown;
> And *Betty*'s prais'd for Labours not her own.
>
> (I, 121–48)

Pope's ideal reader would, of course, not only catch the general allusion to the typical epic scene in which the hero dons his work clothes, but would also probably have caught many of the detailed allusions; "glittering spoil," for example, is Dryden's translation for Virgil's description of armor captured in battle. For the careful modern reader who lacks the classical education, the expansiveness of the passage should suggest something like epic quality.

There is drama in the opening line of the passage, with the sudden unveiling of Belinda's dressing table; the "unveil'd" hints that the toilet has an altar-like quality, a hint Pope expands almost immediately. The perfumes and ointments are laid in "mystic Order," and Belinda, "rob'd in White" like a priestess, "adores" those wonderful powers that enhance a woman's loveliness. As if in response to her adoration a "heav'nly Image" appears, and the "Rites" begin.

Like a true epic hero who arms himself only with the best the world has to offer, Belinda dons the "Off'rings of the World"; the couplet

> This Casket *India*'s glowing Gems unlocks,
> And all *Arabia* breathes from yonder Box

suggests that whole nations have been plundered so that Belinda might appear even more lovely. Even nature co-operates; the ivory of the elephant and the shell of a tortoise are magically transformed into combs for Belinda.

The sylphs, the mock epic counterpart of real epic gods and goddesses, help arm Belinda. Just as an epic hero has the aid of supernatural beings—which often includes a gift or armor—so the sylphs, led by Ariel, put the final touches on Belinda's beautification. But if the hero of an epic has the protection of some divine beings, he also arouses the hostility of others. One feels in reading a classical epic that not only are the earthly events so important that even the gods are involved, but also that those events somehow reflect the total relationship of man and the supernatural. Belinda, having performed the "sacred Rites of Pride," has earned the protection of the sylphs, spirits who were once beautiful women and whose vanities, as their most essential parts (in the technical philosophical sense of *essential*) have lived on. A sylph, then, becomes a kind of guardian angel whose job is to lead a still active coquette through the intricacies of social life and threats of serious love.

The last is especially important because by the nature of the game the coquette is obliged to arouse the passions of her admirers and avoid both serious emotional involvement and lovemaking, for to surrender to a man either emotionally or physically is to lose one's status as a coquette. It is, therefore, especially appropriate that the Baron prays to "Love," that serious archenemy of coquetry. Just as appropriately, Love, as a deity, has the power to grant part of his prayer despite the protection of the sylphs. And, obviously, Belinda's and the Baron's supernatural allies are natural enemies. Belinda's rites are of pride, and pride, especially as developed in this poem, is excessive self-admiration; it is opposed to love because love is primarily a feeling for someone else.

According to the conditions described by Ariel, a fallen coquette becomes a gnome; after Belinda's lock is cut, Ariel must retire as the presiding spirt in favor of the gnome Umbriel, "a dusky melancholy Spright" (IV, 13). Unlike Ariel, whose region is "in fields of Air" (I, 66), the gnome roams earth "In search of Mischief" (I, 64). Mischief lives in the Cave of Spleen, a mock heroic equivalent of the epic Hades. "Spleen" in the eighteenth century was a rather general complaint that could have some physical symptoms (often described much like an upset stomach) but which more often appeared in women as a kind of shrewishness. The Cave of Spleen is a fitting hell for a former coquette because its effects are precisely those which will make her least attractive. The goddess of spleen is described as a hypochondriac, hiding from the light, constantly sighing about her pains, attended by wrinkled "Ill-nature" and an overly made-up "Affectation" (IV, 27–31). The ruler of spleendom is also the queen of "Female Wit" who gives "th' *Hysteric* or *Poetic* Fit" (IV, 59–60), and presides over the giving of pimples to beautiful faces, cuckoldry, embarrassment, and loss of reputation. Like most heroic visitants to the underworld, Umbriel is there on a mission; he has to get the magic trappings that will aid the hero. The trappings include sighs, sobs, passions, shrieking, babbling, fainting, tears, and the whole arsenal of the most unattractive female weapons.

Having gathered such arms, he releases them over Belinda and her companions so that the battle may rage. Belinda, inspired by Umbriel, "burns with more than mortal Ire" (IV, 93), and Thalestris, like Nestor in *The Iliad,* spreads discord. Epic heroes must also fight over a prize of great value, "this Prize, th' inestimable Prize" (IV, 113) Pope calls it, of Belinda's lock. Pope's problem here is to keep the epic tone while still showing the paltriness of the quarrel, and he accomplishes both by having the participants over-react. Thalestris imagines the Baron displaying the lock as a love trophy and Belinda as a "degraded Toast" (IV, 109); Sir Plume of "round unthinking Face" (IV, 125) is so upset he can only blurt out incoherencies. The Baron himself enters into the spirit of the comic epic by acknowledging the importance of the "sacred Lock" (IV, 133) and vowing that he shall wear it always. As in *The Iliad,* where all the minor combatants must have their contests before the appearance of the greatest of heroes, Achilles himself, appears, so here Belinda enters the quarrel only after the others. Pope very neatly preserves our respect for Belinda, despite her foolishness, by attributing her mood to Umbriel who, like a vindictive epic god, enters the action to increase the perplexity of the hero.

By the end of Canto Four and the start of Canto Five, mortals seem to have done all they can. Belinda has been reduced to almost absolute dejection, delivering a mock heroic lamentation that says, in effect, "Alas that I was ever led to live such a life as this." Clarissa, the voice of reason, has had her say; she has pointed out that coquetry must end sometime and that "Merit" or virtue is better than mere charm. After this lull, the battle begins with even more vigor than before. Thalestris calls Clarissa a prude:

> To Arms, to Arms; the fierce Virago cries,
> And Swift as Lightning to the Combate flies.
> All side in Parties, and begin th'Attack;
> Fans clap, Silks russle, and tough Whalebones crack;
> Heroes' and Heroins' Shouts confus'dly arise,
> And base, and treble Voices strike the Skies.
> No common Weapons in their Hands are found,
> Like Gods they fight, nor dread a mortal Wound.
>
> (V, 37–44)

The achievement of the delicate balance that a mock epic requires is remarkable in this passage. Most of the diction would be suitable for an eighteenth-century description of a truly heroic battle; Pope suggests the quickness, the fierceness, and even the confusion of intense military combat. Yet, buried in the middle of the passage, "Fans clap, Silks russle, and tough Whalebones crack," a reminder that these are not warriors but elegant ladies; the "tough Whalebones" is an especially fine touch, yet typical, since it invokes both the majestic size of the whale and is literally and realistically accurate—in the commotion of the quarrel the ladies' stays snap. And the final line has the true epic touch, with again the proper realism; real gods and their epic favorites do not die, and realistically the fight will kill neither Belinda nor the Baron.

The passage immediately following (ll. 45–56) recalls *The Iliad* with a direct comparison to Book XX (11. 91 ff. in Pope's translation) where the gods take sides in the struggle. But the epic reminder only underscores the fact that this is a mock battle; in a fine operatic touch an "expiring Swan" (V, 66) sings as he dies.

Sir Plume is killed by Chloe's frown, but her smile revives him immediately. Again, after the lesser warriors have had their struggle, Belinda and the Baron meet in combat, Belinda armed with a bodkin whose ancestry is described much as is the ancestry of Agamemnon's scepter in *The Iliad*.

As happens often with classical heroes, the end of the battle is not the end of the story. Heroes are born to struggle and then to be taken among the gods. Belinda's lock, the symbol of her beauty, is mysteriously transported to heaven where it becomes "a sudden Star" (V, 127) to which lovers will pray. Like Pope's use of other heroic details, the ending is appropriate on several levels. It reminds us that Belinda and her friends have won their place in the stars not for their fierceness but for their charm. Practically, it turns Belinda's fear that the Baron would keep her lock as a love trophy into a graceful compliment; the god of love triumphs by gaining a new brightness in the sky, a new source of inspiration for lovers. And, of course, *"this Lock"* as Pope calls the poem in his final couplet, has indeed immortalized Belinda.

The success of Pope's use of the mock epic conventions lies not in the general reminders of the differences between the heroic age and the Augustan, the over-all contrast between the life and death passion of one age and the superficial refinement of another, but rather in Pope's ability to turn those characteristics of the genre most clearly designed to inflate the subject into a precisely balanced mixture of mockery and admiration. There is no hint in the poem that Pope had to choose between, for example, advancing the action or describing the characters and carrying on his epic imitation; the seams simply do not show. Each of the devices Pope uses fits neatly into its place in both the form he has chosen and the content he has to deal with.

Verse Patterns as Literary Determinants

We have already seen how Pope met two of the requirements he set himself in *The Rape of the Lock*—that of using the epic conventions precisely and effectively, and that of using an actual occurrence as the basis of his poem. Pope imposed still a third limitation upon himself (or more accurately, his habitual preference for the heroic couplet and its dominance after Dryden imposed it); he tells the entire story in heroic couplets, an exceptionally tight form in which the poet has only twenty syllables in which to complete a thought, and in which the metrical scheme must be heavily iambic with a rhyme after each five accents.

The test of a poet who chooses to write within a metrical pattern such as the heroic couplet, the sonnet, the rondeau, or whatever, is obviously not whether or not he can produce something in that particular pattern; even the most unskilled amateur can hammer out a few closed couplets or a sonnet. The real test is whether the poet can use the pattern to enhance what he has to say. Somehow, he has to fuse the stanza pattern and the content so tightly that the reader feels that his manner of expression is inseparable from his matter.

The following poem, W. H. Davies's "What Is Life," * fails almost totally because of the lack of relevance of what is said to the way it is said:

> What is life, if full of care,
> We have no time to stand and stare.
>
> No time to stand beneath the boughs
> And stare as long as sheep or cows.
>
> No time to see, when woods we pass,
> Where squirrels hide their nuts in grass.
>
> No time to see, in broad daylight,
> Streams full of stars, like skies at night.
>
> No time to turn at Beauty's glance,
> And watch her feet, how they can dance.
>
> No time to wait till her mouth can
> Enrich that smile her eyes began.

* Copyright © 1963 by Jonathan Cape Limited. Reprinted from *The Complete Poems of W. H. Davies* by permission of Jonathan Cape Limited and Wesleyan University Press, publishers.

> A poor life this, if full of care,
> We have no time to stand and stare.

The short, four-beat couplet stanza the poet chose distracts from his meaning because it commits him to developing an image in two lines; in effect, he says, "Let's look at the lovely things in nature; life isn't worth much unless we do. Take a quick look at the stars there, they're worth sixteen syllables." The words, of course, do not say this; but the stanza pattern does convey an impression of haste and so contradicts the effect the poet tries to achieve.

If we look at the first quatrain of Donne's Holy Sonnet 7, we can see several of the ways in which a poet uses a stanzaic form to increase the effect of what he has to say:

> At the round earth's imagined corners, blow
> Your trumpets, Angels, and arise, arise
> From death, you numberless infinities
> Of Souls, and to your scattered bodies go.

The feeling behind the statement in these lines is exceptionally bold; Donne, a mortal, commands the angels at the last judgment to blow the doomsday trumpet and the souls of the dead to arise and return to their bodies. Donne's problem is to exploit the form so that it convinces the reader of the speaker's boldness and of the grandeur of what he is commanding be done. This is not the place for a thorough analysis of the lines, but we might note some of the fairly obvious details that contribute to the tone. To help capture a sense of the catastrophic power of the end of the world, Donne deliberately makes the meter jar; instead of the smooth iambic that one expects in a sonnet, Donne's line scans,

> x x   /   / x / x / x   /
> At the round earth's imagined corners, blow

with two very weak stresses followed by two strong stresses and the expected iambics filling out the rest of the line. But the variation in the first four syllables makes the later iambics seem harsher than they otherwise would. If we change one word in the line and rearrange the first four words, we get:

All round the earth's imagined corners, blow,

in which the initial iambic seems to inform the ear that this is to be a conventional and fairly tame line, so that the accents in the last part are not to be hit as hard as in Donne's original version.

Furthermore, the pause in the line comes unusually late. Usually caesurae, or pauses, in English poetry fall about in the middle of the line unless some special effect is wanted. The part of the line before the comma is difficult to pronounce partly because of the way Donne has handled the metrical pattern and partly because of its length; when we get to the comma, we take a breath and so are physiologically ready to explode the next word, "blow." Since the word means what it does and since it comes at the end of the line, it is all but impossible to avoid pronouncing it forcefully. And instead of the rest that we often get at the end of a line of poetry, we have to continue on immediately with "Your trumpets," especially since the vowel ending of "blow" blends so smoothly with the beginning sound of "Your"; it simply does not sound right to pause between the two words. The result is a kind of dynamic, explosive quality about the passage that perfectly matches the meaning of the lines. Then, suddenly, Donne varies the caesura pattern, giving us three quick pauses in succession, with the accented syllable in two cases coming just after the pauses; all this forces an especially harsh and emphatic reading of the lines.

Although it would be inaccurate to say that Donne could not have been so forceful in any other form (we simply do not know what would have happened had he decided to handle his topic in another form), we can say with some certainty that in this quatrain at least the potentialities of the meter have been exploited fully. The details in the pattern draw attention to the relevant details in the statement.

It is possible, however, to go much too far with this kind of analysis and to claim too much for it. We cannot predict flatly that a given theme, subject, or tone can be expressed only in a given form. Nor can we claim that the form itself is responsible for the excellence or badness of the performance. We must work from the finished poem—from that idea, that attitude, that experience, expressed in just that way. We can comment only on how well or how badly the parts fit together.

Nor ought we assume that certain poetic devices always produce certain poetic effects. Since Chaucer, for example, iambic pentameter has been recognized as the closest metrical approximation to the language that most of us use, and probably correctly so; but Donne's use of iambic pentameter in Holy Sonnet 7 is hardly conversational, and other meters may at times sound conversational. The quadruple assonance of "a's" in Donne's sonnet produced a harsh and powerful sound; they do not in "and angels arabesqued airily." In discussing versification, we must always remember that the effect is a product of all of the elements in the poem working together. The effect of any particular literary determinant is conditioned by its relation to all of the other literary determinants that comprise the total work.

Versification, Word Order, and Meaning in *The Rape of the Lock*

One of Pope's chief problems in *The Rape of the Lock* is to take an unusually limited form, the heroic couplet, and without violating its basic pattern, to express (a) extended and almost lyrical descriptions of the lovely Belinda, (b) swift narrative movement, (c) exposition, as in the lectures by Ariel, (d) a variety of tones of voice as different characters speak, (e) sharp and incisive social commentary, (f) individual lines that meet three sets of conditions—showing what has to be shown for the sake of the narrative, implying the attitude of Belinda and her group, and implying Pope's own more mature attitude. The twenty syllables have to express everything from gentle devotion to irrational anger, appropriately to describe everything from an elegant dressing table to a kind of Alice-in-Wonderland hell. And, of course, Pope had to meet the most important requirement made of all writers—

not to bore his readers. This last is no mean task when one considers that Pope has to repeat the persistent iambic pentameter couplet almost four hundred times. Since rhyme scheme, basic thought unit, and meter are set, Pope has to achieve his variety through use of varied sentence patterns, devices of sound, and striking word placements.

One of the most effective ways to avoid the monotony of the repeated five-beat line pattern is to break the line in various ways by changing the position of the caesura from line to line. Pope begins this kind of variation in the first lines of the poem:

> What dire Offense from am'rous Causes springs,
> What mighty Contests rise from trivial Things,
> I sing—This Verse to *Caryll,* Muse! is due;
> This, ev'n Belinda may vouchsafe to view:
> Slight is the Subject, but not so the Praise,
> If She inspire, and He approve my lays.
>   Say what strange Motive, Goddess! cou'd compel
> A well-bred *Lord* t'assault a gentle *Belle?*
> Oh say what stranger Cause, yet unexplor'd,
> Cou'd make a gentle *Belle* reject a *Lord?*
> In Tasks so bold, can Little Men engage,
> And in soft Bosoms dwells such mighty Rage?

Although this is not Pope at his best, it is still readable and nicely avoids the rocking-horse sound that heroic couplets often fall into. In the first two lines there is no marked caesura; in the third there are three distinct pauses—after the second syllable, after the seventh, and after the eighth; in the fourth line, the single caesura occurs after the first syllable; in the fifth line, after the fifth; in the sixth line, after the fourth; in the seventh line, after the fifth and seventh; in the eighth line there is no marked caesura; in the ninth the caesura comes after the sixth syllable; in the tenth line it is unmarked again; in the eleventh, after the fourth syllable; and in the twelfth it is once more unmarked.

The positioning of pauses in a line may seem to be a very minor detail, but it is the kind of matter that Pope gave attention to. By putting his pauses in various places in the lines and by having some lines without internally marked pauses (one line does not even have an end stop), he manages to keep the regularity of the iambic pentameter without the creation of a heavy-footed "da-dum, da-dum, da-dum" beat.

Yet the avoidance of monotony is a minimal, perhaps even a negative virtue; it helps prevent our boredom without positively interesting us. Much of the positive interest in Pope's technique, as distinguished from his ideas, stories, and so on, depends upon his ability to surprise the reader. The pattern is both a hindrance and a help because it limits what the poet can do as it sets up the expectations of the reader. It is, after all, rather difficult to surprise someone who does not know what to expect; it is much easier if some fairly precise expectations have been aroused and then somehow altered but not frustrated. The reader must feel surprised; but after the surprise, he must also feel that whatever has been substituted for what he expected is better than what he expected. It is this constant ability to lead the reader to anticipate one thing, then delight him with something even better, that is the basis of Pope's technical mastery as a versifier.

Perhaps the most prevalent kind of surprise in *The Rape of the Lock* is the intrusion of a discordant word into a series. In lines 137 and 138 of the first Canto, Pope gives the reader this picture of Belinda's dressing table:

> Here Files of Pins extend their shining Rows,
> Puffs, Powders, Patches, Bibles, Billet-doux.

Ordinarily, a series of nouns, all with the same grammatical function, would indicate that the objects included are to be thought of as roughly equal in significance. Pope contributes to this expectation by presenting a visual image of parallelism in the first line of the couplet—the files of pins stand erect and are all alike and equal. The first three items named in the second line, and the last item, are all appropriate for the dressing table of a coquette; the Bible is the unexpected item, and with it Pope says much about Belinda and much about himself. The mention that Belinda keeps it alongside her tools of vanity is Pope's way of telling the reader that she considers the Bible no more important than her pins and powders. Also, the couplet occurs in a mock religious passage in which Belinda is attending to the "sacred Rites of Pride" (I, 128). The pins and puffs and patches are thereby raised to the rank of sacramentals. Pope, with the clever placement of a single word, has been able to show the reader the confusion within Belinda's own value system and at the same time, by making the contrast between the cosmetics and the Bible so apparent, to suggest that by Pope's own standards that confusion is seriously wrong.

As if this were not enough, "Billet-doux" also works in a variety of ways. For an age of believers, there would be something sacrilegious in equating the word of God with a personal note from a lover. Yet Belinda treats the two as if they were equally important. Also, the rhyme links "Billet-doux" with "rows," implying that the letters lined up on her table are as numerous and as unimportant as her pins. It is a minor touch, and quite subtle, but it reminds the reader that the worst thing about the coquette's value system is that it treats persons as objects, for a coquette is a woman who uses men to gratify her vanity. The positioning of "Billet-doux" works yet another way; if a series of parallel grammatical elements has been presented, we expect some kind of order. Pope seems to work up to a climax, from "Puffs" to the Bible; but the final element in the series forces a double-take. Is "Billet-doux" a climax or an anti-climax? Actually, Pope has it both ways. Within the coquette value system, nothing is more important than letters of tribute from conquered males. For Belinda, in other words, the order is climactic. But Pope and his readers, at least the non-coquettes, sense the anti-climax. Through the simple positioning of a noun, Pope has suggested both Belinda's way of seeing things and his criticism of her perspective.

The same technique works in Pope's famous implied comparison of lovers and lap dogs:

> Now Lapdogs give themselves the rowzing Shake,
> And sleepless Lovers, just at Twelve, awake.
>
> (I, 15–16)

Here Pope presents two roughly parallel lines, instead of a series of parallel nouns, but the effect is equally complex. The basic comparison is apt. For the coquette, lap dogs and lovers are alike pets, both creatures kept to satisfy the coquette's need to be loved while feeling a minimum of emotional involvement. The lap dogs may even be better off than the lovers, for they at least sleep near their mistresses. The effect is further complicated by the fact that sleepless lovers cannot awake. The whole routine is a complicated game which requires that lovers pretend insomnia. Pope also manages to suggest in the second line the absurdity of lovers all over London simultaneously springing to life when the clock strikes twelve.

At times Pope reverses the technique, seeming to give a double meaning and offering only a single, as in Ariel's question:

> What tender Maid but must a Victim fall
> To one Man's Treat, but for another's Ball?
> (I, 95–96)

The conjunction 'but" ordinarily introduces a contrast, as it quite clearly does in the first line of the couplet. But in the second line there is no contrast between "Treat" and "Ball" since both are part of the same social whirl. The result is highly compacted meaning. Literally, the lines say that the social whirl prevents the lady from falling. But the implication is that she never really escapes; at best she merely passes from one dangerous situation to another. Virgins cannot indefinitely go on enjoying hairbreadth escapes.

The great couplet,

> Here Thou, Great *Anna!* whom three Realms obey,
> Dost sometimes Counsel take—and sometimes *Tea.*
> (III, 7–8)

uses rhyme to comment devastatingly on Belinda's society. The Queen herself, it implies, sees no distinction between affairs of state and social events. And the rhyming of "obey" and "Tea" further suggests that the Queen's subjects follow her lead without question. This is not merely an isolated witticism, for Pope's essential criticism of the society is that it confuses the important and the petty. With this quick glance at the court, Pope hints that the confusion of values is not peculiar to Belinda and her spoiled friends; it radiates out from the center of government itself. The whole society has replaced common sense with comfort, virtue with elegance.

In describing the effect of Pope's couplets, words like "hint" and "imply" have been used repeatedly. Part of the strength of Pope's couplets is that they tend to compress ideas and images and so force associations that a looser form would have to make explicit. Pope is a master at packing two ideas side-by-side within the couplet so that the reader must associate, say, lovers with lap dogs; the comparison does not have to be made overtly, for the compression within the couplet juxtaposes the ideas tightly enough so that it comes naturally. It would, of course, be wrong to say that the heroic couplet leads inevitably to the kind of meaningful compression Pope attains; poets can be as prolix in rhymed iambic pentameter as they can in free verse. But the form does contain within itself potentialities for significant compression, and Pope brilliantly actuates that potential. No poet can do more with the form he has chosen.

Thematic Determinants: The Social Theme

Although the preceding essays on the techniques and background of *The Rape of the Lock* are useful for an understanding of the poem, a critic must at some point be prepared to state what they add up to. *The Rape of the Lock* is a picture of and a judgment on a society. We have noted in a general way what Pope's judgment is—that his society had sacrificed common sense and virtue for comfort and elegance—but that description of the theme is neither sufficiently specific nor qualified quite fully enough to be an accurate statement of the theme.

One of a critic's first questions as he attempts to formulate the theme of a narrative is the appropriate level of generality for his thematic statement. Some works seem to describe a condition applicable to all men everywhere, or at least to all men at a certain stage of their lives. The kind of experience Keats presents in the "Ode on a Grecian Urn" is possible to man regardless of the time or the place in which he lives. In other works, authors spend significantly more effort localizing the theme. Hemingway's *The Sun Also Rises,* for example, describes the sense of loss after the First World War. A part of Hemingway's intention is to show that the protagonist, Jake Barnes, is unlike anyone who existed before; instead of being an everyman, he is the peculiar creation of an abnormal moment in history. Jake's physical loss is a result of a castrating wound suffered in the war. Because Jake is in love with Lady Brett Ashley, a woman who cannot live without physical love, the physical loss is also an emotional loss. And because of the physical and the emotional loss and because Jake lives in a world of persons whom the war has wounded in one way or another, he has also lost his sense of values. The over-all pattern of *The Sun Also Rises,* the tone, the accumulation of details, all indicate that the reader's proper response is to feel that never before was there a period of history in which man had lost so much and lost it so completely. The theme of such a work does not have to do with all men, or even with a certain kind of man, but with a certain kind of man living under specific conditions. Although there is no widely recognized terminology for the distinction I am making, we can say that the "Ode on a Grecian Urn" has a relatively universal theme, *The Sun Also Rises,* a social theme.

The distinction is, of course, not clear cut; the presence of a theme on one level does not mean that themes on other levels will be completely absent. The matter is one of emphasis. In *The Sun Also Rises,* to continue with that example for a moment, we can extract the universal theme that "war causes loss." It is a sensible theme, for war does indeed cause loss. But as Hemingway writes his novel, he seems to be choosing his material so that it will imply most strongly that "this particular war at this particular time caused this particular kind of loss." To state the theme of *The Sun Also Rises* as a universal, then, would not be wrong, but it would place the emphasis on the wrong level. If the best criticism is that which most accurately reflects the literature, a critique that changes the emphasis of a work blunders seriously. The critic has to look where the author tells him to look and to try to see what the author has tried to make most obvious.

The Social Theme of *The Rape of the Lock*

Although we know that the specific occasion of *The Rape of the Lock* was an attempt to patch up a quarrel between the Fermors and the Petres after Lord Petre had cut a lock of Miss Fermor's hair, Pope's poem is also a critique of the values of the aristocratic society of his period. As Pope tells his readers in the mock epic introduction, the narrative will show why a lord assaulted a "gentle Belle" and why the Belle rejected a lord.

Perhaps the first thing to note is that the Belinda of the poem is not the Arabella of real life. Pope has done a masterful job of transforming Arabella into an idealized gentle belle; one of the subtleties of the poem is that Belinda is so convincingly attractive and yet so little described. Readers for over two hundred years have been astonished at her beauty and yet unable to describe her in any detail. We see her carefully preparing herself at her dressing table, we see all London looking at her adoringly, we see her triumphing over young men, we see her eyes flashing in anger; yet Belinda is curiously not an individual in any real sense. In making her the complete coquette, Pope has made her completely coquette.

As if to tell his reader that Belinda is a type, Pope lets the mechanism of the sylphs suggest that a whole supernatural apparatus, complete with ranks of spiritual beings and a heaven and a hell, has been created for young ladies like Belinda. For the most part, although there are exceptions, Belinda is surrounded by persons like herself, by "Fair Nymphs, and well-drest Youths" (II, 5). Belinda's life is presented as an endless series of treats and balls; it is a life of social intercourse made possible only by the participation of large numbers of persons as light-headed as Belinda. Yet even though Pope makes it abundantly clear that Belinda is typical of a certain kind of young lady, he makes it equally clear that she is not an "everygirl." Quite early in the poem (I, 59 ff.), Pope has Ariel explain to Belinda that there are different kinds of woman—"fiery Termagants," "Soft yielding Minds," "The graver Prude," and "The light Coquettes," and among the coquettes are those who reject mankind and those who eventually accept mankind.

Like most narratives that hold the reader's interest, *The Rape of the Lock* has as its climax or turning point a turning point in the life of its protagonist. On the day described in the poem, Belinda's career as a coquette is threatened. Can she remain a coquette, forever rejecting mankind, or will she fall? And since Belinda does fall, and since she is a typical coquette, the question is really, "Why do coquettes fall?"

The various possible answers are all involved in one assumption constantly in the background in *The Rape of the Lock:* the society is so completely artificial that it makes unnatural and therefore impossible demands on the coquette. To begin with, there is no such thing as an old and attractive coquette, and Belinda will age. Although not identified as an old coquette, Affectation, Spleen's handmaid, has all the characteristics; she,

> with a sickly Mien
> Shows in her Cheek the Roses of Eighteen,
> Practis'd to Lisp, and hand the Head aside,
> Faints into Airs, and languishes with Pride;
> On the rich Quilt sinks with becoming Woe,
> Wrapt in a Gown, for Sickness, and for Show.
> (IV, 31–36)

Although Ariel has promised Belinda that the coquette becomes a sylph, it is more likely that she will end like Affectation. Somewhat later, Clarissa points out that no amount of primping can stop the ravages of age.

In fact, Ariel fails precisely because Belinda is getting older and more mature. Nothing is lacking in Ariel's plans for the defense of Belinda; he marshalls his forces, assigning defense perimeters to the various sylphs, with the skill of a leader of an epic army. At the decisive moment, Ariel seemingly has control of everything, but,

> Just in that instant, anxious *Ariel* sought
> The close Recesses of the Virgin's Thought; . . .
> Sudden he view'd, in spite of all her Art,
> An Earthy Lover lurking at her Heart.
> Amaz'd, confus'd, he found his Pow'r expir'd,
> Resign'd to Fate, and with a Sigh retir'd.
>
> (III, 139–46)

Ariel is powerless because, whether Belinda is aware of it or not, "An Earthly Lover" lurks in her heart. As soon as Belinda falls in love, she has outgrown the game that she and her friends have been playing.

The game is unnatural; Belinda is bound to lose because she must be sexually attractive, attract everyone, and be touched by no one. The card game, which is a realistic enough description of a hand of Ombre, reflects the action. In this woman-dominated society, Belinda determines what will be trumps—that is, what will be of most value. In the opening stages of the game, most of the cards are described as masculine, and Belinda, like a true coquette, wins by playing man against man, as Pope has said earlier,

> What tender Maid but must a victim fall
> To one Man's Treat, but for another's Ball?
>
> (I, 95–96)

In the combination card-courtship game, the Baron wins points by playing his diamonds (then as now a girl's best friend); he shows his manliness with clubs and his gentleness with a display of hearts. Within the card game, as within the courtship game, there are casualties; the "*Knave* of *Diamonds*. . ./wins (oh shameful Chance!) the *Queen of Hearts*" (III, 87–88). To make us see clearly the comparison between the loss of the Queen and the seduction of the coquette, Pope shows Belinda at that moment trembling "at th' approaching Ill,/Just in the Jaws of Ruin, and Codille" (III, 91–92).

Ruin, or seduction, is the constant threat in the world in which Belinda lives. As a result, there is much concern with honor, for along with the assumption that women are lovely goes the assumption that they are frail. If, "When Musick softens, and Dancing fires" (I, 76), a coquette does not weaken it is not because of her own strength; what men call honor, Ariel tells Belinda, is the protection of a sylph—an airy nothing. Three times in the poem a coquette's virginity is compared to a China jar (II, 106; III, 159; IV, 163). Because the honor of a coquette is so precariously preserved, Thalestris is not entirely wrong when she exclaims that Belinda will be dishonored if the Baron keeps the lock.

Thalestris' reaction, given the premises by which her society operates, is inevitable. But as Pope points out in various ways, those premises are false. Clarissa, who as her name tells us sees things most clearly, knows that coquetry is not an end in itself. Her speech is worth quoting at length:

> Say, why are Beauties prais'd and honour'd most,
> The wise Man's Passion, and the vain Man's Toast?
> Why deck'd with all that Land and Sea afford,
> Why Angels call'd, and Angel-like ador'd?
> Why round our Coaches crowd the white-glov'd Beaus,
> Why bows the Side-box from its inmost Rows?
> How vain are all these Glories, all our Pains,
> Unless good Sense preserve what Beauty gains:
> That Men may say, when we the Front-box grace,
> Behold the first in Virtue, as in Face!
> Oh! if to dance all Night, and dress all Day,
> Charm'd the Small-pox, or chas'd old Age away;
> Who would not scorn what Huswife's Cares produce,
> Or who would learn one earthly Thing of Use?
> To patch, nay ogle, might become a Saint,
> Nor could it sure be such a Sin to paint.
> But since, alas! frail Beauty must decay,
> Curl'd or uncurl'd, since Locks will turn to grey,
> Since painted, or not painted, all shall fade,
> And she who scorns a Man, must die a Maid;
> What then remains, but well our Pow'r to use,
> And keep good Humour still whate'er we lose?

> And trust me, Dear! good Humour can prevail,
> When Airs, and Flights, and Screams, and Scolding fail.
> Beauties in vain their pretty Eyes may roll;
> Charms strike the Sight, but Merit wins the Soul.
>
> (V, 9–34)

Clarissa makes two main points here: the first, which we have already considered, is that a coquette cannot remain a coquette all of her life. The second is that beauty and charm are less important than "merit."

Although Clarissa does not define "merit," Pope does suggest what it is at least negatively in his descriptions of Belinda and her group. Primarily, Belinda's society is egocentric; its highest values are those which gratify the vanity of the individual. Belinda at her dressing table participates in "the sacred Rites of Pride." And if we read the dressing table scene as if it were described from Belinda's point of view (with, of course, the addition of Pope's ironic tone), we see that Belinda takes it for granted that all nature and all society exist to gratify her. The British navy and the commerce of the world exist so that Belinda will have gems from India and scent from Arabia; because Belinda needs a comb, "the Tortoise and the Elephant unite." Belinda believes that the world revolves around her lovely self.

The same kind of egocentricity is present in other characters. Thalestris misunderstanding the honor involved in the theft of the lock is bad enough; even worse, however, is her self-centered statement that she will not let her friendship for Belinda damage her own reputation. Like Belinda, but totally without Belinda's charm, Thalestris values objects and persons only as they touch her reputation. This condemnation of egocentricity is also the basis of Pope's more general charges against his society. If judges hurriedly sentence criminals so that they might dine early, they have assumed that their personal comfort is more important than the life of another individual; if Queen Anne does not perceive the difference between taking tea and an affair of state, it is presumably because she feels that her mere presence makes either occasion equally important.

The antidote to such egocentricity is love, a willingness to involve one's self seriously in the feelings of others. Pope does not stress love as a corrective of society as a whole, for to do so would throw the focus off Belinda; but he does make love the instrumental force in Belinda's growing-up. We have seen that in preparing for the fateful day, Belinda's world revolved around only her pride. But here are the Baron's preparations for the day:

> For this, ere *Phoebus* rose, he had implor'd
> Propitious Heav'n, and ev'r'r Pow'r ador'd,
> But chiefly *Love*—to *Love* an Altar built,
> Of twelve vast *French* Romances, neatly gilt.
> There lay three Garters, half a Pair of Gloves;
> And all the Trophies of his former Loves.
> With tender *Billet-doux* he lights the Pyre,
> And breathes three am'rous Sighs to raise the Fire.
>
> (II, 35–42)

Belinda was described as a goddess who adored her own image in the mirror; she regarded the puffs and love notes on her table as fitting tributes. The Baron is described as a mere suppliant whose thoughts are intent not on himself but upon Belinda and whose worship is not of Pride but of Love; even the mementoes of his life as a beau are seen not as trophies but as sacrifices. Although Pope's touch in the two descriptions is light, the contrast is obvious.

Because the Baron is selfless, at least in contrast to Belinda, Clarissa sides with him in the quarrel. The Baron has realized that it is time to stop the childish game of coquettes and beaux. The difference between Belinda and the Baron is that the Baron is a slight step ahead of her; the Baron has willingly sacrificed his toys, but Belinda is still fighting to preserve what Pope called the "Toyshop of her Heart" (I, 100).

Yet for all her egocentricity, Pope does not entirely condemn Belinda. He condemns, instead, those who should know better— Queen Anne, the judges who thoughtlessly condemn poor wretches to hanging, the Sir Plumes and Thalestrises. Belinda escapes Pope's condemnation for numerous reasons. The most basic is that Pope wrote the poem to charm the real-life Belinda into common sense, not to enrage her; but the charm works because of the framework Pope created. Belinda can be forgiven in part not only because she is beautiful, but also because she is young. Clarissa speaks for "good sense" to "preserve what Beauty gains," and the gains of beauty are real gains; Pope does not for a moment deny their appeal. But Pope, through Clarissa, is willing to accept the social world of the coquette with one important provision—that the coquette sometime grow up. As a leader of a great nation, Queen Anne *should* know the relative values of taking tea and counsel; judges *should* understand that a man's life is more important than dinner; Sir Plume and Thalestris, as an established married couple, *should* address themselves not to Belinda's vanity but to her common sense. Belinda, however, is still young. Pope has captured her at just that moment when she should be passing from coquettish charm to womanly wisdom. She does not finish the transition within the poem; but with "An Earthly Lover lurking at her Heart" she is almost ready to accept her new role, if only the Sir Plumes and the Thalestrises of the world will let her.

Further Possibilities

The study of a major work of art is never complete. After five essays on *The Rape of the Lock,* we have really only begun to explore the poem. Much could be learned about Pope's artistry and way of working by analyzing closely one of its several set pieces. A study of the sylphs, for example, and the paraphernalia surrounding them, with special attention to their source in Rosicrucian belief and the changes Pope made, would permit the student to see first-hand how an artist uses certain kinds of material. Equally informative would be similar studies of the game of Ombre, or a comparison of the mock epic battle scenes with battle scenes from real epics.

Although it would be rather time-consuming, a study of a typical day in the life of an early eighteenth-century belle or beau would make more clear the kind of life Pope describes. A reading of the memoirs, diaries, and letters of the period would give the student a sense of both the elegance of the age and of the frustration that an intelligent person must have felt in observing large numbers of bright young people becoming Sir Plumes and Thalestrises. An understanding of a work of literature includes an awareness of the world from which it came.

Since *The Rape of the Lock* was revised extensively, a comparison of the two versions would aid in clarifying Pope's final intention in the poem. We may assume, when an author revises a work, that he tries both to make it more interesting and to make more clear his purpose in writing it. Such a study requires that the critic not only show what the significant revisions were, but that he also account for them in relation to the intention of the whole poem. A major addition in the revised version of *The Rape of the Lock* is the sylphs. Exactly what does the supernatural apparatus permit Pope to do that he had not done before? What does the addition clarify that earlier was vague?

Within a long work, certain key motifs are likely to recur frequently. The motif might be a recurring word, image, situation, or a cluster of images and ideas. Such motifs not only help unify a work by providing a thread which holds it together, they are also often chosen consciously or unconsciously because they reflect the major concerns of the author. "Honor" is mentioned repeatedly in *The Rape of the Lock;* if the reader can determine precisely what it means to each of the characters who uses it by studying the contexts in which it occurs, he will go far in understanding what Pope is saying about his society. In addition, there are frequent references to things being ruined—new brocade, tea cups, the Queen of Hearts—that cumulatively give the impression that Belinda lives in an exceptionally fragile world where things of value are constantly in danger of breaking. Similarly, throughout the poem are frequent *doubles-entendres,* beginning with the *"Rape"* in the title. The sexual allusions occur so regularly that a reader ought to sense a kind of undertone, a feeling that for all Belinda's innocence, the coquette's game is chiefly one of arousing sexual passion and frustrating it.

It would be possible also to analyze Pope's technique much more fully than we have. There are, for example, some passages in *The Rape of the Lock* that are primarily narrative—that is, passages in which the chief intent is to advance the action as rapidly and as smoothly as possible; other passages describe persons or objects; still others are speeches of this or that character. Is there any difference rhythmically, syntactically, or in any other way among such passages? If there are differences, what details in the make-up of the lines account for them? Or, a different kind of technical question, precisely how does Pope let us know how he, as narrator of the poem, feels about his subject? There is throughout *The Rape of the Lock* a steady, identifiable tone of voice. How does a reader recognize it, how does he describe it, and what in Pope's choice and arrangement of words creates that tone of voice?

III

Sophocles' *Oedipus Rex*

Literature in Translation

Most American students are seriously handicapped by their inability to read a foreign language comfortably. To go beyond English is for most to stumble through Virgil, Baudelaire, or Thomas Mann, propped up somewhat feebly by a dictionary and a memory of a sophomore language course. Ideally, all students of literature ought to acquire at least a second language, and perhaps a third or fourth. Actually, however, most of us will have to make do with translations, and most often with translations that have been assigned in class. The student ought, therefore, to know something about translations generally.

Most importantly, there is no such thing as a perfect translation of a work of literature; languages are simply not mutually compatible enough so that complete equivalents of complex expressions can be found. The inadequacy of translations is most obvious in poetry, but the factors that make translations of poetry inadequate also affect translations of prose. Donne's "The Ecstasy," for example, begins,

> Where, like a pillow on a bed,
> > A pregnant bank swelled up to rest
> The violet's reclining head,
> > Sat we two, one another's best.

> Our hands were firmly cemented
> With a fast balm, which thence did spring.

The lines are what they are because of a particular combination of
(1) the rhythmic and pitch patterns, (2) the literal meaning of the
words, (3) the tone, including the level of usage, and (4) the
metaphors ("pregnant bank," "hands firmly cemented," and so on)
and rhetorical turns ("one another's best"). In order to produce
an equivalent passage, the translator would have to reproduce all
of these elements in precisely the same proportions they have in
the original. The German word for "pillow," for example, is *"Kopf-
kissen";* a translator would have to decide whether to preserve the
denotative meaning of "pillow" and change the sound of the line,
or to approximate the sound and change the idea slightly. In addition, the Donne passage is in iambics, a meter which sounds relatively natural in English poetry but less natural in other languages;
ought the translator preserve the iambic meter as far as possible,
and thereby make the translation seem somewhat strained metrically, or ought he change the iambics to a more natural meter?

In most drama and fiction the language is relatively less complex
than it is in poetry and the translator's problem correspondingly
simpler. Yet many of the subtle nuances which, for example, distinguish one character from another in conversation or suggest that
a character is using a certain tone of voice, result from the small-
scale things that happen in one language but not in another.

Not only do the details of the languages make translation necessarily imperfect, the difficulty is further increased by the fact that
different languages reflect different cultures. In Russian, for example, to mention that a character wears a certain type of boot
identifies him as a native of a particular region and places him in
a certain economic class; since the word will have no equivalent in
English, does the translator simply use the word "boot," anglicize
the Russian without explanation, or work into his translation all
that the word implies? Or again, Russian has an elaborate system
of suffixes which imply specific attitudes—affectionate, belittling,
and so on—which often set the tone of a passage but which become
awkward when translated into their English equivalents. Although

these details are relatively insignificant in themselves, they are examples of the countless decisions a translator must make.

Not only is there no such thing as a perfect translation, there is also no such thing as the best translation. At most, a translation is "best" for a particular purpose. A literal translation attempts primarily to be a word-for-word equivalent of the original. The translator will usually attempt to write readable English and to preserve as much of the flavor of the original as possible, but when he is faced with a choice of reproducing the literal meaning of the original accurately or making a more readable version in his own language, he will choose in favor of the original. At the other extreme is the very loose translation in which the translator assumes that he has assimilated the original completely—tone, implications, meaning, etc.—and attempts to create something in English that produces the effect of the original. In this kind of translation the writer will feel free to change words, or images, or perhaps even to transfer the story from pastoral Greece to pastoral England, and so on. In general, the difference between the two extremes is one of giving either the exact denotative equivalents of the original or the feel of the original. Most translations fall somewhere between these extremes. Usually, rather than write an atrocious English sentence, the translator will alter the original somewhat; and rather than make a major change in the original, he will let an ungraceful sentence stand.

Because translations are not completely accurate re-creations of the originals, certain kinds of study obviously ought not be made of translations unless the critic also knows the original language. For example, any study that relies heavily upon detailed linguistic analysis will give conclusions about the translation, not about the original. In some translations of *Oedipus Rex* the translator avoids having Oedipus say "I understand" to have him say repeatedly "I see." Without knowing Greek, a reader of the translations has no way of choosing among three possibilities: (1) every time the the English says "I see" or some variant, it is a literal translation of a Greek word meaning "to see," (2) it is usually a translation of a Greek word meaning "to see," (3) the translator has simply taken advantage of the fact that in English "to see" is an acceptable substitute for "to understand" and used it to emphasize the sight motif in the drama. Any argument to the effect that the constant repetition of "to see" helped unify Sophocles' *Oedipus Rex* not based on a knowledge of the Greek text would be worthless. Or, to give another example, in the Fitts and Fitzgerald translation of *Oedipus Rex,* the first antistrophe begins, "The tyrant is the child of Pride." In English "tyrant" is an emotionally loaded word because it suggests the worst possible kind of ruler; the Greek word meant merely a ruler who had not inherited the throne. To decide whether "tyrant" or merely "ruler" would be the best translation of the original Greek word would require a thorough knowledge of the play, the character of Oedipus, and Greek feelings about rulers.

A student who does not know the original language can sometimes gain an insight into a foreign work by comparing translations. If, for example, most of the translations of *Oedipus Rex* maintain a constant repetition of "to see," it is highly probable that the Greek used a verb meaning both "to see" and "to understand." It is not a proof, however, it is simply a probability. Although at times translators rely too heavily on their predecessors, as a general rule a reader comparing translations may assume that the original is a kind of center around which all variant translations will revolve; those matters of language on which different translations tend to agree are probably present in the original. Where there is widespread disagreement, the translators have probably had to make choices and have made them on different bases.

Because the kinds and qualities of translations differ, the student ought not to let any one translation dissuade him from reading a work; if one translation seems stilted, or dull, or verbose, another might be better. Translations generally follow the spirit of the period in which they were made. Each age has its own version of the best style, its own pattern of emphasis and avoidance, its own interpretation of what another nation or another time ought to be like. The eighteenth century has Homer, for example, as a remote, god-like figure who wrote of a world of supermen for a world of supermen, and the ideal verse form as the heroic couplet; the eighteenth-century translations of Homer reflect those views.

In the middle of the twentieth century we, rightly or wrongly, see Homer as a kind of bard, a primitive predecessor of television and the movies, and we tend to assume that the best language is that which comes naturally. And, of course, within a period, the satisfaction a translation can give will depend upon the ability of the translator, his purpose in translating, and the reader's expectations.

On Reading Drama

Although all literature should be read actively and imaginatively, with the reader constantly re-creating in his own mind the world described by the author, reading drama poses special problems. Except for closet drama, plays are written to be performed. Dramatists assume that trained actors will speak their lines, that the actors will use the appropriate facial expressions (or masks) along with whatever gestures and movements are called for, that there will be some scenery—no matter how conventional or scanty— and that all of this will be in view of the audience. The poet or novelist furnishes the materials for a world to be built within the imagination of the reader; the dramatist counts on his world being physically present for the spectator. To read drama intelligently, we must try to feel the play as it would be performed, especially as it would be performed on the stage for which it was written.

There are many styles of staging drama. Most of the standard dramas of whatever period have been performed in modern dress, and Shakespeare's characters have appeared in Greek togas and ten-gallon hats. A student attempting to understand a play, though, would do well to imagine it as it was originally performed. The theater of each period and each place has certain conventions that determine what a dramatist may or may not do.

One of the quickest ways of realizing the contrast between different styles of staging is to compare the opening pages of Shakespeare's *King Lear* and O'Neill's *The Hairy Ape,** paying particular attention to the stage directions. Shakespeare's characters are described briefly—"Lear, King of Britain; King of France; Duke of Burgundy; Edmund, bastard son to Gloucester," and so on. Stage directions consist of such brief comments as "Enter Kent, Gloucester, and Edmund"; "Sennet. Enter one bearing a coronet, King Lear, Cornwall, Albany, Goneril, Regan, Cordelia, and Attendants," with little or no attempt to describe the characters or the scene. On the other hand, O'Neill sets his stage very carefully:

> SCENE. The firemen's forecastle of a transatlantic liner an hour after sailing from New York for the voyage across. Tiers of narrow, steel bunks, three deep, on all sides. An entrance in rear. Benches on the floor before the bunks. The room is crowded with men, shouting, cursing, laughing, singing—a confused, inchoate uproar swelling into a sort of unity, a meaning—the bewildered, furious, baffled defiance of a beast in a cage. . . .
>
> The treatment of this scene, or of any other scene in the play, should by no means be naturalistic. The effect sought after is a cramped space in the bowels of a ship, imprisoned by white steel. The lines of bunks, the uprights supporting them, cross each other like the steel framework of a cage. The ceiling crushes down upon the men's heads. They cannot stand upright. This accentuates the natural stooping posture which shoveling coal and the resultant over-development of back and shoulder muscles have given them. The men themselves resemble those pictures in which the appearance of Neanderthal Man is guessed at. All are hairy-chested, with long arms of tremendous power, and low, receding brows above their small, fierce, resentful eyes. All the civilized white races are represented, but except for the slight differentiation in color of hair, skin, eyes, all these men are alike.

O'Neill is quite obviously writing for a stage with comparatively full physical resources. The setting requires that something like a firemen's forecastle of a ship be built on stage, complete with bunks, benches, and presumably the other gear one would find among a crew of ship's stokers. And not only is the stage setting supposed to give the impression of a ship's forecastle, it must also suggest that the steel in the room crushes down upon the men. And the men themselves are to be definite physical types.

All of the detail that O'Neill gives is designed to enhance not only the visual effect, it is also an important part of the theme. One of the governing ideas in *The Hairy Ape* is that modern society, with its hardness and steel and constant drudgery, has reduced the working man to almost ape-like status.

Shakespeare wrote for a barer stage; the scenery was probably limited to a few painted trees and shrubs for outdoor scenes, an ornate chair would suggest a throne for court scenes, and so on. Nor could he, if he had been writing *The Hairy Ape,* rely on central casting in a nation of over two hundred million persons to provide him with a roomful of actors of the same physical type; his actors were part of a company that regularly worked together. Consequently, Shakespeare must create his characters and scenes differently from O'Neill. O'Neill's stage has the resources to build the scene to suggest even the symbolic overtones he wants; Shakespeare, lacking the elaborate stage equipment, has to work more like a novelist; he has to create a scene for the audience to imagine rather than see. When Kent, in Act II, scene ii, of *King Lear,* meets Oswald, Oswald asks: "What dost thou know me for?" and Kent replies:

> A knave, a rascal, an eater of broken meats; a base, proud, shallow, beggarly, three-suited, hundred-pound, filthy, worsted-stocking knave; a lily-livered, action taking knave; a whore-son, glass-gazing, superserviceable, finical rogue. . . .

The frankness of speech is, of course, appropriate for Kent and for the scene, but it also tells the audience how to imagine Oswald. In the second scene of Act III, Lear says:

> Blow, winds, and crack your cheeks! Rage! Blow!
> You cataracts and hurricanoes, spout
> Till you have drenched our steeples, drowned the cocks!
> You sulphurous and thought-executing fires,
> Vaunt-couriers to oak-cleaving thunderbolts,
> Singe my white head! And thou, all-shaking thunder,
> Smite flat the thick rotundity o'the world!

These are obviously the ragings of an embittered and hopeless old man, but it is also Shakespeare telling his audience that Lear is outdoors in a howling storm. A modern dramatist or movie writer would have rain falling on the stage, wind-machines howling, and his lighting crew working feverishly.

Before attempting to come to any thorough understanding of a drama, the student should first inquire into the stage conventions of the period. And then perhaps the best strategy is to imagine himself directing the play, fully responsible for setting the stage (within the conventions of the period), for approving the casting, for deciding on the costumes of the actors, for determining where each actor is to stand on stage, how he is to gesture, what his tone of voice is to be. At the opening of *King Lear,* for example, the retiring king has asked two of his three daughters for flattery in return for their share of the kingdom; he then asks his favorite, Cordelia, "What can you say to draw/A third more opulent than your sisters? Speak." Cordelia replies, "Nothing, my Lord." Is her tone haughty, confused, or loving? To answer an apparently simple question like this, we have first to answer the immensely more complicated question of precisely what kind of woman Cordelia is and just what her relationship with her father is. Conversely, an understanding of Cordelia will depend upon how we interpret large numbers of such small-scale elements as a tone of voice or a look. If at the beginning of the play we imagine Cordelia saying "Nothing, my Lord" in a completely cold, haughty tone of voice, we have begun a misinterpretation of the character that will probably take a considerable amount of time and effort to undo. Plays are written to be staged by trained directors and performed by trained actors; the reader of a play must accustom himself to making the kind of decisions directors and actors have to make. In no other way can we hear and visualize the performance with the completeness necessary for full appreciation.

Oedipus Rex and the Greek Stage

Although the detail is unimportant in itself, a student reading the following scene from *Oedipus Rex* should sense that he is in a new world. Oedipus says:

> I have sent Kreon,
> Son of Menoikeus, brother of the queen,
> To Delphi, Apollo's place of revelation,
> To learn there, if he can,
> What act or pledge of mine may save the city.
> I have counted the days, and now, this very day,
> I am troubled, for he has overstayed his time.
> What is he doing? He has been gone too long.
> Yet whenever he comes back, I should do ill
> Not to take any action the god orders.
>   PRIEST: It is a timely promise. At this instant
> They tell me Kreon is here.

If this scene were played in modern drama, it would probably merit a laugh, for it is a not very clever variant of that hallmark of amateur writing in which the first character says, "I think John will telephone," and the second immediately says, "Yes, I hear the telephone now." In modern drama we laugh at this kind of overly hasty promise and fulfillment largely because it is so unrealistic that it shows too clearly what the author is trying to do. Yet we accept it in *Oedipus Rex*. Why?

The answer involves understanding a philosophy of the theater entirely different from ours in the twentieth century. A fourth-century Greek attending a performance of *Oedipus Rex* did not expect realistic drama because he had no tradition of realistic drama. The stage that he saw as he sat in the open air consisted of a platform on which the actors stood and a backdrop consisting merely of a wall with a central door through which the actors could come and go, with an altar further in the background. On either side were structures used for whatever machinery the plays called for.

As if to increase the formality of the performance and the aesthetic distance between actors and audience, the orchestra area, in which the chorus danced, was located between the first row of seats and the stage. There was no roof on either the stage or the orchestra, and no special lighting.

The great aesthetic distance thus achieved was fitting for Greek tragedy, for the tragedy was part of sacred ritual. The tragedies, including *Oedipus Rex,* were written as part of the annual spring festival for Dionysus, the god of wine and a good harvest, whose priest was present at the play and whose statue overlooked the drama. Although the relationship between the worship of Dionysus and the development of tragedy is too complicated to discuss here, and although we have no way of knowing for certain how much of the ritual feeling was due to the religious occasion and how much to the drama, the physical make-up of the stage certainly reminded the audience that the drama was more than a simple afternoon's entertainment. In addition, the plots of the tragedies were intended to further religious feeling. The constant theme of Greek tragedy is man's relation to the gods; although the terms of that relationship change from play to play, the spectator is seldom permitted to forget man's complete dependence upon the gods.

Oedipus Rex is typical in this respect. The inciting force of the drama is a plague sent by the gods in punishment for Thebe's failure to avenge the murder of King Laios; but the king's murder is in turn the working out of a prophecy of Delphi that his son would kill him. As the drama develops, Oedipus and Jocasta, wife and mother of Oedipus, express growing defiance of the oracles through which the gods speak to man, and the chorus constantly reminds the audience that no man may safely defy the gods. In a very real sense, then, the tragedy is a depiction of man's dependence upon the gods.

Moreover, Dionysus himself, the god in whose behalf the festival was held, was a god who, like Oedipus, died to remove a plague. Although versions of the story are numerous, the primitive worshipers of Dionysus apparently chose a man to represent the god, because they believed that the only way to remove the blight of winter was to slay the old god and to scatter the remains in the fields so that their crops would prosper through the coming spring and summer. Involved in this ceremony is the notion of the scapegoat, the creature who can take upon himself the sins of those around him and whose death or punishment can expiate those sins. Since the expiation had to be perfect, it meant in earliest times that the sacrifice had to be a god or the god's incarnation; later the king would do, then any physically perfect human being, and finally, as mankind began to find human sacrifice repugnant, a physically perfect animal. Oedipus, as King of the Thebans, is the perfect figure to draw on himself the sins of the city and to expiate them.

Oedipus, then, is both a dramatic figure—a human king of Thebes—and a ritual figure. The costuming of the Greek actors tended to emphasize the non-human. The actors wore masks designed to stylize and to exaggerate the emotions they were to express. With the masks, of course, any play of facial expression was totally impossible; an actor could not, by facial expression, create an individual character. At the end of *Oedipus Rex,* for example, Oedipus wears a mask of exaggerated anguish; we are to feel that this is not a particular person suffering, but that Oedipus is somehow more than a man suffering something more than anguish. Since the masks also probably served as megaphones, much of the individual tone of voice was lost, making the whole performance even more formalized. Stylized tunics worn by the actors eliminated individualization in dress, and the elevated shoes added to the impression that these heroes were indeed larger than life.

The chorus underlined the solemnity of the performance. Although we shall discuss its functions in some detail later, the chorus danced or moved across the stage in one direction as it chanted the strophe, and back as it chanted the antistrophe. Only one fragment of such choral music exists, but we know that the song and its movements were stately and designed to elevate whatever mood was appropriate to that moment in the drama. The leader of the chorus, the Choragos, served as spokesman, responding in situations where it would be awkward for the entire chorus to speak.

The strict injunction against violence on stage further increased the solemnity. Although the reasons for prohibiting violence on stage are uncertain, the effect of having it reported—as when the messenger reports the death of Jocasta and the blinding of Oedipus —is further to separate the audience from the action, to emphasize the ritual drama rather than the human drama.

Although there are exceptions, it may be said that the tendency of Western drama since the Middle Ages has been to draw the spectator into the play; the chief exceptions are those neo-classical works of the seventeenth and eighteenth centuries which admittedly attempted to re-create the spirit of Greek drama. The audience is generally expected to feel that there are human beings on stage, and that the characters live in a world with human dimensions. Even Shakespeare's magnificent tragic heroes live in a world in which winds blow, rain falls, dogs bark, and cocks crow; it is a world that we could conceivably live in. The tendency in Greek drama, on the other hand, was to stress the ritualistic, the larger-than-life. If Oedipus, for example, seems long-winded for speaking in paragraphs rather than in sentences, it is because Sophocles creates a world in which ritual is more important than the everyday reality of a drunken porter answering a knock on Macbeth's castle door.

Characters as Dramatic Functionaries

Dramatic characters are not real persons. They are created by an author to do something in the over-all play (this, by the way, is true of any narrative). In real life if I ask why a friend did a particular thing, I am actually asking about his motivation. What factors, objective and subjective, caused him to decide to take a specific course of action? I might very likely want to know more about his past, especially the experiences he had in childhood; and I would also want to know what long-range consequences he expected the decision to have. In life, it is legitimate to look at the complete context in which the decision is made because the world goes on before, after, and around the decision. But in drama, or narrative generally, we have only the world the author created. If a flesh and blood human being has Hamlet's problem, a psychoanalyst might want to inquire into his boyhood relations with his father. But as a dramatic character, Hamlet has no boyhood; he has only the life that the dramatist gives him in the play, only the scattered bits of a past that Shakespeare lets us know of. Any speculation about how Hamlet as a boy felt about his father is only speculation; it may be interesting, it may even have a use, but it remains guesswork.

In trying to understand a dramatic character, the most useful question to ask is not "Why did he do this?" but "Why did the author have him do it?" This latter question has the advantage of recognizing that the character exists not as a person, but as a function in the narrative.

To begin with an obvious example, in the Sherlock Holmes detective stories there is always an abundance of material centering on Dr. Watson. Although a chance remark by Watson sometimes gives Holmes the insight he needs to solve the case, Watson's active role in the action is usually too small for the amount of attention given him. This raises the interesting question of why an experienced writer, working in a genre in which rapid story development is essential, should seem to waste time creating an unnecessary character. The answer, of course, is that Watson is necessary—not for the story, but for the author and for the reader.

In the Holmes stories, Conan Doyle has the problem of making absolutely clear to the reader the thought processes of a master detective whose sense of observation and logical power far exceed the reader's. How does one create a character who can think more accurately and more rapidly than the reader, and who will nevertheless be understood? There are a number of solutions; the most obvious and amateurish (although even this may be handled well) is to have the narrator report in some detail what is happening in the mind of the unusually brilliant character. Or the author may do what Doyle did, create a character who is likable but slightly dense, make him the hero's companion, and, whenever the hero's mind clicks too rapidly for the reader to follow, our Dr. Watson can ask a question. When the device is working well, Watson's question is the question most readers would ask at that point in the narrative. And, of course, in answering Watson, Holmes really explains his deduction to us. Even though Watson may himself be interesting at times, he is less a character in his own right than a representative of those of us who are not quite as mentally alert and agile as Holmes, and who therefore need some help in following Holmes's logic.

Actually, Watson is one of a large number of literary confidants, of characters whose purpose is to be told things so that the audience may understand them. It is a rare fictional detective who lacks someone to show off to. One of the several functions of Horatio in *Hamlet,* to move to more serious literature, is to listen to Hamlet give necessary background information about the situation in Denmark.

Quite often, a major function of a character may be simply to respond for the reader or the audience, and by his response, to show the reader the proper response. Holmes, for example, is supposed to be as brave as he is logical—no shriek in the night, no attack by armed assailants, no torture, can frighten him. The fearlessness makes Holmes a more perfect hero, but it also makes problems for the author. If your hero does not show fear, how do you indicate that he is in a situation in which ordinary men like ourselves would be afraid? Again, various techniques would do, but one of the most satisfactory and most used is to put an ordinary man, a Dr. Watson, on the scene, and let him register fear. When Watson says in terror, "My God, Holmes, what is it?" the reader knows that if he were there, he too would feel the terror.

Obviously, not all function characters serve as on-the-scene substitutes for the audience. If the world of the narrative is at all complex, it will be filled with messengers, grocers, porters, and what have you. Such functionaries are usually treated callously by the author. In *Hamlet,* to use that familiar example again, Shakespeare does a magnificent job of directing our sympathies. He has succeeded in making four hundred years of audiences feel that a young man who insults his mother, is responsible for the death of

a boatload of men, stabs an old family retainer, arranges that another person will be killed in his place, drives a young girl crazy,
and kills her brother, is really a sympathetic hero. Shakespeare
arranges his action so that, with the exception of Ophelia and
possibly Gertrude, we cannot feel sorrow when the other characters
die. Minor characters are to be thought of as necessary functions
of the story, not as human beings.

Perhaps the "foil" is the most widely recognized function character. The purpose of the foil is to compare and/or contrast with
another character, usually the protagonist. In *Hamlet,* as we noted
earlier, Fortinbras and Laertes share with Hamlet the loss of a
father; their responses to that loss help the reader better to evaluate
Hamlet's response. Even Dr. Watson is, in addition to our man
on the scene, a foil for Holmes; when Watson reacts in amazement
or terror and Holmes with comprehension or courage, we are to
note the difference and to increase our respect for Holmes.

There are, of course, other kinds of function characters, but it
would be pointless to attempt to classify them all. We might just
note three of the more important types, which we can typify by
citing the porter in *Macbeth,* Fortinbras in *Hamlet,* and Clarissa in
The Rape of the Lock.

One technical problem a writer of narrative has that the casual
reader is likely to be unaware of is that of pacing his story. Most
comedians, for example, have some "filler," some rather quiet
material to put between the jokes because they realize that the
audience cannot hear a joke if it is laughing. Comedians also realize
that, in many situations, a joke is funniest if its punch line comes
unexpectedly, so they tell an anecdote filled with mild humor and
diversionary material, then pleasantly surprise the audience with
the punch line. Authors of serious narrative use the same technique.
In *Macbeth,* Shakespeare has just given his audience a very intense
moment with the murder of the king; another tense moment has
to follow almost immediately. But two such moments coming one
after the other would tend to cancel each other out, or at least to
produce a diminished effect; hence, in *Macbeth,* the drunken porter
provides a bit of comic relief, giving the audience time to regather
its emotional strength before it is racked again. The porter may,

of course, have other functions, but a major reason for his presence is to pace the action so that Shakespeare can get the maximum emotional reaction from his audience.

The chief duty of the Fortinbras kind of character, as we are discussing it now, is to end a narrative action. Although some modern narratives end openly—that is, with no clear and definite conclusion—most traditional narratives end with a very distinct resolution of all the conflicts that have raged throughout the action. One way of writing an ending is to have someone within the action, however remotely, responsible for ending the conflicts. When Fortinbras appears on stage at the end of *Hamlet,* we may rest assured that Denmark is now in good hands, and that all the problems likely to be caused by the death of the king and the heir to the throne are resolved. Malcolm at the end of *Macbeth* and Kreon at the end of *Oedipus Rex* function in much the same way; their presence assures the spectator that the specific problems posed at the start of the play have been resolved and that those same problems will not recur.

The Clarissa character is a spokesman for the author. In didactic literature especially, an author may want to be absolutely certain that his ideas reach the reader with a minimum of distortion. One of the many ways of helping the reader perceive clearly what the author wants to say is to create a character whose obvious good sense, whose understanding of what has happened, qualifies him for the reader's trust. Sometimes the trustworthiness of the character can be established merely by a name—Clarissa, Trueman, All-worthy—but at other times the writer has to work relatively hard to create the necessary trust. But once it is created, we may accept that character as the author's representative.

Although fictional characters are not real people, an author will usually try to give his creations the illusion of life, and will usually provide them with adequate motivation and consistent reactions. When Horatio delivers his farewell speech to Hamlet—"Now cracks a noble heart. Good night, sweet Prince/And flights of angels sing thee to thy rest!"—the words are perfectly consistent with Horatio's character; they may even be the words that a real Horatio would have said if a real Hamlet had died. But within the play, they are said not only to show Horatio's reaction, but also to tell the audience as directly and as clearly as possible that the play is about to end, that they ought to react with sorrow to Hamlet's death because he was indeed a "sweet Prince" and a "noble heart," and that the sorrow ought to be eased somewhat because the troubled Hamlet is now at rest. If this kind of analysis seems cold-blooded in implying that Shakespeare, who created such life-like characters, calculated the reactions of his audience instead of shedding tears with Horatio, it is nevertheless probably accurate, at least from a critic's point of view. When drama works, it works not because the author has created a structure of perceptions, emotions, and actions that satisfy his characters, but because he has created a structure that satisfies us, his audience.

The Function of the Chorus in *Oedipus Rex*

For all practical purposes, the chorus and its leader, the Choragos, may be considered a single character in *Oedipus Rex*; * when the Choragos speaks, he speaks as a representative of the chorus. And the chorus, in turn, represents at varying times the citizens of Thebes, Sophocles' audience, and Sophocles.

Perhaps the most single telling indication of the Choragos as spokesman for the chorus and thereby for the people of Thebes occurs in a curious exchange early in the first scene. Oedipus has just given his solemn oath to seek out the murderer of King Laios and to punish both the murderer and all who aid him; the Choragos replies immediately, "I swear/I did not do the murder, I can not name/The murderer." A modern audience is likely to find it strange that Oedipus then leaves off questioning the citizens of Thebes and tries another line of investigation. We would expect a modern investigator to go from door to door asking questions. Oedipus, however, does not have to do so, for when the Choragos asserts

---

* Excerpts from *Oedipus Rex* translated by Dudley Fitts and Robert Fitzgerald are reprinted by permission of Harcourt, Brace & World, Inc., and Faber and Faber Limited. Copyright 1949 by Harcourt, Brace & World, Inc.

his innocence, he speaks for the entire population of Thebes; the citizens have already been polled.

This is, of course, merely a detail, but it indicates sharply the way the chorus and the Choragos represent the Theban citizenry. Their full role in the play may best be seen, however, by analyzing the choral odes, including the parados.

In the parados, the chorus expresses its complete dependence upon the gods—even when the gods are angry—and their hope that the gods will once more favor them. They have just heard Kreon deliver the oracle and Oedipus vow to carry out the oracle's wishes; nevertheless, despite the promise of Oedipus, they ask whether Apollo "Will . . . send doom like a sudden cloud, or weave it/Like nightfall of the past?" The next part of the parados, the antistrophe, prays to Apollo's twin sister, Artemis, and asks for salvation. "No man," the second strophe reminds the audience, not even Oedipus, "fights off death with his mind." The third strophe ends with a plea based on the conviction that only the gods can save Thebes. In what must be one of the high points of choral drama, Oedipus enters, presumably from the center door at the rear of the stage, just as the chorus ends the parados with the cry,

> Whirl upon Death, that all Undying hate!
> Come with blinding torches, come in joy!

As these lines are chanted, it is easy to imagine the chorus whirling dramatically to face Oedipus, who is himself not death but who is the center of the infection which is killing Thebes and who, at the end of the play, will be blinded.

If we look at the parados more closely, we find that it does several things. It states, like a "Clarissa" character, the proper attitude toward the gods, and it is necessary that that be established early. Even within the prologue, there is some indication that the great ones of the city—Oedipus, the embodiment of temporal power, and the priest, the embodiment of spiritual power—have doubts about the power of the gods. Something is not quite right if the priest comes to Oedipus because he believes Oedipus to be the man "wisest in the ways of God" and addresses him with the god-like title, "O mighty power." The priest is not impious, but as a priest he should place more trust in the gods and less in a mortal. Oedipus, too, is overly ready to accept the priest's estimate of his ability. Although near the end of the prologue he acknowledges that he will need the help of the gods, he has already shown his pride by saying, "Then once more I must bring what is dark to light." Both the priest and the king seem uncertain of how much power is the gods' and how much man's. In the immediately ensuing parados, the chorus does not doubt; its function here is to let the audience know clearly that the gods have all power. The wisdom of Oedipus will not help, for "no man fights off death with his mind"; and the chorus's immediate request to the oracle is very likely an implied rebuff to the priest, who as a priest should seek the aid of the gods rather than the aid of man.

The chorus will retain this thematic function throughout the play, as it will its function of telling the audience how the people of Thebes feel about the events. The suffering of the Thebans was seen only indirectly in the prologue; the chorus gives a first-hand report of its agony:

> The plague burns on, it is pitiless,
> Though pallid children laden with death
> Lie unwept in the stony ways,
> And old gray women by every path
> Flock to the strand about the altars
> There to strike their breasts and cry
> Worship of Phoibos in wailing prayers:
> Be kind, God's golden child!

It is a telling picture of a suffering people.

In the first ode, the chorus adds to its functions that of pacing the emotions of an audience who already knows the outcome of the drama. Thematically, it is significant that here, even after Oedipus has begun tracking down the slayer of King Laios, the chorus realizes that the killer will be found not by Oedipus, but by the Furies, instruments of the gods, and that "Holy Parnassos' peak of snow" will blind "that secret man."

Nevertheless, at this point the chorus is confused, and its confusion is necessary to suggest the proper reaction on the part of the audience, for Sophocles in this drama has an especially difficult problem. The Greek audience for whom he wrote knew the story of Oedipus thoroughly. Yet despite their foreknowledge of the events, Sophocles had to keep their emotions from racing ahead. To put this more generally, one of the many interrelated strands that make up the structure of a drama is a structure of emotions; a drama fails if the audience laughs where it should cry or feels secure where it should feel apprehensive. A writer must make certain that his audience feels the emotion proper to that particular moment in the play; an audience knowing the complete story of Oedipus is likely to let its knowledge of what *will* occur color improperly its response to what *is* occurring. One of the tricks Sophocles uses to keep the emotions of the audience apace with the play is to have the chorus respond as the audience should. The job of the chorus at this point in the play is to express the tension the audience should feel about the guilt or innocence of Oedipus and to remind the audience that it is possible still to side with Oedipus even after he has insulted the prophet Teiresias. "No man," the chorus says, not even Teiresias,

> can judge that rough unknown or trust
> > in second sight,
> For wisdom changes hands among the wise.
> Shall I believe my great lord criminal
> At a raging word that a blind old man let fall?

The central issue here is the validity of prophecy—if a prophet says that Oedipus is a criminal, shall he be believed? This issue of the power of prophecy, of human interpretation of the will of the gods, is perhaps the most important issue in the play; the confusion of the chorus here permits the audience to feel it as an issue, and their allegiance to Oedipus is a clue to the audience that the proper reaction at this moment is to side with the king.

The second ode occurs just after a quarrel between Oedipus and Kreon in which Oedipus has acted badly, the Choragos has acted as a mediator, and Jocasta's recapitulation of the story of the killing of King Laios has made Oedipus doubt his innocence. The scene ends with Jocasta, with good reason from her point of view, denying the authority of the oracle, and Oedipus responding, "You may be right." This expression of doubt about the veracity of the oracle is a step further than the chorus had gone in the previous ode; the chorus had doubted the word of a single individual, not the word of the oracle itself. The chorus sorrowfully turns away from Oedipus and Jocasta. The opening lines in the second ode are a prayer that the chorus may be "reverent in the ways of right," and the closing words a rebuff to their King and Queen:

> Our masters call the oracle
> Words on the wind, and the Delphic vision blind!
> Their hearts no longer know Apollo,
> And reverence for the gods has died away.

During the ode, the chorus has accused Oedipus of drinking "from his sickening cup/Recklessness and vanity" and prophesied that "Any mortal who dares hold/No immortal power in awe/Will be caught up in a net of pain." The chorus here is both reminding the audience of the theme and cueing its reaction to Oedipus and Jocasta.

The third ode functions chiefly to keep the audience apace with the play. In the previous scene, Oedipus has learned that he might truly be the slayer of King Laios; Jocasta has begged him not to inquire further and Oedipus, who fears that Jocasta may be asking him to cease for fear that they discover he is of lowly birth and so not worthy of her, ironically concludes that he may be the child of Luck. In effect, the ode at this point tells the audience to forget briefly what it knows about the birth and fate of Oedipus and to imagine for a moment that Oedipus is indeed the child of Luck. By forcing the audience to see for a moment the possibility that Oedipus might in fact be lucky and to imagine his fortunate birth in some detail, the chorus heightens the emotion brought about by the "unlucky" fall of Oedipus.

By the fourth ode, speculation about the identity of Oedipus is

impossible; the full story of his birth has been told, and everyone
realizes his complete guilt as foredoomed by the gods. What remains for the chorus is to sum up once more, to state the theme
and to draw the universal application. The magnificently moving
elegiac ode concludes:

> But all eyes fail before time's eye,
> All actions come to justice there.
> Though never willed, though far down the deep past,
> Your bed, your dread sirings,
> Are brought to book at last.
> Child by Laios doomed to die,
> Then doomed to lose that fortunate little death,
> Would God you never took breath in this air
> That with my wailing lips I take to cry:
> For I weep the world's outcast.
> I was blind, and now I can tell why:
> Asleep, for you had given ease of breath
> To Thebes, while the false years went by.

This ode, which begins, "Alas for the seed of men," is the full
acknowledgment of man's helplessness before the gods. No one—
not Oedipus, not the chorus, not the audience—can escape what
the gods will. If Oedipus has been blind in the enjoyment of his
good fortune, if he has mistakenly believed that he was the "child
of Luck," the chorus in its own less heroic way has been guilty of
the same errors. The first antistrophe of the final ode described
Oedipus in his glory as "True king, giver of laws,/Majestic Oedipus!/
No prince in Thebes had ever such renown,/No prince won such
grace of power." The ode ends with the recognition that like Oedipus himself, the chorus has been blind "while the false years went
by." Less heroic than Oedipus, the chorus has not risen so far
and so does not have so far to fall, nor have they followed Oedipus
and Jocasta very far into doubt of the prophets of the gods; but
like Oedipus, they took the step, and they must follow Oedipus
their own short way in his agony.

The Idea of the Tragic Flaw

Although classical tragedy may have had its roots deep in primitive ritual and so emphasizes the human less than does modern drama, it nevertheless is usually concerned with the sufferings of a man. In attempting to describe the kind of hero appropriate for tragic suffering, Aristotle, generalizing upon the tragedies he knew, argued that the tragic hero had to be better than ordinary men and yet not so good that his fall would strike the audience as unjust. If an ordinary man falls, we are likely to feel that the fall has been from too slight a height to be consequential; if a worse than ordinary man falls, we will probably feel that he got what he deserved. Neither is the proper response for tragedy. But if an unusually good man suffers, then the normal emotions for an audience to feel are the emotions Aristotle felt to be most suitable to tragedy—fear and pity. If a man as good as Oedipus can fall, what about us, who are so much less? And if a man as admired as Oedipus must fall, must we not pity him?

Although Aristotle requires the tragic hero to be better than the normal run of men, he may not be perfect. Aristotle knew that despite the Greek belief in fate or the gods, the proper emotion at the fall of a perfect man is anger with the powers that be rather than fear and pity. Consequently, he reasoned that the ideal tragic hero ought to be better than other men generally, but with a single fatal flaw. The tragic hero, as Aristotle defined him, was an ideal man except for a single defect of character. This is not the place to enter into an abstract discussion of the nature of the tragic flaw; most of the commentators on Aristotle who have tried to describe it abstractly have argued that it is, depending upon the critic's own bias, either pride or an error in judgment.

The issue of the tragic flaw is interesting because it illustrates how a concept that is far too limiting in itself may lead to a fuller understanding of a literary work. If accepted literally, the concept is limiting because it implies that the tragic hero can be characterized by a single trait—pride, rashness, ambition, bad judgment, or whatever. It tends to take the fully rounded figures that are the greatest tragic heroes and to make one-dimensional figures of them. To use an earlier example, it is easy to use the concept to reduce Hamlet to a stock figure who shows the evils of procrastination, or immaturity, or rashness, or mother fixation; any number of tragic flaws may be assigned to a Hamlet or an Oedipus and defended because, although art is not life, most great art is modeled after life, and in life man usually falls because of a number of things rather than because of a single kind of thing. The great tragic heroes could not give the illusion of being complete human beings if their falls could be fully explained by any single vice. Hamlet dies because he procrastinates in killing the king, because he has some of the impracticality of youth, because he is excessively concerned with his mother's remarriage, and because his rashness in stabbing Polonius arouses the court. Without a great deal of difficulty, it would be possible to find other flaws in Hamlet's character and to show that without any one of them, the tragedy could not take the shape it does—which is merely another way of saying that the complete tragedy grows out of the complete character of the man and that neither great tragedies nor great heroes are likely to be simple.

The problem with the notion of the tragic flaw, then, is that it is reductive; accepted literally, it forces the reader to look for simplicity where he should seek complexity. Nevertheless, it does call the reader's attention to the fact that, in most tragedies, the hero is flawed. It may not be a single flaw, but still a part of the responsibility for the fall of the hero belongs to the hero. How large a part will naturally depend upon the playwright and upon the philosophy he and his times accept. A discussion of the ways— and the plural is important—in which the tragic hero is imperfect will explain much about the theme of the tragedy.

Oedipus and the Tragic Flaw

There is a sense in which the tragic flaw of Oedipus is pride, but pride can manifest itself in so many ways that it is all but useless in distinguishing one tragic hero from another. A look at Shake-speare's great tragedies shows that all of his heroes are guilty of pride in some form or another: Hamlet believes that he is man enough to save Denmark; Lear foolishly believes that he is loved by all three of his daughters; Macbeth thinks he ought to be a king; Antony believes that his personal feelings for Cleopatra are more important than his duties to the state. All of these are mani-festations of pride (and also, by the way, of intellectual blindness), but they differ so much in their causes and effects that to say that each hero possesses the same tragic flaw evades the real issues.

Moreover, especially in classical drama, what appears to a modern reader as pride may not be pride. Modern manners call for a false humility. If an actor wins an Academy Award or an athlete makes All-American, he thanks his parents, his friends, all of his associates, and seemingly half of the world's population. For the actor or the athlete to say that he worked hard and deserves the award is considered shocking pride. Sophocles' Greeks would not have understood our attitude. Much of what we see as pride in Oedipus, the Greeks would have seen as a legitimate estimate of his worth. For example, when Oedipus, in his opening speech, says, "I have come myself to hear you—/I, Oedipus, who bear the famous name," he is merely stating a fact; the Greek view would have been that his name is famous, he made it so, and that there-fore he has every right to say so. If he is confident that he can find the murderer of King Laios, it is in part because he has already solved the riddle of the Sphinx when not even the wisest of the Thebans could.

In fact, one of the most consistent features of the drama is Sophocles' repeated partial exoneration of Oedipus. Oedipus, for example, seems to be at his worst in the scenes in which he attacks Tieresias, the blind prophet, and Kreon, Jocasta's brother; and arguments that Oedipus has a tragic flaw—whether it be pride, impetuousity, irascibility, or whatever—rely heavily on these scenes. Yet Sophocles very carefully builds into the drama sufficient motivation to justify, partly at least, the anger of Oedipus at Kreon and Tieresias.

The conflict with Tieresias comes just after Oedipus has solemnly vowed that he will seek out and punish the murderer, and has threatened banishment for anyone who refuses to tell what he knows of the murder. Tieresias then appears; their exchange begins this way:

> OEDIPUS: What is troubling you? Why are your eyes so cold?
> TIERESIAS: Let me go home. Bear your own fate, and I'll
> Bear mine. It is better so: trust what I say.
> OED: What you say is ungracious and unhelpful
> To your native country. Do not refuse to speak.

Several lines later, Tieresias says,

> No; I will never tell you what I know.
> Now it is my misery; then, it would be yours.

Oedipus is engraged by this answer, and since tragic heroes are supposd to have a tragic flaw, the temptation is to use this scene to prove the pride, impetuousity, etc., of Oedipus. Yet Sophocles has constructed the scene—with the vow by Oedipus followed almost immediately by the confrontation with Tieresias—so that the anger of Oedipus is justified. Oedipus has just given his sacred promise to the people of Thebes that he would banish anyone, "no matter who he is," who withheld information. For Oedipus to be less than enraged with Tieresias after he admits that he has the solution to the oracle would not only be unheroic, it would be cowardly.

Again, in the confrontation with Kreon, Sophocles has prepared a partial justification of Oedipus. Tieresias has just accused Oedipus of being the "damned man, the murderer of Laios"; Oedipus believes that he is not the murderer for very good reason —he simply does not remember killing the old king. There must be some reason for the accusation, so Oedipus suspects a political plot involving Kreon, since it was Kreon who both reported the oracle and suggested that Tieresias be sent for. For Oedipus to be totally unsuspicious in this situation would require great stupidity.

In a similar way, Sophocles, relying upon the legendary story of the killing of Laios, partly exonerates Oedipus for the killing of the king. Oedipus describes the scene:

> And there a herald came towards me, and a chariot
> Drawn by horses, with a man such as you describe
> Seated in it. The groom leading the horses
> Forced me off the road at his lord's command;
> But as this charioteer lurched over towards me
> I struck him in my rage. The old man saw me
> And brought his double goad down upon my head
> As I came abreast. . . . I killed him.

If one visualizes the scene, he sees the charioteer trying to bump Oedipus, perhaps taunting him with a near miss, and Oedipus striking out in anger; then Laios attacks Oedipus with a weapon, and Oedipus defends himself, killing the king. Although Oedipus acts hastily here, Sophocles has chosen to remind his audience that Oedipus was literally goaded into the murder.

Before trying to discover why Sophocles builds his scenes so that Oedipus at his worst moments is at least partly justified, it will be well to look at another possible tragic flaw in Oedipus—his so-called intellectual blindness. The charge certainly has merit; Tieresias, who has second sight, says that Oedipus is blind to the truth, and much of the time Oedipus is. In fact, critics have long been amazed at the slowness of Oedipus in recognizing his guilt. It is admittedly difficult to explain why Oedipus did not know of the murder of King Laios; it would seem that a king should certainly be curious about the fate of his predecessor. Yet that ignorance is one of the givens of the play; Sophocles accepts it without question, never once hinting that Oedipus is slow witted or unnaturally uncurious, presumably because that is the way it was in the legend which Sophocles had as his source. Some critics feel, however, that as soon as Tieresias makes his accusation, Oedipus should say, in effect, "Yes, I remember now; just before coming to Thebes I killed an old man—it was probably Laios." Others feel that when Jocasta attempts to comfort Oedipus by telling him of the original prophecy and her version of the death of the king, he should remember; and that he should certainly connect his name, "Swollen foot," with the pierced ankles of Jocasta's child. He does not, and a part of the explanation lies in the fact that for Sophocles, that is the way the story was. Modern military analysts may wonder, for example, at the incredible stupidity of the British in wearing red coats while marching through Indian country in colonial times, yet any account of British-Indian warfare simply has to accept that as a given—it was the way it was. Sophocles undoubtedly felt that way about his material.

Even so, as with the various possible instances of pride, Sophocles has built the play partly to exonerate Oedipus of any charge of intellectual blindness. He has Oedipus, midway in the second scene, give a capsule autobiography that serves a number of functions— not the least of which is that of reminding the audience that Oedipus is firmly convinced that he is the son of Polybos of Corinth and Meropê of Doria. The charge of intellectual blindness would be more certain had not Sophocles given his audience an Oedipus who was absolutely, albeit mistakenly, convinced of his own identity. This certainty, which is thoroughly justified from the point of view of Oedipus, in large part explains why he cannot believe Kreon and Tieresias.

Moreover, Sophocles is very careful to install a false clue to further justify Oedipus' slowness to recognize that he is the killer of King Laios. The eye-witness who reported the crime said that the king was attacked by a band of robbers; Oedipus, on the other hand, knows that he was alone when he killed on the crossroads before coming to Thebes. Sophocles thereby makes it unlikely that Oedipus would connect himself with the murder of Laios.

There is one other possible charge against Oedipus, one other possible specification of his tragic flaw—impiety. The charge cannot be refuted entirely because the entire action of the drama and its sources are acts of impiety. King Laios orders his son killed in order to escape the will of the gods; Oedipus flees Corinth to prevent an oracle from coming true. From the moment of Oedipus' birth, those who knew of the oracle tried in every way possible to deny the gods' will. And, as we have seen, Oedipus openly denies the voice of the gods, both as it speaks through Tieresias and as it speaks through the oracle. In scene three, after apparently learning that the oracle could not possibly be true, Oedipus says, "Why should a man respect the Pythian hearth or/Give heed to the birds that jangle above his head?"

But despite the strength of the charge of impiety against Oedipus, Sophocles permits the reader to feel some justification for Oedipus' actions. In fleeing from Corinth, for example, Oedipus believes that he avoids the commission of a double sin—the murder of his father and incest with his mother—and the avoidance of sin is a kind of piety. Moreover, as we have seen, Oedipus has every reason to believe neither Tieresias nor the oracle; Tieresias has accused him of a crime he does not remember committing, and his most direct blasphemy comes just after the messenger's information has made it seem that the oracle could not possibly be fulfilled. If Polybos is dead, Oedipus cannot possibly kill him; it is not the fault of Oedipus that he does not know that Polybos is not his father.

Why does Sophocles make it so difficult to assign any single tragic flaw to Oedipus and why does he suggest in each case a partial excuse for the appearance of the flaw? Perhaps the best answer relates to the theme of tragedy as a genre (which will be discussed in the next essay), but the question can be answered more narrowly in terms of the stature of the tragic hero. To answer the first question, a tragic hero is too large to be undone by any single vice; Aristotle said that the tragic hero is somehow better than ordinary men. A man dominated by a single vice is not better than ordinary men—he is a man obsessed. An Oedipus who was merely impetuous, or irascible, or proud, or intellectually blind, or impious, would be a fitting character for a Ben Jonson comedy of humors. The tragic hero needs to have his evil grow out of the situation, not out of himself. Oedipus is not impetuous, but he acts impetuously when the occasion demands; he is not irascible, but can be goaded into anger; he is not impious, unless he has apparently good reason for his impiety. This also explains why Sophocles partly excuses Oedipus for each of his faults; the actions of a true tragic hero cannot be motivated by a vice, they must be motivated in a way that the audience can accept, and this means that he must have a reason, an excuse, for what he does.

On the other hand, Oedipus cannot be exonerated completely of his responsibility for his fall, and Sophocles makes no attempt to do so. In Oedipus' long and magnificent speech at the end of the play, he acknowledges that "This punishment/That I have laid upon myself is just." A part of the paradox of Oedipus, and a part of the paradox of every orthodox tragic hero, is that man is both fated and responsible. As Oedipus says of himself, Apollo "brought my sick, sick fate upon me./But the blinding hand was my own!" Oedipus has come to see himself as the instrument of his own fate, suffering because the gods have decreed that he suffer and because he is the kind of man he is.

The Question of Tragedy

There are as many definitions of tragedy as there are critics who write about tragedy; tragedy can be defined by its structure, the kind of action it portrays, the emotions it produces, or the themes it embodies. Like all definitions, any definition of tragedy is useful in that it sets up a category and permits objects so categorized to be studied for their basic similarities and differences. Extreme purists, and there are not many of these any more, would limit "tragedy" to certain classical dramas and their strict imitations; others would say that any serious narrative, dramatic or not, in which the protagonist suffers a reversal of fortune is tragic; still others would contend that the essence of tragedy is the production of tragic emotions, usually fear and pity; and others would contend that tragedy is characterized by its thematic pessimism (or by its optimism, since it involves often a restoration of order).

The underlying feature of all these definitions of tragedy, however, is the awareness that tragedy is concerned with human suffering, and that the best tragedy is a serious inquiry into the causes of human suffering. To put this another way—more clear, but one which many critics would object to—tragedy basically is concerned with this single question: "Why does man suffer?" But it must be pointed out immediately that tragedy does not give a clear and simple answer to the question. In fact, one of the major weaknesses in the notion of the tragic flaw is that it makes the answer to the problem of man's suffering entirely too easy by saying, in effect, that man suffers because he has a single flaw in his character. No serious tragedy can provide so simple an answer, for any reasonably intelligent audience knows from its own experience that man suffers because he accidentally contracts a disease, because he tries to do good and harm inadvertently results, because others make him suffer, because he makes an error in judgment, and so on. There is no neat answer to the question of why man suffers, and to expect tragedy to give a neat answer would be to expect tragedy deliberately to lie about life.

If serious tragedy cannot give us an easily formulatable answer, it can give us the materials we need for wondering at the universe in which we suffer. To oversimplify somewhat, there are three categories of explanation that account for man's suffering: man himself is evil or imperfect, man is at the mercy of inhuman forces outside himself (the gods, fate, nature), man is a victim of his society. The remarkable thing about the greatest tragedies is their acknowledgment of all of these causes in one form or another. Hamlet's call to action, for example, is supernatural; yet Hamlet himself has faults which hasten his downfall and he lives in a society hostile to his values; Macbeth acts as a result of a prophecy (the supernatural), but also because he weakly listens to his wife's advice and because conditions seem right for Duncan's murder. Modern tragedy tends to minimize supernatural influence but in its place may emphasize anything from archetypal fears (O'Neill's *Emperor Jones*) to inherited venereal disease (Ibsen's *Ghosts*).

And, of course, although great tragedy tends to include in itself all the causes of man's suffering—the individual himself, inhuman forces outside himself, other human beings—the proportions will naturally vary from age to age, depending upon the ethical, philosophical, and psychological attitudes prevalent in the author's society. A nation with a strong belief in the gods will have a tragedy that emphasizes the role of the gods in determining man's fate; Renaissance Christianity, with its belief that man is a moral agent who determines his own fate, creates tragedy which emphasizes the character of the protagonist.

Despite the fact that emphases may change as the societies that shape the views of tragic writers change, the one thing that great tragedy cannot do is to offer a simple answer to the problem of why man suffers. A completely Freudian play, for example, one which attempted to show that its protagonist suffered because his sexual training was repressive, would probably be accepted only by Freudians; only Marxists were able to accept the Communist dramas that argued that the only source of evil in man's life was his economic system. Tragedy at its best is not designed to answer the question it asks; it is designed to help us better understand fully what is involved in the answer. As we watch the tragedy of an Oedipus, or a Hamlet, or a Willie Loman, the seriousness with which a mature audience can accept the tragedy will depend largely upon the honesty of the representation of the suffering of the tragic hero and the avoidance of a facile and unconvincing explanation of it.

Oedipus Rex and the Question of Tragedy

If one asks why Oedipus suffers, it should become clear rather soon that there is no single and easy answer. In fact, *Oedipus Rex* reads like a compendium of answers to the question of why man suffers —the gods are powerful, Oedipus himself is evil, and the plague must be removed from Thebes. Rather than pick one cause as the most important, it may be wise to name a single abstract factor that involves all of the above, and then to analyze that. The overriding factor in Oedipus' suffering is that he lives in a tragic universe, a universe in which the man who would be a hero is constantly called upon to make decisions in which the choice is not between alternate goods, nor even between a good and an evil, but between two evils.

Why the universe is so is not the question of tragedy, nor is it the question Sophocles asks, although Sophocles does provide gods who meddle in man's life, a hero ambitious to be a hero, and a state that must be purged. But within *Oedipus Rex* we never see a major figure offered any choice but that between two evils.

The decision to murder the infant Oedipus is such a choice. King Laios has been told by the oracle that if he and his wife have a child, that child will eventually be guilty of patricide and incest. King Laios believes the oracle, so he must choose between slaying his son and being slain by him. Within the drama the story behind the original oracle is not explained, and even if one traces the legend back to discover why the family of Laios must be punished, the problem does not change—man, confronted by a choice of evils, cannot but make an evil choice.

The same kind of dilemma that faced Laios faces Oedipus throughout the play—both in the main action and in the exposition. As we have noted, the decision to leave Corinth seems at the time to be the best decision Oedipus could make; his only alternative would be to remain in Corinth in the household of the persons he believed he was destined to sin against. The decision to kill Laios—if it can be called a decision—was a choice between acting heroically and fighting back against an attack, or acting cowardly and letting the king pass without responding to being driven off the road; most Greeks would have approved of Oedipus' anger.

Within the main action of the play, Oedipus' choices remain choices between evils. In an earlier section, we saw that he had no real choice during the impassioned scene with Tieresias. To have been less than angry with Tieresias after he had vowed to prosecute anyone who withheld knowledge of the king's murder would have been unthinkable. A hero does not break a public and solemn vow in order to protect a man, no matter what his reputation, whose silence may be responsible for the destruction of his city.

In fact, one of the most moving aspects of *Oedipus Rex* is the manner in which the world constantly closes in around Oedipus despite the good intentions of Oedipus and those near him. After the scene with Tieresias, the next step in his downfall occurs in the exchange with Jocasta, who tries desperately to comfort Oedipus by retelling the story of the murder of King Laios as she knows it;

as she tells the story, she mentions the survivor, who must be sent for.

The messenger from Corinth similarly tries to comfort Oedipus, who still fears that he may commit incest with Meropê, whom he believes to be his mother. Fate, or the gods, or whatever, here plays another trick on Oedipus. The messenger is the very same person who received Oedipus as a babe from a shepherd and gave Oedipus to Polybos and Meropê. This almost unbelievable coincidence may simply be an attempt on Sophocles' part to avoid introducing additional characters; nevertheless, it does occur, and it does provide another link in the chain which binds Oedipus to his fate. Hoping to free Oedipus from his lingering fear of incest, the messenger tells the true story of the adoption of Oedipus, and once more a seemingly good choice turns out badly. Fate or the gods play the final trick when the shepherd, the survivor of the slaying of Laios, appears and is discovered to be the same retainer whose duty it had been to abandon the infant Oedipus and who instead gave him to the messenger from Corinth. The shepherd's choice is between telling the truth and death.

Most fundamentally, of course, it must be remembered that the major choice of Oedipus—whether to pursue the inquiry into the murder of the king, even when it becomes clear that it could result in proof of his own guilt, or to abandon the search—is itself a choice between two evils. We know what happens when Oedipus chooses to continue the inquiry. As Sophocles reminds the audience, to abandon the search is to make Oedipus a moral coward afraid to discover his own identity, a weakling who is not willing to sacrifice himself to save his people.

Looked at in another way, all of the choices of Oedipus are the decisions of a hero. Throughout the play, Oedipus is contrasted with lesser men. When Kreon first returns from the oracle, he suggests caution in telling the public of the oracle's message, and Oedipus gains stature over Kreon with his reply, "Speak to them all,/It is for them I suffer, more than for myself." In the first scene, even Tieresias, a prophet, shies away from telling the truth while Oedipus, unheedful of the consequences, demands it. Especially, though, Oedipus towers over the chorus, the representative of the ordinary people. The chorus and the Choragos constantly recommend the safe virtues; in the quarrel with Kreon the Choragos reminds Oedipus that "a prudent man" would ponder Kreon's words, for "Judgments too quickly formed are dangerous." After the quarrel between Oedipus and Jocasta (who also recommends caution), the Choragos says, "I fear this silence:/Something dreadful may come of it." Such fear is fitting for ordinary men, for non-heroes; Oedipus replies, "Let it come!" After Oedipus has blinded himself, Sophocles continues to contrast the attitude of the Choragos and that of Oedipus; the Choragos is generally sympathetic and wishes that Oedipus had never found out his guilt; Oedipus rejects sympathy, and although he wishes that he had never been born, he admits the justness of his punishment. As he says at the end of a long speech in which Sophocles cleverly shows both his suffering and his courage, "Of all men, I alone can bear this guilt."

The last lines of the play, probably chanted by the Choragos, leave the audience with a chilling reminder of its differences from and likenesses to the great. The Choragos says:

> Men of Thebes: look upon Oedipus
>
> This is the king who solved the famous riddle
> And towered up, most powerful of men.
> No mortal eyes but looked on him with envy,
> Yet in the end ruin swept over him.
>
> Let every man in mankind's frailty
> Consider his last day; and let none
> Presume on his good fortune until he find
> Life, at his death, a memory without pain.

Perhaps, after the play has followed the fate of Oedipus through his suffering and the Choragos has had his say, the particular answer to the question of why man suffers is oblique rather than direct. Perhaps the assumption that guided Sophocles in the choices he had to make in writing *Oedipus Rex* was the assumption that, after all, good luck is at best a matter of not suffering. To be great is to attract the attention of the gods, it is to be in a position where impossible decisions cannot be avoided, it is for Oedipus and for tragic heroes like him to accept the suffering of an entire nation as his own. The ordinary man, the man whom the Choragos represents and speaks to, whose "mortal eyes have looked on [Oedipus] with envy," will never attain a hero's glory. The hero, especially the tragic hero, must "presume on his good fortune," must run risks. And, as the Choragos reminds his audience, good fortune is not measured in glory, but rather, in a tragic universe, in the negative reward of finding "life, at . . . death, a memory without pain."

Further Possibilities

Drama itself, and especially tragic drama, is such a splendidly complex and rich form that the approaches to it are all but endless. Greek drama especially poses numerous problems, some solvable and some not, but all worthy of consideration.

Questions about the background of *Oedipus Rex* are of special interest. In the preceding analyses, for example, we have just barely touched upon the problem of the survivals of primitive ritual in Greek tragedy. Precisely what were the rites of Dionysus out of which tragedy grew? To what extent is classical tragedy as we have it a reflection of its origins, and precisely how do those origins affect it as drama? The ritual of Dionysus, for example, involved the purgation of the demons of winter and the sacrifice of a victim; to what extent does that ritual shape the content of *Oedipus Rex* and—to broaden the inquiry—the general development of classical tragedy? The beginning student is unlikely to find definitive answers to these and similar questions, but a study of them does throw light upon the literature.

Or one could ask about the continuation of the story of Oedipus and his family as it carries through Sophocles' *Antigone* and *Oedipus at Colonus.* Since Kreon appears in a quite different light in *Oedipus Rex* and *Antigone,* a comparison of the two Kreons offers the student a chance to see the way the need to shape a dramatic character for a conflict forces specific kinds of characterization upon a dramatist—or upon any teller of a narrative. The Kreon that is appropriate for *Oedipus Rex* would not be appropriate for *Antigone*. Or, one might look at *Oedipus at Colonus,* a play which shows Oedipus finally purged of his sin and of his suffering, accepted by everyone as a man so holy that his final resting place will bring good fortune to the city of his burial. Despite the length of time between the composition of the two plays, probably about twenty years, is it justifiable to consider the early play in the light of the later? If so, and it is certain that Sophocles' audience knew the story of *Oedipus at Colonus* long before Sophocles wrote the later play, is it proper to assume that the theme of the one modifies the theme of the other? Alone, *Oedipus Rex* suggests that suffering redeems the community but not the individual; taken together, the two plays imply that suffering properly accepted also redeems the individual.

It would be equally illuminating, though in different ways, to inquire into sources from which Sophocles worked, including several of the variants of the Oedipus legend, in an attempt to discover what elements Sophocles accepted and why. How, for example, does Sophocles compress the long and complicated story of the family of Cadmon into the events that transpire in only one day and still make the entire story comprehensible? Thematically, what versions of the stories of the family of Oedipus did he either ignore or minimize in order to suggest the theme he does suggest? Dramatically, why does Sophocles choose the scenes he chooses? In short, it might be helpful to consider the finished version of Oedipus in the light of one or more of the literary determinants we used in the analysis of *The Rape of the Lock*.

It would also be instructive to consider *Oedipus Rex* in relation to Aristotle's *Poetics*. No work of literary theory had so much influence as *The Poetics,* and the single play that seemed to Aristotle to embody the tragic materials and form most fully and properly was *Oedipus Rex*. In considering Oedipus as a tragic hero, we have seen one small facet of Aristotle's theory of tragedy. Attempts to illustrate Aristotle's definition of "action" by an analysis of the play, or the interrelationship of action and character, attempts to analyze the structure of the play according to the pattern set by

Aristotle—all of these would be instructive in showing how the parts of the drama fit together.

A student could also learn something of the way drama is put together by examining the way Sophocles handles the expository passages in *Oedipus Rex*—particularly those passages that refer to action that took place before the main action of the play. Why, in particular, does Sophocles introduce each piece of information in just that particular place in the drama? Or why is the same expository material repeated several times during the play—in particular, for example, why does the chorus in its final ode repeat information that has already been given several times? For a study of dramatic pacing, the first scene is a masterpiece in its presentation first of the complete majesty of Oedipus as he vows to discover the murderer, then the lull, almost an interlude, in the bit when Oedipus speaks to the Choragos, followed by rapidly mounting and intense anger building through the rest of the scene.

Some of the considerations taken up in the earlier sections might well be discussed with a different emphasis. We saw, for example, that the tragic world of Oedipus is a world in which the hero does not have an opportunity to make the right choice; the tragic hero constantly makes what seems the best choice given the information he has, and it turns out badly. There is a way, then, in which the universe of the tragic hero is ironic—what appears to be the better is usually the worse. A look at the details of *Oedipus Rex* will show that the world of Oedipus is pervaded with ironies, perhaps the most striking of which involves the reversal of roles between Oedipus and Tieresias. Oedipus derides Tieresias for his physical blindness and becomes physically blind himself; in becoming physically blind, he acquires some of the insight of the prophet.

And, of course, the play on blindness may be treated in relation to the other ironies in the play, or it may be treated as part of the theme of the distinction among kinds of wisdom, a distinction that runs throughout the play. Oedipus is "wisest in the ways of men" but obviously not wisest in the ways of the gods. Precisely what is the difference between the two kinds of wisdom as Sophocles draws them? Does Jocasta attempt to make a false distinction between the wisdom of the prophets and priests, and the gods, and so fall into blasphemy? Such an analysis might also carry further than we did earlier the distinction between the wisdom of the Choragos, representing the average citizens of Thebes, and the heroic "wisdom" of Oedipus.

IV

Shakespeare's *Henry IV, Part I*

Literature and History

In the discussion of *The Rape of the Lock* we saw that a knowledge of the situation upon which the poem was based could corroborate an interpretation of Pope's poem. Unfortunately, most real-life events are not as tidy as the snipping of Belinda's hair and the subsequent quarrel. Since Aristotle, critics have known that events happen with a randomness, an improbability, and an inconclusiveness that do not make for great literature. In *The Poetics,* Aristotle argued that tragedies ought preferably be based on history (or legend) because audiences can accept what they know to have happened more readily than they can accept a purely imaginary story. The assumption behind Aristotle's argument is that the emotions the audience of tragedy is supposed to feel, fear and pity, will not be roused by a plot which contains events the audience thinks improbable. This line of argument eventually led Aristotle into a discussion of whether an improbable—i.e. unbelievable—possibility is dramatically preferable to an impossible probability; for reasons we do not have to go into here, Aristotle concluded that it is more important that the events in tragedy be credible than that they be true. Although the phrase "impossible probability" seems contradictory, by it Aristotle most likely meant an event in a narrative that is probable given the premises upon which the narrative is based, even though those premises themselves lead to impossible situations. *Alice in Wonderland,* to take an obvious example, is based upon impossible premises that lead to impossible situations; but, granted the premises, what happens in it is probable.

Later critics, particularly Shakespeare's contemporary Sidney, complicated and deepened the notion of literary or artistic probability by combining it with the notion that art depicted what Sidney called a "second nature," a "golden world." The second nature is an ideal world in which all the imperfections of the real world are *overcome*—not eliminated, for that would be to eliminate the conflict necessary to narrative, but confronted and overcome. Literature, Sidney argued, is the ideal instrument with which to teach man to be more human. Philosophy is perhaps better for ascertaining ethical principles, but philosophy is by nature cold and unemotional, and therefore does not incite man to do what it teaches him is right. History, literature's other rival, is exciting because it is the actual record of men living and dying. Yet history (and implicitly reality) fails as a teacher because evil historical characters often die prosperous and happy, and good historical characters often die in misery. Suppose, Sidney asks, there were an art that combined history's power to excite, to motivate action, with philosophy's power to abstract and to reach ethical conclusions; that art, Sidney concludes, would be man's best teacher.

If we consider both Aristotle's and Sidney's views, we see that we have two plausible justifications for an author's distortion of historical fact. Reality ought to be used as a basis of drama, Aristotle argues, because it is believable, and therefore it ought to be used only when it is believable; if a historical situation will not seem probable to an audience, Aristotle condones inventing a situation that will seem probable, even if it is not literally accurate. Sidney makes such invention a moral duty of the author. The author's prime responsibility is to envision and to communicate a second nature, an ideal world, in which the moral law determines the fates of the characters and in which each detail is calculated to improve the reader. It should be added immediately that Sidney was not arguing for a narrow literary didacticism; the view that literature ought to reflect moral law (however that was conceived) has been the dominant view from which Western literature has been written until only recently. Sophocles showing us the fate of Oedipus, Fielding giving his good young heroes good marriages, or Faulkner tracing the blood guilt of the South through several generations—all of these operate within Sidney's conception of literature as showing a second nature in which universal moral imperatives are irrevocably enacted.

The views of Aristotle and Sidney represent, in effect, a variation of the notion of literary determinants. Put in our terms, Aristotle and Sidney both argue that historical accuracy as a literary determinant ought not override other possible literary determinants, and that where the author must choose between literal historical accuracy and either the effectiveness of a passage or its thematic value, he ought to be willing to sacrifice the historical accuracy.

History and *Henry IV, Part I*

Henry IV, Part I, is based upon the main events in the first years of the reign of King Henry, roughly the period from 1400 to 1403. Although complicated and dramatic, the events are relatively easy to understand. Henry IV had recently ascended the throne of England after deposing Richard II. Historically, Henry's revolt seems to have been popular, at least at the start, largely because of the growing incompetence of Richard II and because Richard had illegally confiscated Henry's estates. Despite the fact that many nobles were willing to help a wronged gentleman back into the property that was rightfully his, they were less willing to support the deposition of a legitimate monarch. Although Richard II was asassinated and many of his supporters were executed, Henry nevertheless left a number of loose ends. Glendower, the fiery and powerful Welsh leader, was opposed to Henry as he had been to Richard; most importantly, however, Edmund, fifth Earl of March and the rightful heir to the throne, was left alive. In 1403

Glendower rebelled; Henry attempted to put down the revolt, then finally returned to London, leaving command of the troops to Edmund Mortimer, uncle of the Earl of March, and Mortimer's brother-in-law, Hotspur. Edmund Mortimer was captured. (Shakespeare, incidentally, confuses the two Edmunds, as does Holinshed, his chief source.) During his captivity, Mortimer and Glendower became friends and Mortimer married Glendower's daughter. The marriage allied Glendower, powerful rebel against the crown, and the family of the legal claimant to the throne.

Meanwhile, Hotspur had returned to his domain in the north of England and there successfully put down an uprising of Scots. In doing so, he captured a number of Scottish leaders, including their chieftain Douglas. At this point Henry IV's problems began in earnest. Henry IV made the mistake of demanding that Hotspur surrender the prisoners to the crown, a demand that was itself illegal. Hotspur countered with an offer to release the prisoners only on the condition that his relative, Edmund Mortimer, be ransomed from Glendower. Fearing to release so powerful a relative of a claimant to the throne, Henry IV refused Hotspur's condition and peremptorily demanded surrender of the prisoners. Hotspur, urged on by his uncle, Thomas Percy, Earl of Worcester, with reminders of Henry's ambition, led a rebellion against Henry IV. At the Battle of Shrewsbury, Hotspur, hampered by the delays of Northumberland and Glendower, was defeated and killed.

Such, essentially, is the history reflected in *Henry IV, Part I,* a history Shakespeare derived largely from the *Chronicles* of Holinshed. There is still another major actor in the history, Prince Hal, the future Henry V. According to Holinshed, Prince Hal had acquired a reputation as a profligate; for the ambitious and proud King Henry IV, who had hoped to establish a glorious British dynasty, the seemingly prodigal heir to the throne was a bitter disappointment. Still according to Holinshed, whose description of Prince Hal is probably based more on legend than on fact, the Prince surprised everyone at the Battle of Shrewsbury, during which he emerged as a gallant, heroic, and popular leader of men. During that battle Prince Hal is said to have first showed the promise that was to make him one of England's greatest kings.

There remains one more character to be accounted for, the semi-historical Falstaff. The original of Falstaff was Sir John Old-castle, a Protestant rebel whom Prince Hal befriended but whom King Henry V had to have put to death. Shakespeare had to change the name from Oldcastle, a name the character bore in a rather inept history play called *The Famous Victories of Henry V* and in the first version of *Henry IV, Part I,* because Oldcastle's descendants objected to the caricature of one of their family. How a member of one of the most puritanical of the religious sects of the period, a member so devout he was willing to die for his convictions, became transformed into the hedonistic, cowardly, but lovable, Falstaff remains one of the unsolved mysteries of literary history. The best guess is that in the bitterness of the religious feeling of the time the popular imagination was willing to attribute any evil to one whose religious opinions were unorthodox; that, coupled with the legend of Prince Hal's prodigal youth and the fact that Hal and Oldcastle had been friends, was apparently sufficient to bend the historical fact.

These, then, were the materials from which Shakespeare made *Henry IV, Part I.* Although the historical events of the early years of the reign of Henry IV are dramatic as history, they did not lend themselves to drama, at least not to effective drama, without change. Henry IV was not a likely candidate for protagonist of a drama for at least two reasons. Despite his courage and his comparative success in realizing his ambitions against great odds, he appears personally to have been an aloof, austere man, totally lacking the irresistible charm of his son. Conversely, the reputation of Prince Hal, the myth that had grown up around him in the years after his death, would tend to lead a popular dramatist such as Shakespeare to draw interest away from the cold Henry IV and to focus it on the warm Prince Hal.

Whatever the reasons for Shakespeare's shifting dramatic interest from the title character to the son, the decision left several problems, and the problems led to some rewriting of history. Most importantly, the historical conflict centered on Henry IV and his struggle to maintain his rule; dramatically, in throwing the focus on Prince Hal, Shakespeare had also to create a new central conflict, one that would revolve around the Prince. The solution was both elementary and brilliant; it consisted of transforming the historical Hotspur into a foil for Hal. Ignoring the historical fact that Hotspur was twenty-three years older than the Prince—and actually three years older than Hal's father—and that the *Chronicles* do not emphasize a rivalry between the two, Shakespeare created a Hotspur approximately the same age as Prince Hal and endowed him with precisely those princely qualities that Hal most seemed to lack at the start of the play.

To show how serious the rivalry between the two men was and to help establish it as a major conflict in the play, Shakespeare has Henry IV wish for a son like Hotspur. In the confrontation between the King and his son in Act III, scene ii, the King says that Hotspur "hath more worthy interest to the state/Than thou the shadow of succession" (ll. 98–99) and calls the Prince "my near'st and dearest enemy" (l. 123). Hal immediately accepts the challenge, vowing to

> redeem all this on Percy's head. . .
> the time will come
> That I shall make this Northern youth exchange
> His glorious deeds for my indignities.
> Percy is but my factor, good my lord,
> To engross up glorious deeds on my behalf.
> And I will call him to so strict account
> That he shall render every glory up.

In Shakespeare's play, Hal fulfills his promise, defeating Percy in single combat; historically, Holinshed's *Chronicles* simply lists Hotspur among the slain at the Battle of Shrewsbury, with no indication of who killed him or how.

Although one cannot say why Shakespeare did what he did, the Hal-Hotspur rivalry makes the inclusion of the Falstaff scenes both dramatically and thematically appropriate. We see Hotspur all seriousness, so completely intent on being the lordly soldier that he has no time for his wife, who is obviously very much in love with him. In contrast, we see Prince Hal abandoning his princely duties to play pranks with and on Falstaff, frequenting taverns, and apparently acting very much the juvenile delinquent. We shall see in a later section that the scenes with Falstaff serve several purposes, but thematically they permit Shakespeare to contrast the comparatively simple Hotspur, obsessed with ideas of knightly valor, and the greatly more complex Prince Hal, so completely in control of himself that even in dissipation he commits no gross or harmful acts, and so psychologically complex that he is able to use even his dissipation as a part of his preparation for his destiny as one of England's most popular monarchs.

To summarize, history as Shakespeare found it did not provide completely adequate materials for excellent drama; the historical focus was on the comparatively uninteresting Henry IV and the conflict was of forces and groups rather than of individuals. In altering history to make the play a more dramatically satisfying experience, Shakespeare also deepened it thematically. The changes permitted Shakespeare to create, in Sidney's phrase, a second nature, a world in which history is ethically meaningful. Prince Hal and Hotspur in reality may not have been intense personal rivals and most probably were not, but by making them so, Shakespeare was able to give his audience a better understanding of the making of a great and popular king.

The Entertainment Bulge

We have seen that Greek tragedy was an outgrowth of religious ritual and therefore highly formal. Although the Elizabethan drama, like the Greek, grew out of religious ritual, the aura of awe and devotion so obvious in Sophocles' kind of drama would have been entirely unsuitable for Shakespeare's stage. Sophocles' audience, as it looked up from the stage for a moment, saw a statue of Dionysus and a priest in his ceremonial robes. Shakespeare's audience had come looking for entertainment; they saw no statues of Christ or the saints, no priest in his vestments. If we may believe contemporary accounts, many of the audience had probably stopped on their way to the theater to watch the gory spectacle of dogs tearing at a bull or a bear; within the theater prostitutes solicited an evening's work and pickpockets the price of their evening meals. The kind of drama that satisfied Sophocles' audience certainly would not satisfy Shakespeare's.

Part of the formality of Sophocles' drama results from the tightness of the construction. In Sophoclean drama all of the emphasis is upon a single, unilinear action, with comparatively little extraneous material. Except for some details of exposition, some repetition, the choral odes, and some necessary pacing within the scenes, most of the material in *Oedipus Rex* is necessary for the action. In even the most serious of Shakespeare's plays, a retelling of the simple story would force the omission of some of the most interesting material in the play.

A number of reasons account for this change in the content of serious drama; perhaps the two most important are the changed conception of man's role as agent in the moral universe and the change in the audience. The first calls for the careful creation of character and inquiry into motivation, since both Christianity and Renaissance humanism stressed man as the creator of his own destiny more than did pre-Socratic Greek thought. Put simply, for Sophocles the action was more important than the man, and since "action" and "story" are loosely convertible terms here, the emphasis in a Sophoclean tragedy is on story. But for Shakespeare, the man was at least as important as the action; hence Shakespeare must slow the telling of his story to include comparatively full descriptions of character and analyses of motivation. To illustrate briefly, one has only to remember that Sophocles gives little space to showing Oedipus in the process of making decisions; most of the space is given to Oedipus proclaiming or enacting decisions already made. The typical Shakespearean hero spends as much or more time making his decision and justifying it as he does acting upon it. Specifically, *Oedipus Rex* begins with Oedipus having made a decision to relieve Thebes of the plague; it takes Hamlet several scenes to be in a position to make a similar decision, and still longer to act on it.

Another way of making the same point is to note that because of changed theater traditions, Shakespeare had available a greater variety of materials with which to satisfy the literary determinant of rhythm. The mere fact that drama, as narrative, requires action, coupled with the fact that Shakespeare's audience was more interested than Sophocles' in character, in itself provides the opportunity for a kind of elementary rhythmic complexity. If we can describe as "bulges" those parts of the narrative where a cluster of elements seems to be distinct from the main line of the story, or seems overdeveloped in its relation to the main line of the story, many of the most interesting bulges occur because Shakespeare needs to entertain his audience. In play after play, he includes a number of sure-fire bits that will guarantee the attention of his entertainment-seeking audience. A sure-fire bit is the kind of scene which in real life a crowd is likely to stop and watch. A noisy drunk, a bit of clever conversation, or a brawl will automatically draw the attention of most persons. All such situations have a kind of intrinsic interest, and even the best authors are not above using such obvious material to hold the interest of the audience. Although much criticism stresses the formal properties of art—the necessity of tight integration of incidents, the organic growth of one scene from another—authors themselves understand that formal beauty is meaningless unless it interests. Even the most serious writer—whether he is trying to show the perfection of his medium or trying to deliver a message that he believes will save the world—realizes that all is for naught unless he captures and holds the attention of those who buy theater tickets and books.

But in a satisfactory narrative, these entertainment bulges are frequently much more than that. A narrative, by definition, is not a series of skits, a collection of sure-fire scenes. It is, rather, more like a network of strands—the story, the theme, the characterization, the imagery, the tone—which must all be woven together. One of the surest indications that a work of art is inferior is the recognition that its author can do only one thing at a time, that in order to entertain us he has to distort his symbolism, for example.

Perhaps the clearest way to talk of this is in terms of "economy." Most theories of art tell us that good art is economical—that it does what it does in the most efficient, brief, way possible. And, of course, this is by and large true; the catch is in the phrase "what it does." If we define what it does too narrowly, say only in terms of action, then even a tightly constructed drama like *Oedipus Rex* has uneconomical moments. The splendid scene between Oedipus and Tieresias, for example, is much longer than it needs to be in terms of the story; if brevity in telling were the only consideration, it would go like this:

> OEDIPUS: Tieresias, tell me what you know of the killing of Laios.
> TIERESIAS: I know everything, but will say nothing.
> OEDIPUS: Then you are a traitor and a wicked old man.
> TIERESIAS: All right. You killed Laios and, furthermore, he was your father and Jocasta is your mother.

These few lines advance the story as much as do the one hundred sixty or so in the original play. But, of course, my rewriting is not economical, it is cheap; it does not take up much time or space, but neither does it do much. Sophocles' scene is economical in the best sense of that word; it advances the narrative, adds an insight into the character of Oedipus, develops the sight imagery, poses an interesting moral question (should Tieresias speak, even though he knows it will ruin Oedipus?), enables Oedipus to make a distinction between the gods and the prophets (an important thematic distinction), and—just as important as any of the preceding —provides the kind of thrill audiences of plays and courtroom scenes seem to relish.

The placing of scenes which are written primarily to be entertaining is naturally extremely important, and there are no general rules. In fact, successful drama can exist without such scenes, but it then needs some substitute appeal. In general, however, such bits occur in one of the following kinds of situations: (1) when it is necessary to get the attention of the audience, especially at the opening of a play before there is anything else to build attention on; (2) as a relief from a long stretch of quiet or intensely serious material; (3) when it is necessary to mark time between the major sequences of the drama.

Such sure-fire bits may, of course, come anywhere in a drama;

and it should be remembered that we are not saying that all dramas must begin with some lively action to catch the attention of the audience. We are saying, rather, that many successful plays do in fact begin this way, and that to understand why Shakespeare spends five minutes or so staging a fight he could have reported in two lines is to understand a part of the continued appeal of his work.

Henry IV, Part I, and the Entertainment Bulge

If we assume that Shakespeare's only purpose in *Henry IV, Part I,* was a retelling of the events that led to the Battle of Shrewsbury and a psychological study of the contrasting characters of Prince Hal and Hotspur, much of what happens in the comic scenes with Falstaff seems grossly uneconomical. In the first two acts, for example, approximately only one-third of the time is given to advancing the main action; the remaining two-thirds is spent developing a practical joke that Hal plays on Falstaff. In terms of the main action of the play, the practical joke is entirely inconsequential. Even in the most dramatic moments of the later scenes Shakespeare permits the comic Falstaff to interrupt the action.

Such "bulges" can, of course, be generally accounted for by Shakespeare's need to entertain his audience and by the need for dramatic pacing. General reasons, however, explain nothing until they are applied to specific instances. What we have to explain is why these particular bulges, with their particular content, appear where they do in the drama. It is not, it must be remembered, a matter of showing why Shakespeare wrote *Henry IV, Part I,* as he did, but rather a matter of showing that the drama is effective because it is as it is. Shakespeare could probably have found other solutions to the same problems; but these are the ones he chose, and they work.

The first scene of the play is chiefly historical exposition in which the viewer learns that Hotspur has won the admiration of Henry IV by his gallantry in putting down a rebellion under Douglas, and the concern of Henry IV by his refusal to surrender the prisoners to the crown. The other main strand in the drama, the Hal-Hotspur rivalry, also begins here, with the king's comparison of the two young men to the disadvantage of his own son. From this first scene, Shakespeare could logically follow with a development of either strand—Hotspur's incipient rebellion or Hal's dissipation. He chose the latter, and dramatically the choice has two beneficial effects.

In the first place, the opening scene is dramatically dull; a modern theater critic would perhaps describe it as talky and static. There is no confrontation of strong personalities, such as we see between Lear and Cordelia, no midnight ghost to whet our interest as in *Hamlet,* nor any of the exciting physical movement that opens *Othello.* As a result, Shakespeare needs some sure-fire entertainment quickly, the kind of entertainment that Falstaff, his cronies, and the Prince can provide in a scene complete with puns, bawdry, and the planning of a practical joke.

Equally important, Shakespeare throws attention to Hal before letting Hotspur on stage. Since the logic of this particular play requires that Hal and Hotspur be contrasted, and that initially Hotspur be shown as admirable, it is dramatically expedient for Shakespeare to introduce Hal first, thereby giving the audience a scene in which the King's estimate of Prince Hal can be partly confirmed and partly rejected, and, more importantly, in which the audience can grow to like the Prince despite his dissipation. To put this in more general terms, if we are told that A and B are opposites and we meet and learn to respect A before we meet B, we are likely to be prejudiced against B. It would have been unwise for Shakespeare to have taken that unnecessary risk.

Act I ends with Hotspur, proudly having met the King, refusing his demands, and deciding on open rebellion. With Hotspur's prayer at the end of Act I, "Oh, let the hours be short/Till fields and blows and groans applaud our sport!" it would seem that the drama is ready to settle down to its main concern, the dramatization of the rebellion and the contrast of character between the Prince and Hotspur. Yet Act II is largely given over to comedy. Of the four scenes in that act, three are largely concerned with the practical joke in which Hal, disguised, robs Falstaff after Falstaff has robbed a group of travelers.

Shakespeare's problem in Act II is one he faced in a number of other plays. One of the characteristic patterns for Shakespearean drama places the main parts of the action in the first, third, and fifth acts. In this pattern, the first act usually gives the exposition; it quite often ends with the protagonist or the antagonist having announced his course of action, at least in general terms, to the audience. The pattern requires, however, that the turning point in the drama not come until Act III, during which an irrevocable decision is made or a fateful act committed—e.g., Othello's heeding Iago or Hamlet's killing of Polonius (thereby missing his chance to kill the King and getting himself exiled), or Hal vowing to his father that he will reform. Act V inevitably includes the resolution of the action. The tendency of such a pattern is to crowd most of the material relevant to the central action of the drama into those three acts, leaving Acts II and IV comparatively devoid of highlights. To put this more briefly, if Act I ends with the announcement of a plan, Act III shows the turning point of the plan, and Act V the resolution, those parts of the play have a guaranteed interest; in Acts II and IV, on the other hand, Shakespeare usually has to reach beyond the primary concerns of the play to interest his audience. The practical joking, the puns, and busy footwork on stage as two robberies are committed, Prince Hal in disguise, the hilarity and human interest of the scene in which Hal confronts Falstaff with a charge of cowardice—all of this is ideal filler, fulfilling the same kind of purpose as the drunk scene, the punning, and the riddles in Act II of *Othello,* for example. They keep the events of the play from rushing together awkwardly while at the same time they keep the audience highly amused. To put this in the terms used in discussing *The Rape of the Lock,* such scenes are one way of satisfying the rhythmic determinant.

Nevertheless, the mark of a literary master like Shakespeare is that while he does one thing, he can do much else. If we look at the entertainment bulges in the first two acts in a slightly different way, we can see that the materials out of which the comedy is made function on several other levels. For example, for thematic reasons Shakespeare had to create a Prince Hal who was in keeping not only with the myth of the profligate prince, but also a likely candidate to become one of England's best kings. As a result, in the comic scenes we see Hal both a part *of* his surroundings and apart *from* them. Perhaps the quickest way to summarize Shakespeare's solution to the problem is to say that the Prince is always in control and always a buffer; he is always there to prevent his dissolute companions from doing any real harm. The main point of Hal's involvement in the practical joke on Falstaff is not that it gives the audience a chance to laugh, but rather that it gives the audience a chance to see Hal in control of a very complicated situation involving highway robbery. Hal's triumph is complete: he turns the robbery into a joke on the robbers, and sees to it that the victims of the robbery suffer no more than temporary inconvenience. As critics since Samuel Johnson have frequently noted, at no time in the play does the Prince commit a vicious act; he may associate with thieves, lechers, and cowards, but at no time is he dishonest, lecherous, or cowardly.

The comic scenes in which the joke is developed, furthermore, contrast brilliantly with a short scene very near the end of the play. The joke, it will be remembered, involves Hal's approval of and participation in a plan to encourage Falstaff to brag of his heroism, then to prove him a coward and a liar. Despite its dramatic purposes, the joke is both immature and pointless. In the later scene, Falstaff once more claims a heroism not his own—he claims that he, not the Prince, killed Hotspur; Hal replies:

> Come, bring your luggage nobly on your back.
> For my part, if a lie may do thee grace
> I'll gild it with the happiest terms I have.
>
> (V, iv, 160–63)

The extent of Hal's change can be measured by the importance he had attached to personally defeating Hotspur. In the climatic Scene ii of Act III he had vowed to redeem himself to his father and to his country by calling Hotspur "to so strict account/That he shall render every glory up" (149–50). Despite the fact that the Prince's reputation seems to rest upon his personally killing

Hotspur, he is willing to let Falstaff take the credit. The similarities and differences between the scenes containing the entertainment bulges and the final battle scenes permit the audience to understand the precise issues involved as Prince Hal abandons his role of profligate and assumes his role as a noble and courageous prince.

Equally as important, the materials out of which Shakespeare builds the entertainment of the practical joke are the central thematic concerns of the play as a whole. One of the questions *Henry IV, Part I,* considers is the nature of those qualities appropriate to manhood. The practical joke shows one way in which a person may be deficient in manliness by showing the cowardice of Falstaff. Cowardice, however, is merely one extreme; Shakespeare creates Hotspur as an embodiment of the other extreme, the extreme of blindly impetuous courage. Similarly, both Falstaff and Hotspur are concerned with their reputations. Much of the comedy that results from the practical joke comes in Falstaff's defense of himself in which Falstaff first claims that he acted heroically and later that he was aware of the joke all along. Hotspur is intensely jealous of his reputation as a soldier. Falstaff attempts to build his reputation on cunning without heroism; Hotspur attempts to build his on heroism without cunning. Prince Hal, however, combines both. After the Prince and Poins have planned the joke, Hal considers his friends and says:

> I know you all, and will a while uphold
> The unyoked humor of your idleness.
> Yet herein will I imitate the sun,
> Who doth permit the base contagious clouds
> To smother up his beauty from the world,
> That, when he please again to be himself,
> Being wanted, he may be more wondered at
> By breaking through the foul and ugly mists
> Of vapors that did seem to strangle him.
> If all the year were playing holidays,
> To sport would be as tedious as to work.
> But when they seldom come, they wished-for come,

And nothing pleaseth but rare accidents.
So, when this loose behavior I throw off
And pay the debt I never promised,
By how much better than my word I am,
By so much shall I falsify men's hopes.
And like bright metal on a sullen ground,
My reformation, glittering o'er my fault,
Shall show more goodly and attract more eyes
Than that which hath no foil to set it off.
I'll so offend, to make offense a skill,
Redeeming time, when men think least I will.

(I, ii, 218–40)

The cunning here is worthy of Falstaff and impossible for Hotspur; but unlike Falstaff, Prince Hal has the courage, the virtue, to enforce his reputation.

It would be possible to consider other comic scenes in *Henry IV, Part I,* in much the same way. The entertainment bulges that may have been necessary to satisfy a rowdy audience are in Shakespeare's best work always more than entertainment. They frequently parallel the more serious scenes, and almost always take as their materials the thematic stuff from which the intellectual value of the drama derives.

Literary Parallelism

We saw in the preceding essay that one of the functions of the comic scenes involving the robbery was to serve as a parallel for a later, much more serious scene, and that the contrast between Prince Hal's reactions in each showed how much he had matured. The technique of suggesting thematic values by creating parallel structures designed to be compared and contrasted is one of the most pervasive of all literary techniques. In the discussion of *The Rape of the Lock* we saw the immense range of implication Pope could achieve through such small parallel units as individual words. Placing the Bible upon Belinda's dressing table along with the powders, puffs, and *billet doux* suggested much about Belinda's world and about Pope's attitude toward it. In Lawrence Durrell's *Alexandria Quartet* the parallel units are at the other extreme of size; they are three full-length novels, each covering roughly the same events (with some necessary changes) from a different point of view. Within these two extremes, units of parallelism come in all sizes—clauses, sentences, paragraphs, chapters, situations, scenes.

Parallelism is an especially useful literary device for several reasons. Most generally, it permits maximum complexity with maximum brevity, and, by asking the reader to compare and contrast the parallel items while controlling the terms of the comparison, it leads the reader to an awareness of meaning instead of stating the meaning for him. In *The Rape of the Lock,* to review for just a moment, Pope creates parallel scenes showing both Belinda and the Baron preparing to go out into the world; Pope heightens the comparison by describing both preparations in religious terms: Belinda performs the "sacred Rites of Pride" and the Baron performs a sacrifice of his tokens of conquest. The effect is to ask the reader to hold both scenes in mind simultaneously and to remember, among much else, that the Baron sacrifices to love, but Belinda worships pride. Belinda's preparation, furthermore, is described in terms of what she takes from nature and society to increase her loveliness; the Baron's preparation is described in terms of what he sacrifices. With both scenes in mind, the reader is supposed to be especially attentive to their differences and to realize that the Baron is somewhat more mature than Belinda. He is ready to grow up; she is not. Because of the parallelism, Pope does not have to state the difference overtly, and because it is not stated overtly, it is more effective.

Parallelism in narrative applies to characters as well as to scenes, and again one of its major purposes is to suggest some of the considerations necessary for the realization of the theme of the work. To return to an earlier example again, Oedipus and Tieresias are both blind; Oedipus falls because he is blind to his own nature, and in his fall becomes physically blinded. By means of the parallel between the King and the seer, Sophocles suggests that inward sight, self-knowledge, is greatly more important for man than knowledge of the external world. Even if, as in some works, the theme is stated overtly, such parallelism helps to "prove" it in the peculiar way that literature proves its themes.

In a sense, the concept of the character of the foil as a literary functionary is a special case of parallelism. The reason that a foil can function as he does is that he has certain similarities with and differences from the more important character. One of the most moving scenes in *Othello,* for example, derives much of its effect from the contrast between Desdemona, whom the audience knows is about to be murdered because her husband wrongly suspects her of infidelity, and her servant, Emilia. Throughout much of the preceding two acts, the audience has been listening to Iago convince Othello that Desdemona is indeed guilty of adultery; because Iago's argument has to be persuasive enough to convince Othello, there is some risk that the audience also might doubt Desdemona's virtue. Yet the whole impact of her death scene will depend upon the audience's awareness that she is innocent. Consequently, just before Desdemona is murdered, Shakespeare places a scene in which Desdemona and Emilia discuss infidelity. Desdemona asks Emilia if she would commit adultery if in return she were given the whole world; Emilia decides that the price is right. Desdemona is shocked, and states that she would commit adultery for no reason. By permitting his audience to compare the attitudes of the two women to the same problem, Shakespeare reminds the audience of Desdemona's absolute purity and thereby greatly increases the tragic effect of the drama.

Literary parallelism is also an effective unifying device, for obvious reasons. The basis of the thematic and emotional effects of parallelism is comparison, and comparison is based upon similarities of scene, situation, character, and so on. By creating parallel elements the author can give his readers the feeling that, despite the complexity of his work, it is indeed all about the same topic. In general, the thematically relevant similarities within the parallel elements reflect a major concern of the work; the dissimilarities reflect the qualifications of the theme, the precise way that the author makes his general idea more precise. We saw, for example, in the "Ode on a Grecian Urn" how Keats creates parallel sets of questions in the first and fourth stanzas, a technique that effectively tied the first and last sections of that Ode together. Yet despite the similarity of the questions Keats asked in the two stanzas, and hence the center of interest in that part of the Ode, the differences in tone are striking—from complete confidence in the urn's ability to answer the questions to a mournful realization that the questions were unanswerable. It is the differences in the parallel elements in this case that complicate and enrich Keats's theme. The parallel situations leading to completely different responses described in the first and fifth stanzas of the Ode work in precisely the same way. Parallel structures permit the author to achieve the greatest unity of impression with the greatest complexity of theme.

Parallelism in *Henry IV, Part I*

Although the most striking parallels in *Henry IV, Part I,* are those between Prince Hal and Hotspur, they are merely the most obvious in a play that abounds in the multiplication of parallel characters and parallel situations. Because Hal and Hotspur will be discussed at length in a later section, I shall concentrate here on the significant parallels among the lesser characters, using Falstaff as a focal point.

We saw when we considered the early comic scenes revolving around Falstaff that the elements which make up the humor are part of the thematic fabric of the play. Falstaff is concerned with precisely those things that Hal and Hotspur are concerned with— courage, honor, reputation. The difference is that he is a clown, perhaps functionally a literal descendant of the court jester who as a wise fool was permitted to challenge the values of those higher than himself, provided he also amused. From Falstaff's lying and boastful account of his role in the robbery through his boasting to have killed Hotspur, the clown parallels the Prince and his noble rival in their mutual ambition for a reputation for honor. As a clown, Falstaff can show two things about reputation that could not be shown in the characters of Hal or Hotspur. Although a nobleman, a man of good birth and blood, Falstaff has lost his reputation; he is known in the court of Henry IV as a wastrel, a fool, a lecher—a totally unfit companion for a young prince. Despite his friendship with Hal, he is obviously most at home not with his peers but with the commoners at the inn. A part of the pathos of Falstaff's character is that his reputation is so far gone that it cannot be redeemed—not by Falstaff's bursts of gargantuan good humor nor by the friendship of a future king. The humor of the practical joke on Falstaff, despite the innocence of Hal's intention, is an extremely bitter humor, for it attacks Falstaff where he is most vulnerable by playing upon his reputation for lack of courage. Without courage, the episode seems to say, man is but a sorry clown.

But with courage, what is man? As a clown Falstaff can also express the other side of the truth. At the Battle of Shrewsbury, looking at the bloody body of Sir Walter Blunt, a nobleman who has just given his life for Henry IV, Falstaff says:

> Soft! Who are you? Sir Walter Blunt.
> There's honor for you! Here's no vanity!
> (V, iii, 32–33)

In the next scene Shakespeare will draw the contrast even more clearly. Douglas, who had killed Blunt, will fight with Falstaff, who will sham death. But unlike the honorable Blunt, the cowardly Falstaff will live to fight another day.

In one of the most brilliant and obvious parallels in the play, Shakespeare has Falstaff, shortly after this scene, rob Prince Hal of the honor of killing Hotspur; and he has Prince Hal, who has set such high store on honor, and staked his honor upon slaying Hotspur, permit Falstaff to take the credit. Shakespeare could have hardly provided a more effective way of telling the audience that Hal has reached a point beyond reputation; his confidence in himself, his knowledge of his own power, is such that he does not need to take Hotspur's honors, as he once threatened to do. Hal's development is further enhanced by the contrast with Falstaff;

Falstaff is exactly as he was in the opening scenes, still attempting to claim honors he has not won.

Much more subtly, however, Falstaff contrasts with both Glendower and Worcester. Just as Glendower and Worcester are the two friends and advisers of Hotspur, Falstaff is a friend and confidant of Prince Hal. Superficially, the relationship between Glendower, Worcester, and Hotspur, on the one hand, and Falstaff and Prince Hal on the other, would seem to be one of contrast. The Prince's companions seem common and dissolute; although Glendower and Worcester will rebel against the crown, they nevertheless seem to have the soldierly virtues. Both apparently are men of greatly more character than is Falstaff. But the "apparently" is important. If we contrast Glendower and Worcester with Falstaff in terms of their actual worth as advisers and friends, none will come off well, but Falstaff will rate considerably higher than either of the others.

Shakespeare (intentionally or unintentionally, for that is irrelevant) underlines the comparison between Glendower and Falstaff by assigning them both essentially the same function in the same part of the play. Glendower is needed in Hotspur's rebellion to provide more troops; Falstaff is used for much the same purpose, albeit on a lower level—he is to recruit men for the army of Henry IV. Like Falstaff, Glendower is a braggart; in the first scene of Act III, he boasts that

> at my nativity
> The front of heaven was full of fiery shapes,
> Of burning cressets; and at my birth
> The frame and huge foundation of the earth
> Shaked like a coward.

> (III, i, 13–17)

Like Hal teasing Falstaff, Hotspur chides Glendower with his boasting; Glendower somewhat later replies with the justifiable boast that he has several times defeated the army of Henry IV. Hotspur naturally assumes that he has in Glendower both a powerful and a trustworthy ally. Falstaff, of course, raises only an army of rabble; Glendower will not be able to get his forces together in time for the battle.

Both Falstaff and Glendower, then, are essentially failures in their tasks of raising support for their leaders. There are, however, two essential differences between the failures of Falstaff and Glendower. Falstaff fails deliberately; he sees the recruiting fee as an opportunity for profit, and he takes his profit. Glendower, despite his boasting of both his military abilities and his supernatural powers, fails for reasons that are not clear. More important, however, neither Henry IV nor Prince Hal depends on Falstaff; no matter how reprehensible Falstaff's actions are, his failure to recruit proper troops causes no real harm. Glendower's failure, coupled with Northumberland's inability to support Hotspur, gives the King's forces overwhelming superiority.

The parallel between Falstaff and Worcester is somewhat different. Falstaff is a liar, a chronic braggart who will stretch and break the truth without provocation. Falstaff's lies, however, are comparatively innocent; they either harm no one (like his lie about the number of persons it took to rob him) or else they are unpremeditated (like the spur of the moment decision to claim Hotspur as his own victim). Worcester's lies, however, are vicious. In the second scene of Act IV, Worcester, Hotspur's ambassador to the King, deliberately lies to Hotspur. King Henry has offered Hotspur liberal surrender terms, so liberal and honorable that Worcester fears that Hotspur will accept them. Belieing his trust as ambassador, Worcester conceals the terms and tells Hotspur tersely, "The King will bid you battle presently" (V, ii, 31).

If audiences for nearly four hundred years have admired Falstaff despite his obvious vices, they have done so not merely because he is a clown; Shakespeare is perfectly capable of creating clowns who have nothing but their humor to recommend them. It is because, despite his buffoonery, Falstaff is very much a normal human being. He is certainly not—like Hal, or Hotspur, or Douglas, or Blunt—the stuff of which heroes are made. But neither is he—like Worcester, Vernon, and Glendower—the stuff of which villains are made. His antics are never of much consequence. No army is defeated because he fails to recruit properly, no men die because he lies. His bragging and his cowardice—unlike the cowardice of Worcester, which prompts his lie—harm no one except himself.

Parallels within a work function in part to refine the theme. The parallels between Falstaff, on the one hand, and Blunt, Worcester, and Glendower on the other qualify the notion of honor presented in *Henry IV, Part I*. Falstaff, commenting on the death of Blunt and later shamming his own death, forcefully reminds the audience of the tremendous cost of honor. Like the chorus, grateful that it escaped the greatness of Oedipus and thereby the suffering of the hero, Falstaff is the ironic voice reminding us of the high stakes that heroes play for. In comparison with Glendower and Worcester, Falstaff is an embodiment of the proof that bragging and lying are not limited to clowns; the viciousness is not in the boast or the lie, but rather in betraying a trust in boasting and lying. Honor and honesty, Falstaff shows, are not the same thing.

Theme and Emotion

In earlier sections we noted in passing that theme emerges from a work not so much on the basis of what is done, but on the basis of the audience's reaction to who is doing it and to whom it is done. Sometimes the emotions are manipulated quite simply, as in "Jesse James," one of the most popular of native American ballads. The ballad praises a thief and a murderer; but somehow Jesse caught the imagination of the people, stories grew around him, and eventually he became a hero. How do you transform a killer into a hero? In the words of another popular song, you "accentuate the positive"—that is, you remind the audience of all the reasons it might possibly have for admiring the dastard. "Jesse James" begins this way:

> Jesse James was a lad who killed many a man;
> He robbed the Glendale train.

> He robbed from the rich and gave to the poor,
> He'd a hand, and a heart, and a brain.
>   CHORUS: Now, poor Jesse had a wife,
> Who mourn'd for his life,
> The children they were brave;
> But the dirty little coward
> They call Mr. Howard
> Has laid poor Jesse in his grave.

There is no attempt in this ballad to deny Jesse's guilt, but there is every attempt to make the audience *feel* that he was not guilty. The first line sets up a kind of David and Goliath situation—Jesse is a lad, a boy, who fights fully grown men, and our sympathies are usually automatically with an underdog. (If one doubts the effectiveness of this trick, let him rearrange the lines: "Jesse James was man/Who killed many a lad"—the change throws all our sympathies against Jesse.) If he robbed, he robbed the railway, a large, impersonal organization which the kind of people the ballad was intended for usually feels deserves robbing. And, of course, Jesse was no common thief; he was a modern Robin Hood. What did Jesse leave behind? Realistically, he left behind a large number of relieved stockholders in banks and railroads, passengers who could now travel more securely, the widows and children of the men he killed, and innumerable lawmen who could breathe a bit more easily. Billy Glashade, who wrote the ballad, knew all of this as well as we do, and his audience knew it. But Billy Glashade's problem was to make the audience mourn for Jesse, so he reminds us only of the poor, mourning wife and of the brave little tikes he left behind. As we hear every time we sing the chorus, which may be a dozen or so times in some versions of the ballad, Jesse's killer is "the dirty little coward." Billy Glashade has done a masterful if rather primitive job of making us minimize all of Jesse's faults and maximize all of his virtues.

Even such a great and classic tragedy as *Oedipus Rex* uses the same techniques to point our emotions in the proper direction. If it is necessary to feel that Thebes has recovered from the plague that threatened it, we must also feel that Oedipus has left the city

in good hands; we must, in other words, approve of Kreon. I
the confrontation with Oedipus early in the play, Kreon is show
to be reasonable, unambitious, considerate of the welfare of th
people, and dignified enough to be king. As a result, our emotior
are properly prepared to be relieved when Kreon assumes contr
of Thebes.

To put this more generally, a work of art may be considere
as a mechanism for adjusting our attitudes toward the variou
qualities the characters represent, the actions they perform, an
so on. Authors know that we are most likely to approve of action
performed by characters we like and to disapprove of those pe
formed by characters we dislike. Conversely, we will probably lik
characters who do good things and dislike those who do ba
things. Simply liking or disliking, obviously, oversimplifies the whol
matter. In a complex work we may be expected to have mixe
feelings about the characters. Nevertheless, by analyzing the emc
tional clues the author gives us, we can often learn more precisel
what he intends us to accept and to reject, and better enjoy th
artistry with which he has achieved his dramatic and themati
effects.

Theme and Emotion in *Henry IV, Part I*

Instead of considering the parallels between Falstaff and sever
other characters in *Henry IV, Part I, we* could have come to th
same kind of thematic conclusions about the notion of honor b
focusing upon the things that Shakespeare did to guide his audi
ence's feelings about Falstaff and by observing their effec
Audiences are willing to tolerate blunter statements about hono
from Falstaff than they would accept from other characters, an
also to feel their justice, because Shakespeare has worked carefull
to make Falstaff a likable character. Because the techniques ar
obvious, I will mention them only briefly. Perhaps most basically
Falstaff entertains us with his humor long and well, and audience
tend to give at least some approval to characters who consistentl

amuse them. Equally as important, however, is that we constantly see Falstaff accused of what others, supposedly his betters, are doing—boasting and scheming to save their lives—without equal disapprobation, and so we accept him as a lovable underdog. Moreover, Falstaff is the close friend of the most attractive person in the play, Prince Hal, and thereby wins a kind of approval by association.

I have deliberately not included Falstaff's personal qualities, except his humor, among the reasons audiences like him because that is precisely the point at issue. If Falstaff were the only liar and coward in the play, if he were disliked by Hal, the probabilities are that audiences would see his vices as vicious; but because we like him, we are willing to make allowances, and those allowances qualify the theme.

The emotions Shakespeare builds in relation to Prince Hal and Hotspur are, however, more directly relevant to the main thematic concerns of the play. *Henry IV, Part I,* is certainly about honor and reputation, but more specifically, it is about the honor of a Prince who is to become one of England's most glorious monarchs. Thematically, the play succeeds to the extent that the audience approves of the future Henry V, for he is the chief positive embodiment of the values that the play is about. Shakespeare had to work within the framework of the myth that depicted Prince Hal as a profligate young man who suddenly burst into maturity. Shakespeare's problem was to create for Prince Hal a dramatically plausible line of development from wastrel to hero. Earlier, we saw how Shakespeare toned down the Prince's juvenile delinquency by never showing him involved in any serious vices and, in fact, righting the wrongs committed by his companions. We have already commented on the development shown by Hal in the parallel scenes in which Falstaff boasts of a heroism not his.

Perhaps, however, the single most important stroke in Shakespeare's control of the audience's feelings about Prince Hal is the transformation of the historical Hotspur some twenty-three years older than the Prince into the Prince's youthful rival. At the beginning of the play Hotspur's fortunes and reputation are at

their highest, Hal's at their lowest—so much that King Henr
IV wishes:

> Yea, there thou makest me sad and makest me sin
> In envy that my Lord Northumberland
> Should be the father to so blest a son—
> A son who is the theme of honor's tongue, . . .
> Whilst I, by looking on the praise of him,
> See riot and dishonor stain the brow
> Of my young Harry. Oh, that it could be proved
> That some night-tripping fairy had exchanged
> In cradle clothes our children where they lay,
> And called mine Percy, his Plantagenet!
>
> (I, i, 78–89)

For a king to prefer a rebellious young noble to his son is indee
a strong indication of the contrast between the two young men.

The following scenes in which Prince Hal appears with Falsta
and his disreputable companions confirm one part of the King
charge and deny another; Hal may live in riot but he does n
live in dishonor. Hal's youthful impetuousity does not harm th
state; Hotspur's simple-minded notion of courage does. Perhap
however, the concept that best defines the contrast between th
two men is "control," both the ability to control self and th
ability to control others. In this sense, even the material concern
ing the practical joke on Falstaff is thematically functional becaus
it shows Prince Hal tricking the trickster—that is, complete
controlling the situation.

Hotspur's first speech is a masterpiece in the subtle way it d
rects the audience's feelings about Hotspur, and, indirectly, abo
Prince Hal. Shakespeare's problem at this point is to create
Hotspur who is a worthy rival for Hal; if Hal is to wrest the hono
from Hotspur, Hotspur must be a man of real merit. On the oth
hand, Shakespeare must also from the very beginning sugge
Hotspur's limitations, and suggest them despite the high prais
given him by King Henry. As Shakespeare builds Act I, Scen

iii, Hotspur is very obviously in a subordinate position. The King has gathered the potential rebels and made his accusation. The first to answer is not Hotspur, but Worcester, whom the King angrily sends away. The King then asks Northumberland, Hotspur's father, to speak, as if to imply that Hotspur is not the man in control of the situation. When Hotspur does speak, he so disingenuously excuses his rebelliousness as justifiable bad temper that Blunt, the King's adviser, accepts his excuse. Nevertheless, the King continues to demand the prisoners that Hotspur has been withholding, and when the King leaves, Hotspur's inability to control either himself or others is shown emphatically. Hotspur vows to keep the prisoners at all costs; Worcester attempts five times to tell him of the plot to gather arms against Henry IV, but Hotspur is obsessed and will listen to no one. His loss of control at this point is so extreme that Worcester says, "I'll talk to you/ When you are better tempered to attend" (234–35), and his father upbraids him:

> Why, what a wasp-stung and impatient fool
> Art thou to break into this woman's mood,
> Tying thine ear to no tongue but thine own!
> (236–38)

Northumberland's words are very much to the point, for in the Renaissance world-view the metaphor of the King as head of the state was accepted seriously, and the charge against women was that they were all emotion; they lacked the head, the rational control, to rule effectively. Probably, moreover, we are to contrast this scene to the previous scene, in which Poins suggested the practical joke to Prince Hal. The Prince, unlike Hotspur, is able to accept advice. Although the advice Hal listens to is trivial and the advice Hotspur pettishly puts off hearing is traitorous, we shall see later it is Hotspur's inability to control himself sufficiently to listen to his counsellors that leads him into a battle he has no chance of winning, and his inability to control Worcester finally permits the battle to be fought.

It is also important in setting the reactions of the audience to the two young men that shortly before we meet Hotspur and see both his merits and his failings, Shakespeare gives Prince Hal a soliloquy in which he announces that he is deliberately playing the delinquent so that, he says:

> My reformation, glittering o'er my fault,
> Shall show more goodly and attract more eyes
> Than that which hath no foil to set it off.
> I'll so offend, to make offense a skill,
> Redeeming time when men think least I will.
>
> (I, ii, 236–40)

The effect of this soliloquy is to remind the audience at a crucial point in the play—just after they have seen Hal playing the fool and before they meet Hotspur—that the Prince is doing so intentionally so that later he can be a more effective leader of men. Shakespeare cannot run the risk of leaving the audience with the impression that Hal is merely a profligate, lest Hotspur, despite his rashness, appear too admirable by comparison. What we discover in the soliloquy is that Prince Hal is not only in full control of his companions, he is also in full control of himself. Although both Shakespeare and his Elizabethan audience would have resented the application of the term to Prince Hal, there is something Machiavellian in Hal's deliberately setting out to use people to create the image of himself that will ultimately be most advantageous.

After the initial exposition in Act I, in which the audience sees both sides of Prince Hal and of Hotspur, the logic of *Henry IV, Part I,* requires that the audience come to admire the Prince more fully as a complete man, and come to see that Hotspur is much less than a complete man. The continuation of the practical joke in Act II permits Shakespeare to do what Hal announced he would do in his soliloquy—to show the world his delinquency so that his reformation will come as a surprise. Hotspur's scene (Scene iii) is one of great delicacy; Shakespeare must continue to show

Hotspur's limitations, but he cannot show them too rapidly lest Hal's rival appear unworthy. The solution is a charming scene between Hotspur and his wife that begins with Hotspur (significantly, in prose rather than blank verse) showing that he is the most courageous and ready for battle of all the conspirators. Lady Percy complains that he has been neglecting his husbandly duties:

> For what offense have I this fortnight been
> A banished woman from my Harry's bed? . . .
> [I have] heard thee murmur tales of iron wars,
> Speak terms of manage to thy bounding steed,
> Cry "Courage! To the field!" And thou hast talked
> Of sallies and retires, of trenches, tents,
> Of palisadoes, frontiers, parapets,
> Of basilisks, of canon, culverin,
> Of prisoners' ransom, and of soldiers slain,
> And all the currents of a heady fight.
> Thy spirit within thee hath been so at war
> And thus hath so bestirred thee in thy sleep
> That beads of sweat have stood upon thy brow. . .
> (41–61)

Hotspur is so completely the soldier, so little the man and husband, that he apparently cannot even hear his wife's charming plea, just as earlier he could not permit Worcester to interrupt.

Within this section, Shakespeare very pointedly uses the Platonic metaphor of the rider and the horse to make the audience aware of Hotspur's limitations. The classic Greek metaphor compares man to a horse and rider; underneath, providing the motive power, are the immensely strong passions. The passions, like a wild horse, are dangerous until controlled by reason, until the rider takes charge. When Hotspur, just after his wife's plea, tells his servant "That roan shall be my throne" (73), he means only that with a good horse he can fight his way to the kingship; Shakespeare, however, probably means that Hotspur is mistakenly trying to ride his passions to the throne—again, a pointed comparison with the completely self-controlled Hal who uses his emotions and the emotions of others to further his own ends. To make sure that the audience does not miss the Platonic implications of the metaphor, Shakespeare carries it further:

> LADY PERCY: What is it carries you away?
> HOTSPUR: Why, my horse, my love, my horse.
> LADY PERCY: Out, you mad-headed ape!
>   A weasel hath not such a deal of spleen
>   As you are tossed with.
>
> (78–82)

Despite the fact that Lady Percy's tone here is probably bantering rather than angry, in accusing Hotspur of being a mad-headed ape and of having more spleen (irascibility) than a weasel, she is saying in effect that he is completely unable to control his emotions. The scene ends with Hotspur refusing to tell his wife his plans because he underestimates her wisdom; in short, he does not understand his wife.

The next scene is Prince Hal's, and it underscores the contrast in several ways, two of which are most effective. Early in Scene iv, Prince Hal parodies Hotspur in a perfectly conceived exaggeration of the scene just played between Hotspur and his wife. The exaggeration shows Hal's complete understanding of both the strengths and weaknesses of Hotspur's character. Perhaps more importantly, however, toward the end of Scene iv, Shakespeare creates a section in which Falstaff assumes the role of Henry IV, and Hal, for a moment, plays himself; then Hal and Falstaff reverse roles, with Hal speaking for his father, Falstaff for Hal. The result is some fine comedy, but it is also a chance for Prince Hal to show his complete understanding of his situation. Hal says, assuming the character of his father:

> Swearest thou, ungracious boy? Henceforth ne'er look on me.
> Thou art violently carried away from grace. There is a devil

haunts thee in the likeness of an old fat man, a tun of man is thy companion. Why dost thou converse with that trunk of humors, that bolting hutch of beastliness, that swollen parcel of dropsies, that huge bombard of sack, that stuffed cloak bag of guts, that roasted Manningtree ox with the pudding in his belly, that reverend vice, that gray iniquity, that farther ruffian, that vanity in years? Wherein is he good, but to taste sack and drink it? Wherein neat and cleanly, but to carve a capon and eat it? Wherein cunning, but in craft? Wherein crafty, but in villainy? Wherein villainous, but in all things? Wherein worthy, but in nothing?

(490–505)

The contrast between Hal and Hotspur is obvious, and it works all to the Prince's advantage. Prince Hal is able to see things clearly and objectively from his father's point of view; Hotspur, even when told clearly by his wife, is utterly incapable of seeing anything from any point of view but his own. Although in the opening two acts Shakespeare has kept Hal involved only in trivialities and Hotspur only in matters of great importance, he has managed to show the Prince as the man with the more admirable qualities—the qualities of control and objectivity that are absolute requisites for a future king.

Perhaps no single element in the play works to shape our attitudes toward Henry and Hotspur with such dramatic subtlety as the contrast between the close of Act II and the opening of Act III. Our last look of Prince Hal in Act II shows him carefully preparing to right the wrong his practical joke has caused and protecting the rascally Falstaff. It is an act of gratuitous mercy worthy of a future king. Act III opens with Hotspur having forgotten the map on which the battle will be planned (Glendower remembered it). By line eighteen of the scene, Hotspur gratuitously insults Glendower to the point where Mortimer tries to interrupt lest Hotspur's bad temper divide the rebels. Hotspur's insults to Glendower continue through half of a rather long scene; when Glendower leaves, Mortimer rebukes Hotspur and gives him good counsel:

> In faith, my lord, you are too willful-blame; . . .
> You must needs learn, lord, to amend this fault.
> Though sometimes it show greatness, courage, blood—
> Yet oftentimes it doth present harsh rage,
> Defect of manners, want of government,
> Pride, haughtiness, opinion, and disdain;
> The least of which haunting a nobleman
> Loseth men's hearts, and leaves behind a stain
> Upon the beauty of all parts besides,
> Beguiling them of commendation.
>
>   (177–89)

Mortimer's analysis of Hotspur is correct, but even when told his faults, Hotspur is unable to change. In the remainder of the scene he unnecessarily insults Glendower's wife about her singing. The contrast between Hotspur and Hal is now all but complete. Hotspur has been shown as courageous but self-centered and unself-controlled, totally oblivious to the thoughts and feelings of others. The Prince, despite his seeming dissipation, has been shown as generous, self-controlled, and totally sensitive to the thoughts and feelings of others.

It is, perhaps, largely because of this careful preparation that audiences, even audiences not familiar with the legend of Henry V, are willing to accept at face value Prince Hal's promise to his father to reform and to acknowledge that Hal's claim of superiority over Hotspur is justified. Hal's speech is the climax of the play; his character is now changed, and the turning point in the drama has been reached. Hal must now rise as Hotspur falls.

Hotspur's fall begins immediately in Act IV, Scene i, with the news first that his father, Northumberland, is ill and cannot add his forces to Hotspur's, and second with the news that Glendower, despite his promises, cannot get to the battle in time. When we next see Hotspur in Scene iii, his chief military advisers, Worcester, Douglas, and Vernon are all urging him to delay the battle; Worcester's troops are tired and Hotspur's forces are badly outnumbered and awaiting reinforcements. Hotspur refuses to listen to the good advice.

Despite Hotspur's arrogance and his apparent dominance of his fellow rebels, his complete lack of control of others in important matters is shown in Act V, Scene ii. Worcester and Vernon, whom Hotspur had sent as ambassadors to King Henry IV, effectively wrest control from Hotspur by concealing the generosity of Henry's peace terms. What has been implicit before becomes apparent here; Hotspur has been put a pawn in Worcester's game.

Although Hotspur dies a courageous death in single combat with Prince Hal, Shakespeare builds the battle scene so that all of the audience's sympathies lie with the Prince. Embellishing greatly upon Holinshed's account of the battle, Shakespeare presents a Prince Hal so wounded that the King wants to send him to the rear; despite his wounds, Prince Hal fights on—even, before killing Hotspur, driving off Douglas from an attack on the King. When the Prince and Hotspur finally meet, the Prince's speech is courteous and generous:

> HOTSPUR: My name is Harry Percy.
> PRINCE: Why, then I see
> A very valiant rebel of the name.
> I am the Prince of Wales. And think not, Percy,
> To share with me in glory any more.
> Two stars keep not their motion in one sphere,
> Nor can one England brook a double reign
> Of Harry Percy and the Prince of Wales.

Hotspur's reply is less courteous:

> Nor shall it, Harry, for the hour is come
> To end the one of us. And would to God
> Thy name in arms were now as great as mine!
>   (V, iv, 61–70)

Henry IV, Part I, ends with Prince Hal doing two generous deeds. One, giving Falstaff permission to claim victory over

Hotspur, has been commented upon earlier. Equally important, however, and parallel to the courtesy to Falstaff, is Prince Hal's courtesy to his brother, John of Lancaster, and to the rebel Douglas. He frees Douglas because of the noble way that Douglas fought in the battle, and gives his brother the "honorable bounty" of formally conferring Douglas's freedom. Hal's acts of generosity to both Falstaff and Lancaster are in effect recognitions that he no longer needs what he once so carefully planned for: he no longer needs the reputation for honor, or courage, or manliness; he no longer needs the reputation for these because he has proved himself.

If we review the structure of emotions that Shakespeare has created in *Henry IV, Part I,* what we find is a series of details carefully calculated to make the audience admire Prince Hal for certain qualities and to define those qualities by comparison with other characters, chiefly Hotspur. What emerges is a prince larger than history but suitable for legend; another way of putting this is to note that Shakespeare has created a "second nature," a universe in which the princely virtues are presented at their most attractive and effective. It is precisely this presentation of the ideal in terms that will win the admiration and emulation of readers that Sidney described as the purpose of literature.

Further Possibilities

Despite giving some attention to the history from which Shakespeare drew his material for *Henry IV, Part I,* we did not attempt to trace precisely what Shakespeare borrowed from either Holinshed or the earlier play, *The Famous Victories of Henry the Fifth.* A better insight into both the thematic and aesthetic intentions of Shakespeare could be shown by such a comparison. Why, for example, did Shakespeare move the reconciliation scene between Henry IV and Prince Hal to *Henry IV, Part I,* rather than keep it in *Part II* where, according to Holinshed, it historically belonged? How does the conception of the characters of Prince Hal and Falstaff differ in Shakespeare's play and in *The Famous Victories?*

A reader curious about history might take one of several other tacks. *Henry IV, Part I,* is part of a series of eight plays ranging from the period of the reign of King John (1199–1216) to the reign of Henry VIII (1509–42) written in various stages of Shakespeare's career. What do the history plays as a group show about Shakespeare's political philosophy? About his notion of kingship and royalty? About his conception of lordly honor? Is the conception static, or does it change from such relatively early plays as Richard III to the later *Henry V?* Or the reader might be less concerned about Shakespeare's conception of history than with intellectual sources upon which that conception of history was based. What qualities would a Renaissance Englishman admire in a leader? Would the qualities for a king be the same as for a lesser nobleman? To what extent did the popular conception of the rulers Shakespeare wrote of determine his portraits of them?

Or, still pursuing the historical interest but changing its focus somewhat, how did Shakespeare conceive of the rise and fall of the house of Lancaster, since six of the eight history plays deal with that subject? Is there implicit in the drama the theme that the original usurpation of Richard II's throne by Henry IV was a kind of original sin that blighted the reign of even so able a king as Henry V? A still different kind of question, in what way did the political situation of England in Shakespeare's time influence the emotional values he attached to his political characters? What parallels were there in the political situation of Elizabethan England with the content of the history plays?

Perhaps the most difficult of the historical topics is a study of the facts of Prince Hal's youth, apart from the specific sources Shakespeare used in an attempt to watch a myth in the making. The *Dictionary of National Biography* describes the real Prince Hal as a youth who at thirteen served in Wales as his father's deputy and who fought Glendower there, after which he successfully invaded Scotland, and then served officially in France. From 1409 to 1412, while his father was ill, he ably ruled England as regent. The real Prince Hal was apparently a serious young man with a high reputation as a soldier, statesman, and leader of men. It would be extremely interesting, but difficult, to attempt to analyze the development of the myth of the prodigal youth that became attached to Prince Hal and to consider Shakespeare's Hal, Falstaff, and Hotspur as characters in the myth of the great king. Such a study would involve wide reading in myth, in folklore, and in early accounts of the career of the Prince to discover how and why elements of the story of the profligate prince became attached to such an exceptional young man as Prince Hal.

Equally interesting, although entirely different in nature, is a consideration of the kinds of problems Shakespeare had to solve in turning a number of quite varied historical persons and situations into effective drama, with special attention to the techniques he used to solve those problems. A play centered on the rather pathetic Richard II and the austere Henry Bolingbroke poses dramatic problems far different from those encountered in a play centered on the rivalry between the colorful Prince Hal and the almost equally colorful Hotspur, and far different from those encountered in a play centered on the psychologically interesting Richard III. Involved in this question would be the question of Shakespeare's maturing technical abilities as a dramatist. What lessons did Shakespeare learn as he moved from one play to another?

The student interested in difficult thematic problems might pay close attention to the final battle scenes. Within the space of a few lines, Douglas saves his life by running away and Falstaff saves his by pretending to be dead. Yet Douglas keeps his reputation for courage, Falstaff his for cowardice. Does the parallel have thematic implications, perhaps suggesting a more ironic treatment of the theme of honor than we have acknowledged so far? Or is this merely a failure to solve the problem of reconciling the objective determinant (Holinshed tells how Douglas vainly sought Henry IV during the battle and of Douglas's survival) with the thematic (Prince Hal must be shown doing heroic things at the end of the play)? An answer to this question would involve a careful reconsideration of the relationship between honor and courage.

In our concern with the functions served by the comic scenes we have slighted an analysis of the comedy itself. On precisely what kinds of comedy does Shakespeare rely in the Falstaff scenes? What, in other words, is Shakespeare's comic range in this play?

V

Conrad's *Heart of Darkness*

Prose Fiction and Biography

Like any other literary form, prose fiction grows from the experiences of the writer, is transformed, and, if successful, enters into the experience of the reader. The extent of the transformation varies greatly from work to work. In *A Portrait of the Artist as a Young Man,* for example, scholars can identify the companions of Stephen Dedalus as associates of the young James Joyce; many of the incidents in the novel actually happened to Joyce, and Stephen's career seems to be blended from what Joyce remembered of his own youth and of his brother's. Faulkner's Yoknapatawpha novels use autobiographical materials somewhat less directly; without putting himself into the series as clearly as Joyce did, Faulkner still uses as his setting the area of Mississippi where he spent most of his life, as his characters the types he knew there, and as his thematic material his feelings about the land and its inhabitants. At a still further remove, Hawthorne based *The Scarlet Letter* not upon personal experience, but upon his research into America's Puritan past, in which his ancestors played an important part, about which he felt a curious mixture of pride and guilt. Or finally, the novel may result from nothing more specifically autobiographical than a lifetime of observing objectively one's contemporaries, as apparently Jane Austen did, and moulding those observations into a form whose only subjective note is the tone of the author's voice.

Obviously, then, a knowledge of the biography of the author will be especially relevant in studying some novels, less relevant in studying others. For example, even though *A Portrait* is usually considered to be an autobiographical novel and contains much that is autobiographical, a reader is likely to understand it better if he recognizes that despite the similarities between Joyce and his hero, there are some very important differences. Although the matter is complicated, in general when we compare what we know about Joyce's life, a fragment of a novel he wroted called *Stephen Hero,* and *A Portrait,* we find that in the process of transforming life into fiction, Joyce deliberately stressed certain things and eliminated or minimized others. Such a comparison enables the reader to see more clearly what Joyce intended in the finished novel. If we do not recognize the autobiographical details in the novel, we are likely to dismiss them—and so to miss an important dimension in it—and if we do not know precisely what is auto-biographical and what is not, we are likely to read the novel too autobiographically—and so to misinterpret completely the character of Stephen and the nature of Joyce's artistry.

Using biographical materials in the analysis of fiction is much more than a matter of noting that Joyce, say, grew up in Dublin at about the same time Stephen was supposed to have grown up there and that Cranly can be identified as J. F. Byrne. That kind of knowledge is only a start. To return to a very basic point, the reality of an author's life, like the reality of ours, is more richly complex than any work of fiction. Joyce's model for Cranly was a human being who ate, slept, drank, smelled and touched things, and felt the emotions that men usually feel; he was not merely the stiff inquisitor-confessor of Stephen that Joyce makes him out to be in the novel.

Another way of making the same point is to remark that even when fiction is most autobiographical, it is nevertheless the work of a man trying to make sense of his own experience. And like scientists, writers make sense of things by separating what is relevant in the total situation from what is irrelevant; if the real-life Cranly was ever in love, married, and became the doting father of a batch of Irish children, that is none of Joyce's concern as the writer of *A Portrait*. Joyce is interested in Cranly only in so far as he, in his character as an unofficial representative of the Catholic Church, forces Stephen consciously to consider certain questions about himself. Joyce seems to be saying that the artist develops as he does partly through the goading of a Cranly, of an adversary who makes choice necessary.

Quite often, the most important thing that a knowledge of the biography of a writer gives us is a clue to how he saw the world about him. To give a simple yet important example, many readers find Dostoevsky's *Crime and Punishment* unconvincing because it ends with the sudden religious conversion of a confessed ax-murderer. The totally uninformed and prejudiced are likely to see the ending as ironic, with Dostoevsky mocking religious values as earlier he had mocked anti-religious values—there is always the temptation to read as ironic what we cannot agree with. Or it might be argued that the ending, although not ironic, is not to be accepted at face value by maintaining that Dostoevsky had written himself into a box he could get out of in no other way. Yet Dostoevsky's biography reveals that he himself underwent a profound, sudden, and permanent religious conversion while a political prisoner in Siberia. Although the biographical information does not *prove* conclusively that Dostoevsky meant the ending of *Crime and Punishment* as a serious reflection of his personal thought, it ought at least warn the reader that he probably did take such conversations seriously.

What we have said about the understanding of biographical information in fiction is merely an elaboration of one of the most basic rules of criticism—the more the critic knows about everything relevant to his subject, the better the critic he will be. One cannot say in advance that an understanding of the author's life will be indispensable in interpreting a novel correctly, but the complete critic will assure himself that he knows at least enough of the biography to know how relevant or irrelevant it is.

One word of warning. The critic cannot assume that because something happened in the life of the writer or because the writer had a particular attitude, that event or attitude will appear in his work. And equally as important, we cannot assume that what appears in the fiction—no matter how autobiographical the work seems—in fact happened to the author.

Conrad and the *Heart of Darkness*

Conrad's *Heart of Darkness,* despite its brevity, is a complex and difficult work; it raises basic questions on every level of man's existence from the most personal through the broadly social and metaphysical. Moreover, it presents the questions as experiences, in terms of ambiguous actions and metaphors, shadowy symbols, and paradoxes. Marlow, who seems the embodiment of and answer to the questions Conrad raises, is a series of contradictions. As he tells the story of the *Heart of Darkness,* he sits in the lotus position, like a Buddhist saint, yet one of the most insistent messages of his gospel is efficiency; he understands that only civilization permits Western man to survive in a hostile world, yet his wisdom has been reached while cut off from civilization; he is a dreamer with an instinct for the practical, a man who hates lies but who does lie. The paradoxes embodied within Marlow can be reconciled within the context of the *Heart of Darkness,* and one preliminary step for doing so is making certain that we understand the value Conrad placed on the materials he used. Because the *Heart of Darkness* is in many respects an autobiographical novel based in part upon Conrad's own employment in the Congo, where he acted in much the same capacity as Marlow, his record of his feelings about the Congo and his experiences there helps the reader sense what Conrad learned in Africa that he wants, through Marlow, to express.

For Conrad and Marlow both, the journey up the Congo river begins in childhood, with a nine-year-old boy putting his finger on that part of a map of Africa which indicated unexplored territory and announcing, "When I grow up I will go there." In his *Last Essays,* Conrad writes that as a boy he saw Africa as "regions unknown" and explorers as "adventurous and devoted men, nibbling at the edges, attacking from north and south and east and west, conquering a bit of truth here and a bit of truth there, and sometimes swallowed up by the mystery their hearts were so persistently set on unveiling." There is a curious double romanticism in the passage, a combination of the usual boyish enthusiasm for adventurous men and deeds and a rather more mature realization that what the explorer must ultimately conquer is not land but truth, coupled with the realization that at times the mystery destroys the explorer.

Much of *Heart of Darkness* grows directly from this double romanticism, for both Conrad and Marlow learn two important lessons from their African journey: they learn to distrust the boyish romanticism and to accept the need for facing the dangerous mystery. Conrad's letters during the early part of 1890, when he was making arrangements to work as a riverboat captain for the Belgian Society for Commerce on the Upper Congo, show a deep desire to go to Africa. Only some remnants of this boyish ambition could account both for the persistent conniving he did to get to Africa and for the sudden and profound disillusionment he felt upon his arrival. Like Marlow, Conrad "set the women to work" to find the right job; an experienced ocean sailor with mate's papers, Conrad had no difficulty in finding work, and indeed even turned down one voyage because of the prospect of an African trip. Only unexplored Africa could satisfy Conrad.

Disillusionment set in almost immediately; by 15 May 1890, while still on route toward Africa, he writes his aunt that man must resign himself to "a little illusion, many dreams, a rare flash of happiness; then disillusion." By the 22nd of the month he arrives at Freetown, Sierra Leone, where he becomes impatient with the secrecy of the company he works for and discovers that only 7 per cent of the workers in Africa can serve out their three years. As a boy, he had romantically imagined African explorers ailing gracefully, comforted by charitable native women, or majestically riding up to a native village and overawing the tribesmen; he knows now that as an African adventurer his lot is less likely to be native women and overawed tribesmen than fever and dysentery—both particularly unromantic discomforts.

Many of the incidents that appear grotesque in *Heart of Darkness* have their source in Conrad's diaries. The first diary begins on 23 June 1890, and although Conrad mentions some individuals favorably, he intends to avoid his associates "as much as possible." By the next day he describes the "prominent characteristic of the social life here" as "people speaking ill of each other." The courageous explorers that the young Conrad had imagined nibbling a bit of truth here and there turn out to be petty gossips not unlike those Marlow describes. His employers, like Marlow's, are small and inefficient bureaucrats: all of the riverboats are out of commission; the manager, Camille Delcommune, has "sordid instincts" and will not honor the verbal agreements made between Conrad and the company. In a letter to his aunt dated 26 September 1890, he finds "everything is repellent to me here. Men and things, but especially men. And I am repellent to them."

Nature and the natives treat Conrad as badly as they treat Marlow. The weather is bad—not romantically bad, as it was in the travel books young Conrad loved, but drearily bad, and the illnesses include four bouts of fever and a five-day attack of dysentery. Not only are the natives unawed, they fight, his carriers argue with him, and one of them even drops him into a mud puddle. The intrepid explorer writes that he is "getting jolly well sick of all this fun."

In addition to his unpleasant companions, the unruly natives, and the weather and disease, the jungle also had its horrors for Conrad. During the trek up-river the diary entries for July mention coming across three corpses and a grave. The first corpse has apparently been shot and there is a horrid smell; the second is "lying by the path in an attitude of meditative repose"; the third is a "skeleton tied up to a post." None of this was a part of the young Conrad's dream when he romanticized African exploration. Yet out of facing what Marlow calls "the abomination" grows a more mature Conrad. Conrad once told his friend Edward Garnett that before his trip to the Congo he was a "perfect animal," by which he meant a man who lived totally unaware of the privilege and the pain of being human.

If one looks at both Conrad's and Marlow's descriptions of their experiences in the Congo, he finds that the common factor is, for want of a better word, "aloneness." Conrad's boat has hardly left France before he feels isolated from Europe. He learns that he, and perhaps all men, are alone with a nature that is at best indifferent and at worst hostile. No animal understands this, and once Conrad does, he has become not "a perfect animal," but a man, a writer capable of creating the enigmatically wise Marlow.

Point of View in Fiction

Although Marlow is a product of Conrad's Congo experiences, Marlow is not Conrad but merely a voice and a character Conrad created to tell *Heart of Darkness* and other stories. In creating Marlow, Conrad chose one of many solutions to the problem of what the relationship should be between the writer and his narrative.

No narrative, not even a non-fiction autobiography, can fully reflect its author. An autobiographer, even if he is determined to tell the truth, cannot tell everything that happened in his life, nor can he tell it in completely neutral terms. He will select both the events and the language, and if he is writing honestly and intelligently, he will select them according to some conception of himself and of his purpose in writing. Consequently, even non-fiction autobiography has as its subject an "I" who is not quite the same person as the author.

The same principle applies in fiction. In a novel like *Vanity Fair,* for example, with a relatively large number of authorial intrusions —that is, parts where the writer seems to express his personal opinion of the action, the morality involved, or whatever—it can be shown that Thackeray the narrator is not Thackeray the man; the narrator in *Vanity Fair* makes statements about the nature of fiction that contradict flatly what Thackeray the man said and wrote. For whatever reason, Thackeray felt the "authorial" intrusions beneficial in *Vanity Fair,* but he also realized that for the purposes of his novel, the intrusions would have to contain statements that he could not subscribe to. Perhaps the most general way of understanding the point is to realize that whenever a writer writes, he has to filter his own personality and views through the requirements of what he is writing; the result is always a narrator who is not the author.

There are numerous ways of classifying narrators, but the most basic is between the *omniscient narrator* and the *limited narrator*. To make the point as clearly as possible, I shall tell the story of "Goldilocks and the Three Bears" from three different points of view.

[A] Once upon a time a girl named Goldilocks went walking in the woods and came to a large house, which she entered. She tried the three bowls of porridge which had been left on the table and found the first too hot, the second too cold, and the third just right—so she ate it all up. Sleepy, she went upstairs to the bedrooms and tried the three beds; the first was too hard, the second too soft, and the third was just right. While she was sleeping, the three bears, who lived in the house and who had gone for a walk in the woods while their porridge cooled, returned. The angry Father bear said, "Who has been eating my porridge?" The gentle Mother bear said, "Who has been eating my porridge?" And the hungry Baby bear said, "Who has been eating my porridge and ate it all up?" After searching downstairs they went up to the bedrooms, where they found Goldilocks sleeping. She awoke in a fright, ran out of the house, and never again entered someone's home without being invited.

This version of the story uses an omniscient narrator; it tells things about Goldilocks that the bears cannot know, and things about the bears that Goldilocks cannot know.

Here is a different version, told by a limited narrator:

[B] Once upon a time there was a girl named Goldilocks who went walking in the woods and came to a large house, which she entered. She tried the three bowls of porridge which had been left on the table and, not liking the first because it was too hot or the second because it was too cold, ate up all

the third, which was just to her taste. Sleepy, she went upstairs
to the bedrooms and tried the three beds. The first was too
hard, the second too soft, and the third just right, so she went
to sleep in it. Opening her eyes slowly, she saw three bears,
one very large and one just plain large, and one very small. The
biggest bear said, "Now I know who tasted my porridge and
tried my bed." The next biggest bear said, "Now I know who
tasted my porridge and tried my bed." And the smallest bear
said, "Now I know who ate up all my porridge and messed up
my bed." Goldilocks, frightened, ran all the way home and
vowed never again to enter a stranger's house without an
invitation.

In this version of the story, nothing is told that could not be told
by Goldilocks. We could do other versions of the story, still using
the limited narrator but limiting the details to what any one of the
three bears would have experienced. Or, the story could be told
in the first person from the point of view of Goldilocks or of any
of the three bears; or the writer could invent a narrator for the
story and introduce him in a frame, in which case it would begin
something like this:

[C] Once when I was traveling through the north woods, I
heard the strange story of Goldilocks. She must have been a
young girl, as you shall see from what she did.

Each way of telling the story has certain advantages and disadvantages. Version A is certainly the most complete in some respects because the omniscient author knows all and can tell all.
Yet suppose the writer were less interested in telling all of the
details than in showing the emotions of the frightened little girl.
He might then well decide to sacrifice the report of what the bears
said when Goldilocks was asleep in favor of concentrating exclusively on what Goldilocks felt. Or suppose that the writer were
interested in showing the differences between two generations and
chose as his case studies Papa bear and Sonny bear; the narrator
might then possibly be the mother, who would in her telling of the

story begin with the bears' walk into the woods rather than with Goldilocks's, limit herself to what the bears discovered when they returned home, and play up the similarities and differences in Papa and Sonny bears' reactions to Goldilocks.

We have, of course, only touched on the most obvious uses of narrators. Authors have been as ingenious in creating different kinds of narrators as they have been in creating different kinds of fiction. Samuel Richardson, for example, pretended that he was merely the editor of *Pamela,* so that in *Pamela* we occasionally have Richardson's editorial voice speaking, along with the voices of the characters who write the letters which comprise *Pamela.* Faulkner has experimented with the technique of using different limited narrators for specific portions of his novels, so that *The Sound and the Fury,* for example, has a separate narrator for each of its four sections. Henry James, Conrad, Ford Madox Ford, and Lawrence Durrell have created narrators who learn during the progress of the work, so that the narrator's perceptions and judgments at the end of the novel are conditioned and usually sharpened by what he has learned in his part in the events. The "New Wave" French novelists have experimented with a narrator who seems little more than a combination tape-recorder and camera, on the theory that the precise and apparently objective registration of physical sensation will give the reader the greatest sense of reality.

It must also be understood that narrators are not always trustworthy. A narrator is just as much a fictional character as anyone else in the novel and may be just as mistaken in his interpretations and descriptions. Perhaps the classical example of the untrustworthy narrator is Gulliver, whose perceptions are sometimes accurate and sometimes totally at variance with the facts. A major part of the theme of a fiction may depend upon the reader's ability to recognize that the narrator's reactions are inappropriate to the situation.

For the beginning student, there is little point in classifying all the kinds of narrators that occur in fiction. The essential thing is to realize that any given story could be told from several points of view, and that the point of view an author chooses will depend almost entirely upon the fictional tradition in which he works and the thematic, artistic, and psychological effects he wants to achieve. The two crucial questions in studying the function of the narrator are: who is telling the story? (or a version of the same question, who is telling which parts of the story?), and why does the author choose the particular narrator he does?

The Narrators of *Heart of Darkness*

Conrad begins *Heart of Darkness* with an unusually elaborate frame in which he carefully introduces the reader to two separate narrators. The first narrator (he has no name) is a rather nondescript character who at first sight seems to exist only to listen to Marlow tell his yarn to the men aboard the *Nellie* and then to pass it on to the reader. The chief narrator is Marlow; it is his story that makes up the bulk of the work as he tells of his experiences in the Congo. Since the story is Marlow's and since the experience we follow is Marlow's, why did Conrad think it expedient to place a narrator between us and his hero? Or, to ask the question more precisely since we cannot know for certain why Conrad chose his method of telling the *Heart of Darkness,* what is accomplished by creating the first narrator?

The technique of the frame for a narrative, and in particular a frame in which the narrator tells a story he once heard, is almost as old as fiction itself. During the period when Hollywood was gushing out B movies, for example, one of the cliché openings was a scene in a fashionable London club, with plush leather chairs and a group of dignified gentlemen sipping sherry and whispering about an especially meditative looking man sitting by himself. One of the group would say, in a hushed voice, "Yes, I knew Adam Stapleton when he was like the rest of us, before the accident in Transylvania. It's a rather strange story, and—well, let's see if you believe it. It started five years ago, on a continental tour." Then a flashback shows our meditative gentleman looking a bit younger and much less thoughtful, and the story begins. Such a beginning, whether it is the cliché opening of a bad movie or the start of a masterpiece like *Heart of Darkness,* tends to do at least two separate things: it aids in what Coleridge called the "suspension of disbelief," and, paradoxically, it creates a sense of mystery and suspense. It does the first by presenting the story as something that even the staid members of a London club might accept and the second by suggesting that there is something extraordinary in the past of the hero that makes him unlike other men.

When a genuine artist—whether he be a Shakespeare or a Conrad—uses a cliché, he uses it with a difference; and the difference is that he usually gets much more from it than does the hack writer. Conrad uses the frame of *Heart of Darkness* to prepare a wonderfully precise introduction to Marlow, his main character. When the narrator describes Marlow in the third paragraph, the description comes after the lawyer and the accountant have been dismissed in a single sentence; Marlow is described in more detail, with "sunken cheeks, a yellow complexion, a straight back, an ascetic aspect, and with his arms dropped, the palms of hands outwards, [he] resembled an idol." If we are reading as alertly as we should be, we ought to wonder at least momentarily why Marlow is singled out for fuller description than the others. The narrator then continues with a romantic revery, rhapsodizing on the glories of exploration and adventure as his listeners look out at the gloom relieved only by London, "a lurid glare under the stars." Only then does Marlow interrupt, "suddenly," with the enigmatic comment, "And this also has been one of the dark places of the earth." Marlow has been standing physically apart from the others on the *Nellie;* his first remark puts him intellectually apart also—he knows something that other men do not know. Much of the import of the following paragraph, a description of Marlow, is that Marlow is an exceptional man, unlike the ordinary seaman who lets the experience of the world pass him by. Marlow then proceeds to counter the first narrator's naïve enthusiasm for exploration with a realistic description of what it must have been like, and his intensity tells us that he has not only experienced much, he has experienced deeply. As the first narrator looks at Marlow, he sees "the pose of a Buddha preaching in European clothes and without a lotus-flower." But the topic of the sermon is completely un-Buddhistic; its recommended virtue is the Western ideal of efficiency.

If we consider carefully what has happened within this frame, we see that the use of the first narrator has permitted Conrad to show Marlow objectively through the eyes of someone else; instead of being told that Marlow is an exceptional human being, we see that the attention of the first narrator is given almost exclusively to Marlow, and we see that in the spectacularly gloomy scene Conrad sets, Marlow is the only person present capable of a non-stereotyped reaction. But, of course, much more also happens. We see how functional the scenery is when we consider that it introduces the basic thematic motifs of light and darkness, civilization and the primitive, and ideals and reality.

Even more important and more subtly, though, the first narrator stands as a mediator between us and Marlow. The narrator's feelings about exploration are naïve, but they are also very much like both Conrad's and Marlow's before their experiences in the Congo. It is not difficult to imagine the first narrator dreaming heroically of exploring the unexplored, of imagining what Marlow called "a white patch for a boy to dream gloriously over." And probably the narrator's feelings about exploration and colonization are like those of most of us, unless we have by some chance seen the bloody business first-hand or read some of the accounts of how the white man butchered his burden.

Just as the African experience changes Marlow, hearing about it changes the first narrator. At the end of *Heart of Darkness,* his youthful optimism has gone. He sees not the river that poured civilization out into the world, but a "tranquil waterway leading to the uttermost ends of the earth . . . [it] seemed to lead into the heart of an immense darkness." At the start of the novel he had exclaimed, "What greatness had not floated on the ebb of that river into the mystery of an unknown earth!"

The first narrator is a part of a complex series of parallel relationships spread throughout the *Heart of Darkness.* As Kurtz is to Marlow, so Marlow is to the first narrator, and so the first narrator is to the reader. As if to make certain that we do not miss the relationships, Conrad makes it abundantly clear that

Marlow's central experience in the jungle is the meeting with Kurtz. Yet despite Kurtz's centrality, he is remembered by Marlow best as a "disembodied voice." The phrase is a striking one, and obviously applies no less to Marlow, sitting apart in the gloom, barely visible, present most certainly to the first narrator as a "disembodied voice." And the first narrator, undescribed, lacking any distinguishing physical characteristics, known only by his style as he retells Marlow's story, is to the reader a "disembodied voice." The implication is that the story told by the voice ought to change the reader, just as it changed Marlow and the narrator. Like the narrator, we have looked, vicariously at least, into the heart of darkness; one of the strongest themes that emerges from the narrative is that the wisdom of a Marlow can be attained only by looking into the darkness.

Conrad uses the frame of the *Heart of Darkness* not only as a means for creating credibility and a sense of anticipation, but also as an essential part of his thematic material.

Fiction and Close Reading

We have seen earlier how the technique of close reading may be applied to poetry and why it is most applicable to short poems. The method is seldom used with prose fiction for at least two good reasons. In the first place, most fiction is usually not meant to be read so carefully; authors know that most readers read prose much faster than they read poetry. Except in a few novels, the language of fiction is not meant to be brooded over, analyzed, and squeezed for every drop of meaning. We can forgive a novel if it is flatly written (Dreiser's *American Tragedy,* for example), provided it has enough else to hold our interest; it is difficult to forgive a flatly written short poem. Second, a close reading of a fourteen-line poem, if fully written out, might take as many as fourteen pages—which is actually a minimum estimate. If the proportion would hold, how long would a close reading of a novel be? Conrad's *Heart of Darkness* runs only about seventy-five pages in most editions; some novels run over twelve hundred pages.

Nevertheless, some novelists do attempt to write a prose that is at times as richly suggestive as the most complex poetry. Such a novel deserves our most careful attention; and, even though the task seems formidable to most students, a novel with a rich verbal texture will repay several readings. Literature, like a fine meal, is not to be gulped down; it is to be savored. The kind of intricate verbal patterns characteristic of rich prose can be perceived but vaguely on first reading. We may, for example, be aware that an image on page 70 that seems especially effective ties together much of what has happened previously, without knowing really what it does tie together; only in a second or third reading, after we have begun to have a firm grasp of the detailed development of the novel, can we appreciate adequately the way it has been put together.

Since a critique based on a close reading of a novel would be an almost impossible task, some method must be found for limiting it. The most profitable kind of limitation, of course, will depend upon the novel. The most often used ways of making a close reading of a novel manageable, however, are by limiting it to the comparison of several scenes, by tracing a single motif or motif cluster, by detailed analysis of a single scene, or by analysis of the details that build up a character, setting, or whatever. Since the technique is selective, the critic's main concern should be to select materials that are either artistically or thematically central to the novel.

The Frame of *Heart of Darkness*
Description as Foreshadowing

We have seen how the frame of *Heart of Darkness* establishes a narrator who will substitute for the reader as he vicariously lives through Marlow's experience. In addition, the introductory section of the frame announces the main motifs of the novel and the main thematic conflict. The conflict may be stated in a number of ways —light versus darkness, civilization versus savagery, the subconscious self versus the conscious self.

In the opening pages of *Heart of Darkness,* Conrad asks his readers to visualize a scene; its components are simple, but richly detailed, and all the details are carefully chosen to point the reader's expectations in a certain direction. At the center of the scene is the *Nellie,* a yawl anchored in a moment of calm and awaiting the turn of the tide. Toward the east, where the Thames empties into the English Channel, darkness has settled; toward the west is London, at the time Conrad wrote the greatest city on earth; the sky is not yet dark over London, but it is darkening and gloomy, and the lights of London make "a lurid glare under the stars."

On first reading, all of this descriptive detail is likely to seem little more than the setting of a mood, the kind of glimmer and gloom scene typical of any number of cheap mysteries. Yet, such is the precision with which Conrad works, many of the major symbols of the novel are introduced here with much the same tension they will have later in the narrative. Most noticeably, Conrad has emphasized the disproportion of light and darkness and described the darkness in heavily emotional terms: "The air was dark above Gravesend, and farther back still seemed condensed into a mournful gloom, brooding motionless over the biggest, and the greatest, town on earth." As if to emphasize the awesomeness of the gloom, Conrad describes the sea and sky as "welded" together. Conrad creates the illusion of a small patch of light representing the greatest town on earth—in other words, a high point of civilization—surrounded and threatened by the natural gloom. The beauty of the passage, and in very large part what makes it convincing symbolically, is that the description is visually realistic. Yet, reading through *Heart of Darkness* for the second time, a reader must surely sense that London on the Thames, enveloped in natural darkness, is an analogue to Kurtz and Marlow in the jungle. If London is the epitome of what civilization has done to the land, Kurtz is an epitome of what it has done to man. Kurtz represents, the reader is told, all the civilized races of Europe; he could have been a musician, writer, politician—in short, a successful member of any profession. Like London, he is surrounded by the darkness; unlike London, he has surrendered to it.

Yet the whole feel of the introduction makes the fate of London, and by implication of civilized man, doubtful. This is, the descriptions tell us in various ways, a time of change. The *Nellie,* like London, appears calm, but it must "come to and wait for the turn of the tide." The wind has died, and after the gloom will come the night. All of nature, Conrad suggests, conspires against the light of London, and this is a decisive time. The only lights, other than London's glare, come from a lighthouse, which Conrad describes deprecatingly as "a three-legged thing erect on a mud flat," and from the ships moving on the river.

Against this background, the first narrator meditates on the glory of former explorations that began on the Thames and reached around the world; since London has been associated with light, his description of the explorers as "bearers of a spark from the sacred fire" implies that civilization has radiated out from London. When Marlow reminds the passengers on the *Nellie* that "this also . . . has been one of the dark places of the earth" he is saying in effect that the darkness exists not only in space, but also in time. Once the Thames was a dark river, the people along it savages, and the world's greatest city elsewhere. The Romans exploring England, Marlow reminds his listeners, were not unlike the Elizabethan Englishmen who explored the New World or the contemporary explorers of Africa. With this historical perspective —which, it should be noted, is as realistic in its way as the description of the sunset—Marlow adds to the immensity of the darkness; where before it had overwhelmed London only in space, now the darkness and the primitive also overwhelm it in time.

By establishing the abiding sense that the darkness, the uncivilized, is present in all times and all places, Conrad prepares his reader psychologically for the experience shared by Marlow and Kurtz. Although the topic merits exploration in its own right, the experience, in its most essential form, is the recognition of the primitive, the darkness, within man. At various times Marlow admits it in himself; when he hears the beating of the native drums, his impulse is to join them, to "go ashore for a howl and a dance." What thrills Marlow about the savages

> was just the thought of their humanity—like yours—the
> thought of your remote kinship with this wild and passionate

uproar. Ugly. Yes, it was ugly enough; but if you were man enough you would admit to yourself that there was in you just the faintest trace of a response to the terrible frankness of that noise, a dim suspicion of there being a meaning in it which you—you so remote from the night of the first ages—could comprehend. And why not? The mind of man is capable of anything—because everything is in it, all the past as well as all the future. What was there after all? Joy, fear, sorrow, devotion, valour, rage—who can tell? but truth—truth stripped of its cloak of time.

The area of darkness has again been expanded; it exists not only in time and space, but also within the mind of man. Not only is man completely surrounded by an external nature that is hostile to him—or at best indifferent—there is a traitor within, an inheritance of the primitive which threatens to break through the safeguards of civilization. The difference between Marlow and Kurtz, to make this very brief, is that Marlow was able to keep the dark side of his mind under control and Kurtz was not.

As if to indicate the existence of the primitive in all men, Conrad presents each of the listeners aboard the *Nellie* (with the exception of the first narrator, who is not described) as having something in common with Kurtz. To begin with the most obvious instance, the Accountant is described as playing with dominoes, or, as Conrad puts it, "toying architecturally with the bones"; Kurtz, who has decorated the fence around his hut with skulls, literally toys "architecturally with the bones." The Lawyer, presumably a dignified old man, is lying down—Kurtz's favorite pose is lying down. And the director of companies, we are told, works "within the brooding gloom," that is, within the heart of darkness.

Because Conrad has chosen to describe these men in terms appropriate for Kurtz, but more importantly because of what happens later in the narrative, Marlow's claim that "none of us would feel exactly like this" is probably ironic. Later in *Heart of Darkness,* we learn that the modern explorers of the Congo are no more efficient than the Romans who explored the Thames. Like the Romans, the explorers of the Congo are, with only few exceptions, "conquerors," men with "only brute force—nothing to boast of, when you have it, since your strength is just an accident arising from the weakness of others."

Rather than merely setting the mood, the materials Conrad includes in the opening section of the frame—even such a small detail as the first narrator's comment after Marlow's first sentence, "No one took the trouble to grunt even," with the "grunt" reminding us of the animality within even the successful and civilized men aboard the *Nellie*—introduce the main symbols and conflicts of the narrative in a sufficiently realistic way that when we meet them in their more fantastic setting in the Congo, we can accept the values Conrad assigns to them. More specifically, one of the reasons that readers can accept Kurtz's disintegration in the jungle and believe in the real danger Marlow faces is because we have felt how precariously London, the world's greatest town, sits threatened by the gloom. And if the fall of Kurtz seems more than a mere horror story about one man going native, it is partly because we have been previously convinced that the darkness that surrounds Kurtz and is within Kurtz surrounds and is within all civilized men.

Characters and Thematic Values

One simple but acceptable definition states that narrative is essentially characters in conflict. A conflict inevitably means a choosing of sides, and one way of interpreting a narrative is to discover who (or what) is on each side and why. The conflict is usually of man against man, although in some works man's antagonist may be nature, institutions, even himself, or all of these.

In considering *Henry IV, Part I,* we examined a number of the technical devices Shakespeare used to make his audience admire the qualities embodied in Prince Hal and deplore those in Hotspur. In a serious narrative, each virtue and each vice will function not only to further the conflict or increase the suspense, but also to say something about man's condition in the kind of world the fiction depicts. Where the conflict in a narrative is chiefly between two or more characters, or groups of characters, the theme will be largely defined by the particular traits those characters possess. In the conflict between Prince Hal and Hotspur, for example, all of Hotspur's deficiencies are qualities which Hal possesses. To summarize briefly, Hotspur's only virtue is soldierly courage; he lacks sympathy for others, the ability to listen to advice, and control over his own emotions—all of which, and more, the Prince has. In the much lighter but no less serious *Rape of the Lock* also the individual virtues and vices of the characters revolve around the thematic center of the poem. The vicious characters are those who perpetuate a blurring of distinctions between the important and the trivial; the virtuous recognize those distinctions. The themes of *Henry IV, Part I* and of *The Rape of the Lock* emerge in part from the reader's recognition that he is asked to admire a certain set of virtues and to disapprove of a certain set of vices.

There are, however, complications, as a quick look at either work will show. Belinda, after all, is not condemned in quite the same way that Sir Plume is condemned, and Prince Hal changes from a profligate to a true nobleman. Such complications are the major reason that great literature is more meaningful than platitudes. Everyone knows that it is better to be sensible than to be empty-headed, and that to mistake the trivial for the important is folly; nevertheless, this bit of wisdom is the thematic basis for *The Rape of the Lock*. But it is merely a basis, merely a foundation on which Pope raises an elegant structure which includes very precise discriminations among degrees of vice and folly. Objectively, for example, Belinda may seem as foolish as either Sir Plume or Thalestris; yet, as we have seen, she is more admirable than her allies because her foolishness is tempered with beauty and youth. Nor are Sir Plume and Thalestris stupid in quite the same ways; Sir Plume seems a victim of natural stupidity, that of Thalestris seems acquired. Not only is the theme narrowed by the ways in which the characters are foolish, it is further narrowed by what they are foolish about. Belinda is upset about the loss of her lock; Thalestris is concerned about her own small conception of honor; and poor Sir Plume enters the fray because that is the empty-headed, officious thing to do. Pope's target in *The Rape of the*

Lock is not folly in general, but the certain kind of folly defined by the characters in conflict.

Just as in some works the reader can gain a more precise understanding of the theme by analyzing various characters, others may be understood better by analyzing the phases through which the protagonist passes. *Oedipus Rex* or *Henry IV, Part I,* for example, could well be reread with the specific purpose of charting the rise and fall of the hero in our estimation and of studying the particular traits that develop to cause that fall. We would see that as Oedipus continues his quest for the murderer of King Laios he becomes so obsessed with the search that he commits repeated indiscretions, ranging through anger, pride, blasphemy, and ending in the complete isolation of himself from the other characters in the drama. Oedipus rises again in the spectator's estimation when he purges himself of those vices in the final moments of the play.

The two methods of analyzing character for thematic values are, of course, not incompatible. A complete study of most works of any complexity would require both approaches. In some instances, it is even valuable to consider subsidiary characters as functions or aspects of the protagonist. Dostoevsky's *Brothers Karamazov* is perhaps the greatest of all works in which characters were deliberately created to reflect aspects of the protagonist. Quite briefly and incompletely, the protagonist of the *Brothers Karamazov* is Aloysha, the youngest of the Karamazov brothers. As Dostoevsky had originally planned what was to have been a trilogy, Aloysha would have begun as a naïvely good young man, then fallen under the influence of Ivan, the intellectual Karamazov, and Dmitri, the sensualist Karamazov, before becoming a maturely good man. Dmitri and Ivan represent aspects of Aloysha's character that he will have to overcome before he can find perfection. Even novels not consciously written with "fragmented" protagonists may sometimes be read profitably that way, since an author will often use secondary characters as foils for his major ones.

In most serious novels the main characters succeed or fail, are admirable or repugnant, happy or unhappy, in part because of the traits they embody. Except in a few works in which the author attempts to show that man's fate depends not upon himself but upon some such impersonal force as society or nature, an accurate reading of the work will depend upon the clarity with which the reader perceives the value systems which the characters embody.

The Gang of Virtue and the Hollow Men

Heart of Darkness is about the Congo experience that made Marlow the man he became, and the emotional center of that experience is his meeting with the remarkable Kurtz, the only man in the novel who has looked into the heart of darkness and "had something to say." Kurtz's final vision, "the horror, the horror," so impresses Marlow that his own sickness and near death seem less significant than Kurtz's final words, which Marlow describes as "an affirmation, a moral victory paid for by innumerable defeats, by abominable terrors, by abominable satisfactions. But it was a victory! That is why I have remained loyal to Kurtz to the last, and even beyond."

In effect, then, Marlow's experience is Kurtz's experience, but lived through by one with more restraint and self-knowledge than Kurtz possessed. Because of the violence of his life and of his final vision, Kurtz becomes a kind of touchstone with which the reader may assess other characters; first, however, it is necessary to determine what Kurtz's vision was and why it came specifically to him.

An understanding of Kurtz begins with a realization that the character of the man changed radically just before his death. If we reconstruct Kurtz's development from the details scattered throughout the *Heart of Darkness,* we find that he was a kind of epitome of western European civilization. All of Europe, we are told, contributed to his inheritance; he was a "universal genius" who could have become a successful journalist, painter, politician, musician, explorer-colonizer, missionary, or whatever he chose. His motives for going to the Congo, as far as he understands them, are the highest. His report to the International Society for the

Suppression of Savage Customs is, Marlow says, "magnificent. . . . It gave me the notion of an exotic Immensity ruled by an august Benevolence. . . . This was the unbounded power of eloquence— of words—of burning noble words." Then something dramatically sudden happens to Kurtz, for scrawled at the end of the report is the denial of all the nobility, the exclamation, "Exterminate all the brutes!"

We can only guess at what happened to Kurtz to cause him to set himself up as a deity whom the natives would fear and worship, but Conrad does give hints. Despite the magnificent eloquence of the report, Marlow finds it "difficult to remember" and remarks that "there were no practical hints to interrupt the magic current of phrases." Kurtz begins as an idealist whose plans for reform of the Congo have no practical basis. In its simplest terms, the final sentence of the report expresses Kurtz's frustrated rage upon find- ing that the practical world resists the ideal world—that he has to pay for his missionary zeal by supplying ivory, that he has to rely upon totally unreliable shipping, that he must live with the natives. The result is the transformation of Kurtz from one of the "gang of virtue" to one who has the fence surrounding his hut capped with human skulls. And Kurtz does become practical, at least on a short-term basis; although his enemies complain that his methods will ruin the ivory trade, he is recognized as the most effective of the traders. But put in terms Marlow or Conrad would use, the cause for Kurtz's degradation is at once simpler and more complex.

Running throughout the *Heart of Darkness* is a contrast between two notions, principle and efficiency; both are introduced by Marlow before the narrative proper begins. Briefly, efficiency saves, principles do not, but each is an attempt to avoid looking into the darkness. When Marlow dramatizes the dichotomy be- tween principles and efficiency in the description of the terrifying journey up-river, he tells his listeners of the call of the primitive and of feeling the "fascination of the abomination" that made the Roman explorer in the introduction go native. He recognizes in that "wild and passionate uproar" that you would, "if you were man enough . . . admit to yourself that there was in you just the faintest trace of a response to the terrible frankness of that noise, a faint suspicion of their being a meaning in it which you . . . could comprehend."

Kurtz came to the jungle armed only with principles, and one of the lessons that Marlow has learned is that "Principles won't do"; they are "rags that could fly off at the first good shake. No; you want a deliberate belief." Marlow does not say what that deliberate belief would be, but earlier he had said that what redeems the exploitation is "the idea only. An idea at the back of it; not a sentimental pretense but an idea; an unselfish belief in the idea— something you can set up, and bow down before, and offer a sacrifice to." The language suggests that Kurtz is that idea, at least for Marlow, for the idea is described as if it were a physical idol, something one bows to and sacrifices to, as the natives did to Kurtz and as Marlow does, though in a much diminished way. Because the belief must be deliberate, it must be accepted in full awareness—not blindly accepted because of principles or fine sentiments. This explains both Marlow's final admiration for Kurtz and our admiration for Marlow; both have looked at the horror, one directly and one indirectly. Kurtz's victory is his final shedding of his principles and his reaction against them, his acknowledgment of the horror of a man living in a universe in which all nature, even his own personal nature, is either indifferent or hostile to him. Marlow's victory is his recognition of this, and his triumph is his survival with that recognition. Man can be saved, these passages suggest, by abandoning the "sentimental pretence of an idea" for the "deliberate belief."

This does not, however, explain how Marlow survived. Telling the listeners aboard the *Nellie* why he did not "go ashore for a howl and a dance," he says, "I had no time. I had to mess about with white-lead and strips of woollen blanket helping to put bandages on those leaky steam-pipes. . . . I had to watch the steering, and circumvent those snags, and get the tin-pot along by hook or by crook. There was surface-truth enough in these things to save a wiser man." A "wiser man," I take it, would be a man who looked more profoundly into things than Marlow does; the implication is that there are two levels of truth—the level at the surface and the level at the heart of darkness—and that man simply cannot give attention to both at the same time. Marlow is saved from going native, from becoming another Kurtz, by his efficiency.

The minor characters in *Heart of Darkness* represent stages in the development either of Kurtz or of Marlow, or alternatives to them. All of the minor characters cannot be discussed in detail, but a look at several will show the way Conrad works and help to define his theme. Other than the first narrator, the character most like Marlow is the Russian. If Marlow can endure his experience in the Congo because of his devotion to the "surface-truth" of things, the same is no less true of the Russian. Despite the fact that he is dressed like a clown and is almost ludicrous in his dog-like fidelity to Kurtz, in his own way he is as efficient as Marlow. The first hint we get of the Russian is the title of the book he left behind, *An Inquiry into Some Points of Seamanship,* which Marlow describes as done with "an honest concern for the right way of going to work." The book, which the Russian obviously treasured, suggests that this harlequin figure has the same kind of interest in "surface-truth" that saves Marlow. The last glimpse we get of the Russian is his flight from Kurtz's territory, during which we learn that his escape had been carefully and successfully planned. In effect, Conrad has bracketed the portrayal of the Russian with clear indications of his efficiency, of his commitment to a workaday interest in surface reality.

Like Marlow, the Russian is also fascinated by Kurtz, but it is a different kind of fascination. Until the end, Marlow is never certain of his feeling for Kurtz; at most, Marlow's acceptance of Kurtz is critical. The Russian admits to recognizing only the side of Kurtz that spouts principles, that talks, as he phrases it, "of love." Sensing that the older and more experienced Marlow suspects a homosexual attachment, the Russian defends Kurtz, only to show his complete innocence and Kurtz's failure as a teacher. The Russian says, "It isn't what you think. . . . It was in general. He made me see things—things."

The emptiness of this—"He made me see things—things"—coupled with the ensuing description of the Russian's complete faith in Kurtz, suggests the Russian's blindness. A person who sees only "things—things," with the word repeated as if it were an explanation, has seen nothing; and a teacher who leads his disciple to see nothing has failed. Through the Russian, Conrad has presented a critique of the traits Marlow praises most frequently in the *Heart of Darkness*—efficiency and a willingness to "bow down before an idea," before a Kurtz. Although these may save a man, as they save the Russian, they alone do not guarantee that he will learn from his experience. Unlike Marlow, the Russian is unwilling to see Kurtz realistically for the horror that he is; his vision of Kurtz is more like the "sentimental pretense of an idea." For all his vitality, his likability, his charm, the Russian remains a very small man, preferable to those who hang around the inner and outer stations, but lacking the strength and the wisdom of those who are able to face the horror.

The Accountant at the outer station may be seen as a kind of halfway figure between Marlow and Kurtz. Marlow respects him because he manages to keep up surface appearances—his hair is brushed, his cuffs neat, his collars clean; he "had verily accomplished something. And he was devoted to his books, which were in apple-pie order." In a curious combination of images, Marlow compares him to a "hairdresser's dummy," then adds almost immediately, "That's backbone."

Yet the backbone is about to crack, and the hairdresser's dummy about to become another hollow man. As the Accountant is working at his books, with Marlow and a dying man in the room, the natives outside make a racket. The Accountant, who has just walked "gently" over to the dying man, says, " 'When one has got to make correct entries, one comes to hate those savages—hate them to the death.' He remained thoughtful for a moment. 'When you see Mr. Kurtz,' he went on . . .'" Conrad has created here a scene that parallels Kurtz's report by showing first the gentleness, the humanitarianism, of the Accountant, followed by an outburst as violent as Kurtz's "Exterminate all the brutes." As if to drive home the parallel, Conrad has the Accountant mention Kurtz immediately and then go on to tell Marlow, in effect, that he is on the side of Kurtz against those in the inner station. His attention to his dress and his appearance, his devotion to his books, are part of a fight against the fate that will overtake Kurtz, and it is a losing fight, as he shows by losing control of himself when the natives make noise. Symbolically, of course, in terms of the geography of the narrative, the Accountant is at the outer station; he has not progressed as far into the darkness as the others.

The two most remarkable characters at the inner station, the Manager and the Brickmaker, present alternatives to Kurtz. The Manager, almost certainly describing his own success, "was once heard to say, 'Men who come out here should have no entrails.'" He has survived because he is the completely hollow man; he originates nothing, he has no genius, and he is never ill. A completely hollow man can survive because there is nothing within him to rot. Curiously, just after Conrad makes much of the good health of the manager, we learn that Kurtz is ill—in other words, Kurtz is not hollow. Kurtz has within him the potentiality to rot, and thereby the potentiality for vision.

The Brickmaker is as hollow as the Manager; at one point Marlow calls him a "papier-mâché Mephistopheles" whom Marlow could poke through with his forefinger and "find nothing inside but a little loose dirt, maybe." But if he is a hollow Mephistopheles, he is nevertheless a real Mephistopheles. Conrad surrounds him with fire. He is a brickmaker whose eyes "glittered like mica disks" and who is the only one at the station who has "a whole candle all to himself." And to show that he is a demon in hell, Conrad reminds us throughout the episode in which he appears that the natives in the background are being punished. Just before the Brickmaker is introduced, "a nigger was being beaten near by." Shortly before we see him for the last time, Conrad sets an inferno-like scene: "Black figures strolled about listlessly, pouring water on the glow, whence proceeded a sound of hissing; steam ascended in the moonlight; the beaten nigger groaned somewhere."

In the portrayals of the Manager and the Brickmaker we have two distinct versions of hollowness. The Manager is intellectually and emotionally hollow; he is a completely dull man who, because of his position as manager of the trading station, unthinkingly and unfeelingly engages in all of the dirty business of colonial exploitation. The Brickmaker, however, is neither dull nor oblivious to what happens around him. His comments on Kurtz and on the idealistic colonizers show, by their irony, a high level of awareness. Kurtz, he says, " 'is an emissary of pity, and science, and progress, and devil knows what else. We want,' he began to declaim suddenly, 'for the guidance of the cause entrusted to us by Europe, so to speak, higher intelligence, wide sympathies, a singleness of purpose.' 'Who says that,' I asked. 'Lots of them,' he replies. 'Some even write that.' " Unlike the manager, he seems to understand the world in which he works and to accept it. There is no indication of the idealism, albeit in the process of being lost, that either Kurtz or the Accountant showed.

Thus far we have discussed only two of the three virtues that Conrad, through Marlow, specifically praises—efficiency and devotion to a deliberate belief. The third virtue is restraint; the hollowness of the Manager and the Brickmaker consists precisely in their having nothing to restrain. Unlike Marlow and Kurtz, they apparently do not hear the voice of the primitive and so are completely safe. But because they are hollow, they literally have nothing to save. They will never achieve even the victory of acknowledging the horror, as Kurtz does, because their hollowness will prevent them from feeling it. Put simply, Kurtz has the depth of character, the passion, necessary to become a great man; he lacks the restraint to control his passion. Marlow has the passion, he recognizes that the voices calling to him from the jungle are human voices to which something in him longs to respond; but despite the longing, he retains his self-control. His efficiency (the surface concern with reality), his restraint (which implies a strength within him that needs restraint) combine to make Marlow the man who survives, and who survives with wisdom.

Psychology and Criticism

Since the start of the twentieth century the study of the subconscious by Freud and his followers has increasingly influenced literary criticism. This is not the place for a detailed description of the various schools of psychiatry—Freudian and Jungian in particular—that have influenced literary study. Any useful understanding of the subconscious, including its motives, its drives, its origins, its most characteristic forms of expression, can come only with long and careful reading of technical psychology. It is possible, however, to outline the general theory briefly and show its relevance to literary study.

The initial assumption is that there is a subconscious, a part of our minds and memories that influences our choices without our being fully aware that we have been influenced; from time to time, most persons react in ways disproportionate to the immediate stimuli. To take a very simple example, most of us know someone we have liked greatly after only a moment's conversation. The usual psychological explanation would be that the immediate stimuli—the appearance of the person and the few words—triggered memories of someone we previously admired, and that the previous admiration has been transferred to the new acquaintance. Neither the memories that have been triggered nor the association of the old and new friends need ever be conscious.

We have seen this principle in operation in our discussion of close reading. In fact, Freud's little book, *Jokes and Their Relation to the Unconscious,* which is based on the notion that unusual uses of language tend to express the subconscious concerns of the speaker or writer, can be read as a psychological justification of close reading. The second principle, though, is radically different from anything we have seen and gives what I shall call generally "myth" or "psychoanalytic" criticism its special content and methodology. The assumption is that the content of the subconscious mind is not entirely personal; it is, for want of a better term, "trans-personal." Because of memories acquired by racial inheritance or broadly human experience—birth, growth, death— we have a need to experience, even vicariously, certain situations and a pre-conditioned ability to respond to them.

To illustrate the trans-personal somewhat more fully without getting into the differences in theory among the psychologists, we can use the example of the person we liked immediately. Suppose we find that most other persons react as we do; the kind of psychology we are considering now would explain the fact (barring some more obvious explanation) by asserting that the new acquaintance appealed to a need that his admirers felt—a need, perhaps, for a father figure. Something about his look, his manner, his way of speaking, reminds his admirers of their *ideal* fathers, no matter how individually different their real fathers happened to be. The appeal of the new friend would not be personal in the sense that it was individually suited to our needs, nor would our needs be individually suited to the appeal; there would, rather, be what we have called a trans-personal quality about both the appeal and the satisfaction.

If the theory is correct, it is especially relevant to the study of art because art is essentially a non-practical and non-rational mode of communication. Although I am using terms somewhat broadly here, because art is both not practical—that is, not directed to some immediate and tangible end—and not rational— in the way that mathematics or philosophy is rational—it may be in part subconscious. And because art, from the consumer's point of view if not from the artist's, is essentially communication, it must, if it is to appeal to many persons for long, have a trans-personal content.

The evidence for a trans-personal psyche is not conclusive, but by assuming it a number of difficult problems can be solved. There are, for example, startling similarities among the myths, legends, and folktales of various peoples, similarities that cannot be convincingly explained away in terms of movements of peoples, dissemination of the stories from a central source, and so on. Stories of younger brothers betrayed by older brothers, of young men who must pass some supernatural test before coming into their inheritance, of the sacrificial death of the old king and his replacement by a new, of women both as workers of black and white magic, of heroic trips to the underworld—all of these are sufficiently widespread geographically and culturally that the hypothesis of a trans-personal unconscious that creates and admires such stories is, at least, tenable.

From the subconscious of the artist, then, may come a level in the work of art which appeals strongly to the subconscious of the reader. To give just one example, most modern readers, if they are responsive, still feel a bit of excitement when Odysseus visits Hades. Consciously and rationally, most moderns do not believe in the underworld, and none believe in it as described by Homer. To put the matter as strongly as possible, when we read of the journey of Odysseus to Hades, we should as rationalistic moderns or as orthodox Christians react with disbelief and perhaps with a bit of annoyance, as we do when other fiction becomes too incredible; that is, we would probably react that way if our reactions were wholly conscious and rational. Whatever the explanation—the descent into Hades represents a desire for and a fear of returning to the womb, the racial memory still remembers and fears the darkness of the caves that were thought to be entrances to the underworld, the pattern of man confronting evil at its most dangerous is impressed upon the unconscious somehow and the unconscious is responsive to it—whatever the explanation, it does seem plausible to say that we sometimes react to what is neither conscious nor personal. Consequently, one of the broadest and most elementary appeals of art might be its appeal to stories, racial memories, or patterns of experience that the reader is not consciously aware of.

Beyond this general basis for myth criticism, methodologies separate and individual psychologists and myth critics separate and quarrel over details. Again, only wide reading will enable the student to pick his way among the types of theory of the subconscious and the details of the critical uses to which they may be put.

Broadly, however, we can separate out three uses of psycho-analytical criticism: the psychoanalysis of the artist, the comparative analysis of individual works and their classification, and the explication of individual works. Since the first and second tend to move away from the particular work of art, they are outside our scope here. Briefly, the psychoanalysis of the artist attempts to use the biographical details of the artist's life and his preoccupation with certain situations, symbols, or whatever, to gain either a fuller understanding of the artist or of the process of artistic creation. Although not its primary purpose, such an understanding may throw light on particular works. The comparative analysis and classification of works attempts to place an individual work within a group of other pieces of literature, myth, folktale, or even ritual; for example, an attempt to show that Hawthorne's short story, "My Kinsman, Major Molineaux" is essentially an initiation story would classify it by showing what it has in common with other initiation stories, myths, and so on. Quite often, this kind of criticism passes over into explication, since the analysis of the story would include an explication and since the comparison with other initiation stories would likely make details in Hawthorne's story clearer. An explication using psychoanalytical materials would attempt to make the unconscious content of the narrative, and its appeal, conscious.

The beginning student must use this kind of criticism carefully, if at all, for to be valuable it requires a great sensitivity to the literary work, an unusually wide reading in folk literature, myth, psychological literature, and related areas, and an absolute refusal to be carried away by simplified interpretations of symbols and partial parallels. In trying to prove a case, there is every temptation to make each cane a phallic symbol and each cave a womb, to make every victim a Christ and every fertile woman an Earth-goddess. Careful criticism means the same for the myth critic as it does for any other critic. It means the use of no material that he is not certain of, the establishment of sufficient positive evidence that a strong proof can be forged, and the patient consideration and justified rejection of any negative evidence.

The Heart of the Darkness

There have been many stories of men losing their sanity in Africa, of the exploitation of natives, of the physical danger of a journey into the jungle, but no other story has had so powerful an effect on so many readers as Conrad's *Heart of Darkness*. Kurtz's dying exclamation—"the horror, the horror"—may be explained easily in several ways, but the easy explanations do not do justice to the impact of the words either on Marlow or on the reader. As an evaluation of Kurtz's deterioration they are a melodramatic reaction of one man to his own failure. As an evaluation of nature's hostility to man, the words are more meaningful, but they might just as well come from Marlow as from Kurtz. Somehow, what Kurtz looks into as he dies is his own nature, and what he sees is the darkness within the heart of man. In this respect, Marlow's journey into the heart of darkness is actually a journey into his own heart; his discovery of the primitive in the Congo is a discovery of the primitive within himself.

I do not want to argue, however, that the *Heart of Darkness* is only an exploration of the human heart; on the contrary, Conrad's genius has created a work that is consistent on several levels. The journey up the Congo is a literal journey up a literal river; the natives are flesh and blood natives; the whites at the stations and in Brussels are real persons with real jobs to do. Likewise, the *Heart of Darkness* has a significant social theme; the presentation of colonial exploitation is as convincing as fiction can be, and Conrad's concern about its effects on both colonizers and natives is clear. But the realistic superstructure of the *Heart of Darkness* exists in connection with a less realistic substructure. At the beginning of *Heart of Darkness* the reader is warned that the meaning envelops "the tale which brought it out only as a glow brings out a haze." The haze which is brought out, I shall argue, is the haze of man's primitive past, a past which Marlow learns to recognize and control.

In fact, the first thing that Marlow tells his listeners, even before he begins the story, is that for the wise man, the past is not dead. "We live in a flicker," Marlow says, and before and after the flicker, there is darkness. As if to prove that the darkness has changed only in location in the roughly two thousand years since the Romans invaded the British Isles, he gives two brief character sketches, the first of the commander of a ship ordered to the Thames, where men die like flies and death skulks in the bushes. He did his job "very well. . . . without thinking much about it either, except afterwards to brag of what he had gone through in his time, perhaps." He looks forward to possible promotion if he can keep his health and if friends in Rome keep their promises. If one adjusts the names and terms from those appropriate to the Roman colonization of Britain to those appropriate to the European colonization of Africa, nothing in the description of the Roman commander's experience is not equally applicable to Marlow's. Even the commander's doing his job "without thinking much about it" previews Marlow's attitude as he takes the ship up-river; and the commander's bragging parallels Marlow's telling of his Congo adventure. The second Roman, the "decent young citizen in a toga" might well be an early version of Kurtz. The young citizen "has to live in the midst of the incomprehensible, which is also detestable. And it has a fascination, too, that goes to work on him. The fascination of the abomination—you know. Imagine the growing regrets, the longing to escape, the powerless disgust, the surrender, the hate." Like the young Roman, Kurtz has come to the primitive world to make his fortune, only to be overwhelmed by it. By making the experiences of the two Romans similar to those of Marlow and Kurtz, Conrad has indicated that the condition of man has not changed; something within man is fascinated by the abomination that has always existed and that still exists. And just as the primitive in man has not changed, the primitive in nature has remained the same; Marlow describes the Thames the Romans saw in language fully appropriate for the Congo.

From the outset, Marlow invests his journey with an almost

supernatural significance. Brussels reminds him of "a whited sepulchre," a place of death; and the image is reinforced by the image of the "grass sprouting between the stones," especially since in the preceding paragraph we have been left with a picture of the slain Fresleven, "the grass growing through his ribs." The detail is impressive; it ties together the geographical space and the human space. The joining of the two is further reinforced by the two witch-like women who guard the door of the Brussels office, but who remind Marlow of death. The episode with the doctor makes the internalizing effect of the preceding section obvious. Marlow, like the reader, expects the doctor to give a routine physical examination; the doctor, however, is an alienist—that is, an early psychiatrist—who tells Marlow that "the changes take place inside." His remark that every doctor should be something of a psychiatrist implies that every patient is exposed in some way to the inner self that Marlow will explore.

All this happens before the voyage begins; the trip itself has a strange, dream-like quality, with the grotesque masks of the natives and the absurd comedy of the puny little ship firing six-inch shells into the huge continent, shells which go "pop," then "give a feeble screech." The trip, Marlow says, "was like a weary pilgrimage amongst hints for nightmares."

The nightmarish quality increases as Marlow pushes deeper into the jungle. Throughout much of *Heart of Darkness,* Conrad describes inanimate things as if they were animate, and animate as if they were inanimate; the boiler at the outer station is "wallowing in the grass" and a truck lies "there on its back with its wheels in the air . . . as dead as the carcass of some animal"; when the natives walk by, Marlow's attention is drawn to them first by the metallic "clinking" of their chains. The landscape of the stations and of the Congo would be nightmarish enough described realistically; Conrad adds to the effect by suggesting a world in which the distinctions between animal and machine, nature and man, primitive and civilized, have broken down.

Although Kurtz's final words make the deepest impression of all Marlow's experience, they are in fact but a summary of what he has learned. In an amazingly complex passage, Marlow seems to drop out of the present and into a primitive past. "We were wanderers," he tells his listeners, "on a prehistoric earth. . . . The prehistoric man was cursing us, praying to us, welcoming us—who could tell? We were cut off from the comprehension of our surroundings; we glided past like phantoms. . . . We could not understand because we were too far and could not remember, because we were travelling in the night of first ages, of those ages that are gone, leaving hardly a sign—and no memories." The ages may have left no conscious memories, but they have left something within Marlow and within us, for "if you were man enough you would admit to yourself that there was in you just the faintest trace of a response to the terrible frankness of that noise. . . . The mind of man is capable of anything—because everything is in it, all the past as well as all the future." Even before his meeting with Kurtz, then, Marlow is aware of the primitive within himself and knows how to control it.

Just before meeting Kurtz, Marlow stresses his sense of isolation; a Freudian psychologist would recognize the description of the stages Marlow goes through here as those that most frequently accompany a patient's final breakthrough to the subconscious material he has been hiding from himself. After the isolation comes a kind of fear, represented in *Heart of Darkness* by the threat of the attack from the savages in the jungle and the cannibals on the boat; the danger, as Marlow feels it, "was from our proximity to a great human passion let loose." In terms that might have been used by Freud to describe the reaction of the subconscious as the patient and his analyst try to make the breakthrough, Marlow admits that the dreaded attack "was really an attempt at repulse. . . . in its essence it was purely protective."

Literally, of course, the natives are protecting Kurtz; in terms of the journey into the heart of man, the forces of the subconscious are protecting Marlow from the full vision of Kurtz, for if Marlow can look into his subconscious and survive, he will have conquered it. When Marlow does anticipate meeting Kurtz, he tells his listeners that he thought not of meeting a flesh and blood man, but a voice; and as he looks back at the meeting he remembers "a voice. He was very little more than a voice." This kind of description of Kurtz that presents him as all but bodiless and constantly brings attention on him only as a voice makes it possible for Conrad to keep the literal and the psychological voyages together throughout this section.

The irony of building Kurtz as the primitive center of Marlow's self and then reminding the reader that "all Europe had contributed to the making of Kurtz" is both subtle and pointed. Psychologically it works, although here the literal and psychological levels come dangerously close to separating. Literally, of course, Conrad is showing how even the most civilized of men may go native; Kurtz is here a developing character, something he could not be if he were exclusively Marlow's primitive self. But in light of the description we get of Kurtz from the people who talk to Marlow after his return from the Congo, it is possible to see Kurtz also as a kind of unguided energy. His accomplishments, so diverse and seemingly so civilized, his political extremism, suggest that even on the literal level Kurtz is basically an undisciplined man, a man of immense but unchannelled energy. And, to refer to Freud once more, this immense but unchannelled energy, this extremism, is characteristic of the id, of that sector of man's mind that is most primitive and that drives him most hard and most mysteriously.

When Marlow argues with Kurtz just before taking him from the jungle, the words he uses still suggest this double focus on Kurtz as literal character and as an aspect of Marlow. Marlow says he was arguing with a "soul," and that Kurtz's last words were "a judgement upon the adventures of his soul upon this earth." If Kurtz does represent the purely primitive part of Marlow's self, the words are fitting because they recognize the absolute horror that man carries hidden within himself.

It is significant that Marlow almost dies when Kurtz dies—that, as Marlow puts it, "It is his extremity that I seem to have lived through," for in this reading of *Heart of Darkness* Marlow has literally lived through the death of Kurtz. It is also significant that Marlow remains loyal to Kurtz. Marlow can no more deny the

Kurtz within him than he can deny that he feels the call of the native drums as he steams up-river. But Marlow has faced Kurtz, and faced him down. Knowing fully what is within himself, Marlow can remain loyal to Kurtz because he knows with certainty that he can control that part of his character. He can never escape it: like Kurtz he will be a strange voice talking in the darkness; when he returns to Europe he will have to lie for Kurtz. He can lie to Kurtz's Intended not because he hates lies any less than he ever did and not because he has been corrupted; he can lie for Kurtz because he recognizes now how much of the primitive is in himself and in others, even in the Intended, and how vitally important it is that only the very strongest look deeply into their own hearts.

Further Possibilities

The preceding essay, tracing Marlow's journey into himself, raises as many questions as it answers. At places in *Heart of Darkness* the literal level seems to contradict the psychological, as when Marlow says, "All that had been Kurtz's had passed out of my hands." Do such passages invalidate the psychological interpretation? If not, how can they be incorporated into it? Is Conrad sometimes forced by the narrative line to choose between the two levels and, storyteller that he is, sacrifice the psychological to the literal? Or does Marlow always interpret events accurately?

The last question raises a more general problem, and one of the most difficult problems in the work. As Conrad sets up the narrative, the mature Marlow tells a story from his relatively immature years; in parts of it he seems to tell the experience as he felt it, without benefit of the wisdom he acquired in the Congo, but in other parts the mature Marlow comments freely upon the experience. When Marlow says, for example, that he set the women to work to get him the Congo job and then goes on to speak of the impractical world that women live in, the action seems to contradict Marlow's assertion that women have no place in the business of the world. The two witch-like women in Brussels who seem to determine the fates of the Congo colonizers and the native woman who alone of all the natives shows courage when Kurtz is taken also seem to act out a role that Marlow's philosophy of women in society cannot account for. Is or is not Marlow always a trustworthy narrator?

The lie that Marlow tells the Intended also raises problems, especially since Marlow so vehemently states on several occasions that he hates a lie. Our psychological reading of *Heart of Darkness* gave one explanation for it, but not the only possible explanation. The dramatic construction of the scene in which the lie occurs shows Marlow's constantly increasing anger and his desire to blurt out the truth about Kurtz; perhaps the lie is not a surrender to temptation, then, but a resistance of temptation showing once more Marlow's restraint. Since the lie does in effect keep the Intended blind, what is the significance of the portrait of her Kurtz has painted?

As a different kind of problem, much could also be done with the historical and sociological background of *Heart of Darkness*. We have seen much of what Conrad recorded in his journals, and a reader can hardly escape feeling the force of Conrad's condemnation of the "pilgrims" and the traders. Furthermore, the psychological reading stressed the nightmarish aspects of the narrative, and some of the horrors that Conrad describes seem almost unnecessary. A study of the conditions that did actually prevail in Africa during the 1880's and 1890's would lead to a better understanding of the realistic basis of *Heart of Darkness*.

In the preceding essays, we have done little with Conrad's use of the natives. There are various kinds of natives who react in various ways to the whites; Marlow admires some, pities others, and feels contempt for some. Strangely enough, he seems to admire those who are still most savage, the cannibals. Is the basis for Marlow's feelings about the natives the same as the basis for his feelings about the whites?

Motifs involving situations, images, and even abstract nouns run throughout the narrative. What is the significance of the fact, for example, that Marlow's predecessor, Fresleven, is killed in a dispute over two black hens, that Marlow almost immediately afterwards describes two women dressed in black, and that there are two women in Kurtz's life, one dark and one living in darkness? The motif of hollowness or restraint could also be traced for insight into the meaning of *Heart of Darkness*.

A study of what Conrad has done to make the story interesting as a story would also be useful. Despite the fact that we know that Marlow survives (he narrates the story), Conrad manages to create a continuing sense of suspense. Precisely how does Conrad keep his readers anxious to discover what will happen next?

A Brief Bibliography of Critical Works

No single short bibliographical essay can adequately survey the wealth of critical approaches available to the student of literature nor, of course, can my few brief comments about the content of a book adequately summarize it. The following list does, however, represent most of the major critical approaches; many of the works mentioned have extensive bibliographies, and others will in other ways lead a student interested in a particular problem to further material.

A. HISTORIES OF LITERARY CRITICISM

The most ambitious recent survey of literary criticsm is William K. Wimsatt and Cleanth Brooks's *Literary Criticism: A Short History* (1959); it is a relatively full consideration of the major critical problems from antiquity to the present. Its pronounced bias, however, makes it advisable to read the concluding chapters first in order to see clearly the assumptions that underlie the history. David Daiches's *Critical Approaches to Literature* (1956) is a useful history of critical problems, but it is much less complete than the Wimsatt and Brooks. The outstanding history of criticism since 1750 is René Wellek's *A History of Modern Criticism: 1750–1950* (1955—); four of the five projected volumes have been published.

B. EARLY CRITICISM

Plato formulated the first coherent critical theory; the *Ion* (*c.* 390 B.C.) and Book X of *The Republic* (*c.* 373 B.C.) are most relevant to modern concerns. Aristotle's *Poetics* (*c.* 330 B.C.) is perhaps even more influential than Plato's work and more directly concerned with literary analysis, especially the analysis of tragedy. Horace's *Ars Poetica* (*c.* 25 B.C.) and Longinus's *On the Sublime* (first or third century A.D.) represent the extremes of Roman literary theory; the former stressed caution and decorum in the creation of literature, the latter emphasized the emotional transport of the audience. Among pre-twentieth-century English critical works, Sidney's "Defense of Poesie" (1583) perhaps best expresses the major aspects of Renaissance literary theory; Alexander Pope's *Essay on Criticism* (1711) and Samuel Johnson's "Preface to Shakespeare" (1765) and the *Lives* of Cowley, Dryden, Pope, and Milton (1779–81) show the main trends in English neo-classical theory. Wordsworth's 1802 "Preface" to the *Lyrical Ballads* and Coleridge's *Biographia Literaria* (1817), Chapters 4 and 13 through 22, state the main issues of romantic criticism. Matthew Arnold spoke for the morally and intellectually serious Victorians in *Culture and Anarchy* (1869) and in *Essays in Criticism,* especially the second series of *Essays* (1888). Oscar Wilde's "The Decay of Lying" (1889) is a delightfully witty expression of late nineteenth-century aestheticism.

"The Philosophy of Composition" (1846) and "The Poetic Principle" (1850) by Edgar Allan Poe, *Nature* (1836) and "The Poet" (1844) by Ralph Waldo Emerson, and the "Preface" to the 1855 edition of *Leaves of Grass* by Walt Whitman show three main aspects of nineteenth-century American criticism. Henry James's prefaces to his works (1907–09) and "The Art of the Novel" (1888) have been among the most influential works on modern fiction; these have been collected in *The Art of Fiction* (ed. R. P. Blackmur, 1934).

C. DISCUSSION OF MODERN CRITICISM

There is an abundance of surveys and summaries of contemporary critical positions. The most complete and best informed by far is René Wellek and Austin Warren's *Theory of Literature* (1949). Its analyses of European criticism are unmatched by those of any other single source, and the bibliography is especially full and useful. John Crowe Ransom's *The New Criticism* (1941) is a generally sympathetic view of the new critics, albeit with some reservations. *The Armed Vision* (1948), by Stanley Edgar Hyman, and *An Age of Criticism* (1952), by William Van O'Connor, are biased and harsh but perceptive surveys. Lee T. Lemon's *The Partial Critics* (1965) classifies recent critical positions, shows their limitations, and suggests a synthesis for contemporary literary theory.

D. INDIVIDUAL APPROACHES AND PRACTICAL CRITICISM

The most influential school of criticism in recent years has been the so-called "new critics," a loosely allied group who emphasized close reading of the text, impersonality in art and criticism, and verbal complexity in literature. The founding fathers of the movement are T. E. Hulme, Ezra Pound, T. S. Eliot, and I. A. Richards. In *Speculations* (ed. Sir Herbert Read, 1924), Hulme argues for poetry that is "hard, dry," and literally accurate. With some qualifications, Pound takes the same line in the *Literary Essays of Ezra Pound* (ed. T. S. Eliot, 1954). Eliot's *Selected Essays* (1951) contains his most important criticism. I. A. Richard's early works, *Principles of Literary Criticism* (1925) and *Science and Poetry* (1926), are his most influential; his *Practical Criticism* (1929), an analysis of critiques written by his students, is especially valuable for the beginning critic. *The Well Wrought Urn* (1947), by Cleanth Brooks, is perhaps the best statement and exemplum of the new critical position. Two essays by W. K. Wimsatt, Jr., and Monroe C. Beardsley, "The Intentional Fallacy" and "The Affective Fallacy," both of which appear in *The Verbal Icon* (1954), support the new critical position by arguing for concentration upon the text of the literary work as opposed to study of either authorial intention or reader reaction. John Crowe Ransom and Yvor Winters, despite their important differences from the new critics, have much in common with them. Ransom, in *The World's Body* (1938), uses much of the new critical vocabulary despite his denial of the formal unity of literary works. Winter's sharp verbal criticism is largely new critical, although absolutist and moralistic in assumptions and tone; his collection of essays, *In Defense of Reason* (1947), contains most of his best work.

The Chicago critics, or neo-Aristotelians, attacked the new critics' emphasis upon verbal criticism and substituted an emphasis on internal structure or, in their terminology, "the intention of the work." The most complete statement of their position is in *Critics and Criticism* (1952), a mammoth collection of essays by the editor, R. S. Crane, Elder Olson, Richard McKeon, and others. Crane's *The Languages of Criticism and the Structure of Poetry* (1953) is perhaps the most coherent statement of the neo-Aristotelian position. Wayne C. Booth's

The Rhetoric of Fiction (1961) is a brilliant application of the Chicago method to the study of fiction.

Critical approaches using the materials of depth psychology, anthropology, and folklore are among the most used currently. The general origin of such approaches is to be found in the work of Sigmund Freud, Carl Jung, and Sir James Frazer. Among Freud's most relevant works are *Totem and Taboo* (1918), *Jokes and Their Relation to the Unconscious* (1916), and *A General Introduction to Psychoanalysis* (1935); Jung's most relevant works include *Contributions to Analytical Psychology* (1928), *Symbols for Transformation* (1956), and *The Archetypes and the Collective Unconscious* (1959). Frazer's *The Golden Bough* (1900; abridged 1959 by Theodor H. Gaster), though out of favor with anthropologists, is by far the most influential study of primitive and classical myth for both modern criticism and modern literature. Other influential works include Joseph Campbell's *Hero with a Thousand Faces* (1949); F. M. Cornford's *Origin of Attic Comedy* (1914); Francis Fergusson's *The Idea of a Theater* (1949); Robert Graves's *The White Goddess* (1948); Jane Harrison's several studies of Greek religion; Gilbert Murray's *The Rise of the Greek Epic* (1907); Lord Raglan's *The Hero* (1936); and Jessie Weston's *The Quest of the Holy Grail* (1913) and *From Ritual to Romance* (1920). John B. Vickery's *Myth and Literature* (1966) is a convenient anthology of essays relating to literature and myth.

Perhaps the most famous of the works of criticism based on Freud's studies is Dr. Ernest Jones's *Hamlet and Oedipus* (1910; 1949). Maud Bodkin's *Archetypal Patterns in Poetry* (1934) is an early and still excellent application of the Jungian method. Lionel Trilling's recent essay, "Freud: Within and Beyond Culture," reprinted in *Beyond Culture* (1965), is a favorable but balanced assessment of Freud's contributions to literature and literary criticism. The archetypal theory of Northrop Frye has achieved wide influence; *The Anatomy of Criticism* (1957) still shows this aspect of Frye's work best.

A number of valuable works are part of no major critical school or group. Kenneth Burke's critical insights are immensely useful both theoretically and practically; *Counter-Statement* (1931) and *The Philosophy of Literary Form* (1941) are his most relevant works, although scattered sections of *A Grammar of Motives* (1945) and *Language as Symbolic Action* (1966) are provocative. Murray Krieger's *The Play and Place of Criticism* (1967) illustrates his "thematic" approach, an approach which attempts to combine rigorous close reading with broadly thematic concerns. Christopher Caudwell's *Illusion and Reality* (1947) remains one of the most stimulating works of Marxist criticism; the Hungarian critic George Lukacs combines a Marxist point of view with sensitivity and wide historical knowledge in such works as *Studies in European Realism* (1950). The extremely practical approach of the Russian formalist critics (*c.* 1917–29) can be seen in *Russian Formalist Criticism,* translated by Lee T. Lemon and Marion J. Reis (1965). Dorothy Van Ghent's *The English Novel: Form and Function* (1953), David Lodge's *Language of Fiction* (1966), and Robert Scholes and Robert Kellogg's *The Nature of Narrative* (1966) illustrate some of the exciting work that is being carried on in the study of fiction.

E. BACKGROUND STUDIES

There are available innumerable excellent biographies, intellectual histories, source studies, textual studies, and so on. The comparative brevity of the following list reflects the difficulty of choosing among riches. Among the most notable biographies is Richard Ellman's magnificent biography of James Joyce (1959) and David Erdmann's *Blake: Prophet against Empire* (1954). John Livingston Lowes's *The Road to Xanadu* (1927), a study of the sources of Coleridge's *The Rime of the Ancient Mariner* and "Kubla Khan," is a model of that kind of scholarship. A careful reading of Harrison Hayford and Merton M. Sealts's recent edition of Melville's *Billy Budd* (1962) is a fine introduction to the problems of textual scholarship. E. M. W. Tillyard's *The Elizabethan World Picture* (1943) is a brief but model study of some of the currents of English Renaissance thought.

Index

239